'Ever since [the] spectacular bankruptcy, Leeson has protested that he has been cast as the scapegoat by blundering buffoons, alias the Baring family, their chief executives and senior officials at the Bank of England. According to Leeson, he was and remains the victim of the stupidity and greed of his superiors. His rollicking autobiography makes a good case for this view'
The Times

'Extraordinary'
Irish Independent

'Paints a vivid, plausible picture of an ambitious, good-natured young trader swept up into a web of deceit in the frenetic, unreal world of the Singapore International Monetary Exchange'
Sunday Telegraph

'Simultaneously entertaining and appalling'
Financial Times

'Coherent and well written . . . Often very vivid, not only about the débâcle itself but also about life as a big-ticket trader on the floor of the Singapore International Monetary Exchange'
Daily Telegraph

'The inside account . . . Gripping'
The Economist

D0252254

ROGUE TRADER

NICK LEESON

with

Edward Whitley

WARNER BOOKS

A *Warner* Book

First published in Great Britain in 1996
by Little, Brown and Company
This edition published in 1997 by Warner Books
Reprinted in 1999 (four times)

A CIP catalogue record for this book
is available from the British Library.

ISBN: 0 7515 1708 9

Typeset in Times New Roman by M Rules
Printed and bound in Great Britain
by Clays Ltd, St Ives plc

Warner Books
A Division of
Little, Brown and Company (UK)
Brettenham House
Lancaster Place
London WC2E 7EN

'The key questions are:

   a) how were the massive losses incurred?
   b) why was the true position not noticed earlier?

Our conclusions, in summary, are:

   a) the losses were incurred by reason of unauthorised and concealed trading activities within BFS [Baring Futures Singapore];
   b) the true position was not noticed earlier by reason of a serious failure of controls and managerial confusion within Barings;
   c) the true position had not been detected prior to the collapse by the external auditors, supervisors or regulators of Barings.'

from the Conclusions to the Bank of England's report
of the inquiry into the collapse of Barings Bank,
published on 18 July 1995

CONTENTS

PREFACE

THIS IS THE PART of the book where you might normally expect to find a short passage dedicating it to
someone. I am not going to do that, as *Rogue Trader*
recounts an episode in my life that I am not very proud
of, and represents a part of my life that I am trying desperately hard to leave behind. I therefore see no point in
devoting the book to anyone or anything.

Having said that, I have used the opportunity the
book presented to set the record straight over a couple
of issues. For example, while I have included references
to the Bank of England's report in the book, I would in
no way like the reader to think that this signifies my
agreement with that report. It doesn't. The Bank of
England's report is a waste of paper and is shamed by
the Singaporean version.

I also believe that very high-level questions need to be
asked both of the Bank of England and of the Serious
Fraud Office (SFO). So far these questions have been
avoided.

There are reasons why I did not return to the UK to

stand trial. I will not pretend to know or understand the machinations behind this decision, but I would like to draw attention to the fact that the Singaporean report states that they were restricted in their access to the majority of evidential documents held in the UK. This is contrary to the views expressed by the SFO throughout my internment in Germany.

This book is not meant as an exposé, and I doubt it will have the sensationalism of the media coverage the reader may be used to. But, unlike some of the media stories, this story is a true one. I have written the book the way that it was and the way that it is. There is a chance that some people will be upset at the manner in which they have been portrayed, but I have read the book over and over again and am satisfied that the impression given is fair. On two occasions I have used pseudonyms to protect identities. These two characters are neither central to the book nor aware that they would be written about, so I feel this is the least I could do.

I would like to take this opportunity to record my gratitude to a few people. I would like to extend my thanks and best wishes for the future to Edward Whitley, who has helped me write *Rogue Trader*. It has not been the easiest of tasks, but the prison authorities were enormously helpful in allowing him to visit. I would also like to thank the legal team, especially Stephen Pollard, Eberhard Kempf and Eva Dannenfeldt, who have been on hand to lead me through the process.

As I entered prison for the first time, one of the first things that was said to me was: 'You'll find out who your friends are now.' Nothing could be more true, and

I have been totally overwhelmed by the level of help and support that I have been offered. I have not been able to reply to all the letters – there were far too many – but my thanks go to each and every one of you who took the trouble to write. I have not received any negative mail, but I have been let down by some people I would previously have referred to as 'friends'.

I would like to thank all of my family and close friends, who have been, and continue to be, an oasis of support. It is their love that keeps me going, and it is only with their love and help that I have managed to get this far. It has not been easy; in fact it has been a slow and arduous process to adapt to the conditions in which I now find myself. But each and every one of you has played a part in pulling me through.

Lastly I would like to thank my wife Lisa, who has been a tower of strength throughout the whole affair. She has kept me going at times when I have been at my lowest ebb, and my only ambition at the moment is to finish the prison sentence and get back to her as quickly as possible. There is no prouder husband than me.

'The recovery in profitability has been amazing . . . leaving Barings to conclude that it was not actually terribly difficult to make money in the securities business.'

Peter Baring, Chairman of Barings,
to Brian Quinn, Director of the Bank of England
in charge of banking supervision
13 September 1993

'It's just a non-transaction. It's an error. It is a back office glitch. Don't worry about it.'

James Bax, Regional Manager of Barings South
Asia, to Ron Baker, Head of the Financial
Products Group
3 February 1995

'I leaned across to Din and told him I was a buyer at 19,000. There was no need to whisper, I could hardly hear myself shout. He looked at me and queried: "What size, Nick?"
"Any size, Fat Boy!"'

Nick Leeson, General Manager
of Baring Futures Singapore
June 1992–February 1995

PROLOGUE

A Weekend at Kota Kinabalu

Saturday 25 February 1995

IT WAS MY BIRTHDAY but the white-water rafting was shut. We'd driven for over two hours to the station, but the cranky old train which should have taken us up along the river had broken down or fallen off the tracks or something. Nobody seemed to know what had gone wrong or when it would start again. It was the same train which had taken soldiers up and down Malaysia in the Second World War, when they were fighting against and then escaping from the Japanese. Those soldiers really knew what it was like to flee for their lives.

Lisa and I went back to the hotel and wandered out to the pool. The Shangri-la at Kota Kinabalu is quite a new place, and the swimming pool is a vast, extravagant crescent surrounded by blue and white canvas umbrellas. I stared across the shimmering water at the pink bodies of the Westerners underneath their parasols, the soles of their feet sticking out towards me as white and soft as cotton wool. They would be brokers, bankers, lawyers, oilmen, and probably traders like me. They were ex-pats, and they liked their beer cold, their chicken satayed, and their women brain-dead and adoring. They also liked their money. I opened my Tom Clancy thriller and tried to concentrate. I could tell them something about money.

A mobile telephone went off behind me. 'Shit!' I said, looking around. 'They've found me!' But then I realised it was someone else's phone; I'd turned mine off and left it in the flat. Nobody could get through to me. I took a deep breath to calm my pulse and lay back down. It'd been so easy to escape: I'd just turned off the phones, packed two suitcases, bought two tickets in cash and we were out of Singapore. I'd once spent a night in a Singapore jail, and I didn't want to spend another.

Thursday 23 February 1995

WHEN the bell rang for the close of dealing at 2:15 P.M. the screaming finally stopped. Everyone had been shouting at me all day. I'd stood in the pit and every dealer on the exchange had screamed at me and I'd screamed back. I'd bought everything the market had to offer. The Nikkei was down 330 points, but had it not been for me it'd have been down a thousand. I'd held out my arms wide, screamed, and grinned, and written tickets, and sent them over to the back office, and gone to the telephones and screamed and signalled to George, buy at 18,100, buy at 18,000, buy at 17,900, buy at 17,800, buy, buy, buy. I'd made the market

2

bounce a couple of times but I'd had the shit kicked out of me all the way down.

I knew I'd still lost millions of pounds, but I didn't know exactly how many. I was too frightened to find out – the numbers scared me to death. I turned off my Reuters screen and the green flickering figures died an instant quiet death. They were just numbers on a screen, nothing to do with real cash. I summed up the day. It'd been hell: I'd bought a falling market all the way down, and whenever I'd tried to sell there'd been someone else in there first. Normally a big ticket trade like 500 contracts happened once every six months – unless it was me – but today there'd been two right in front of me and they'd butchered the market. I was sure our phones were tapped: it was just impossible that so many big tickets could get in front of me. They'd beaten me by less than a second every time. I'd lost more money, God knows how much more. I'd gone in trying to reduce the position and ended up buying another 4,000 contracts. I tried to clear my head: today was Thursday, and my birthday was just two days away now. SIMEX would make a margin call tomorrow for at least another $40 million. It could never happen. I was giving up the fight.

I slipped away from the trading floor and walked quickly outside. I nodded and grinned at a few people. I noticed a lot of astonished, elated faces staring at me, sweating and flushed as if they'd just come off a dance floor. Traders looked at me and knew I'd done an amazing volume of trade; they marvelled at the sheer amount of business I'd got through. They wondered whether I was dealing for myself or for clients, and whether I'd hedged, protected my position. But they knew – as the whole of Asia did – that I'd built up an exposure to over £11 billion worth of Japanese shares. They were doing their sums and they reckoned I was well long: it was hard to conceal it when you stood for over 40 per cent of the Singapore market. The rest of the market had smelled what Barings back in London were completely ignoring: that I was in so deep there was no way out.

Back at the office, the phones started ringing again. It was the *Nihon Keizei Shimbun* newspaper, which monitors the Nikkei 225 index, and they wanted to know what I was going to do with my position.

'We're calling it "The Baring Overhang",' the reporter said.

'Call it what you want,' I answered cheerfully. 'We've got a great position and we don't have a problem with it.'

'Does it all expire on the 10th of March?'

'You'll have to wait and see,' I said. 'I'm not sure what all the clients are going to do yet.'

'But the market'll never rally until you've unwound it,' the reporter pointed out.

'That's all,' I broke him off, 'I've got another call to take. Speak to you later.'

I slammed the phone down and yelled out to anyone who was listening: 'I'm not taking any more calls. Not one.'

Two more telephones started ringing and I waved them away. Let them draw their own conclusions. Nisa, one of the back office girls, came up and handed me the latest statement for Error Account 88888. I didn't even bother looking at it. It scared me to death. I hadn't looked at it all month, and I knew that the position had got worse and worse. I'd been trying to get out of the market, had ended up supporting it to stop it crashing around my ears, and was now another 4,000 contracts deeper in trouble – and these, together with my total position, had lost more money today.

I looked around to see if anyone was coming and then unlocked my desk drawer. From beneath the pile of scraps of paper, the scissors and glue and cut-up letters which I knew I should throw away, I found the print-out of the 88888 account. I scribbled in the latest day's trading and drew a line beneath it: at today's Nikkei close of 17,885, I was long of 61,039 Nikkei 225 contracts, short of 26,000 Japanese Government Bond contracts (JGBs) and had a mixture of Euroyen and Nikkei option positions. I dreaded to think how much money I'd lost.

'Nick!'

I swivelled round and gathered my papers in one move. It was Tony Railton, Senior Settlements Clerk from the London office. Good old Tony. He was a big, bulky man, running a little to fat, and always anxious to please. I'd see if I could fob him off with another pointless chore.

'How you doing, Tony? Good day?'

'Great day, Nick, great day. How was the market?'

'Brilliant.' I flashed him a smile which unambiguously spelt out that I'd made a lot of money.

'I've been trying to get you all day.'

'I'm sorry. It was crazy out there.' I nodded and let him draw his own conclusions.

'It looked that way,' he smiled with admiration.

He was another one who'd been fed the Nick Leeson success story in London, and I couldn't disappoint him.

He was no nearer finding my account than he was a week ago, and he'd been ferreting around the office for a month now. It was pathetic.

'Nick, I was talking with Simon about this hole in the balance sheet – I'm so sorry to bore you with it – but we wondered whether you could make a quick meeting this afternoon? And then James wants a meeting on Saturday, as you know.'

'God!' I leaned back in my chair. 'Look, Saturday's out. I mean, it's my birthday, and Lisa and I want to enjoy it. Sunday would be fine,' I tried to appease him, 'but not Saturday. And sure, let's meet later this afternoon. Lisa's just called to say that she's sick right now so I'm going home to check on her. I'll get back to you about 4:30?'

'Thanks, Nick.' Tony, pleased as punch, ducked his head down as he concentrated on some more papers. He'd got his meeting.

I turned back to my desk and looked again at the column of figures in my hand. If Tony Railton had been able to read upside down – or if he'd been able to carry out just one simple checking device, which any auditor should do first thing in the morning when they switch the machines on – he'd have seen some figures which would have given him a heart attack. I just couldn't believe that he'd been in Singapore for a month, sitting right next to my desk, and he still hadn't carried out a basic reconciliation of the positions I held. It was the most fundamental thing to do, and it would have shown him exactly what I was in for. As soon as I'd heard that he was coming out, I knew everything was over, but each day I'd hung on and he hadn't twigged. He'd sat there at my left elbow, listening to all my telephone conversations with Brenda Granger, when I'd asked for more cash from London, he'd seen the SIMEX letters about the 88888 account, he'd known about some missing money – and he still hadn't put two and two together. I'd almost begun to believe that we could stay on until Lisa's sister came to visit us in March. But tomorrow was bonus day, which meant that I'd have to get out of here.

The phone rang again. Christina Lim held her hand over the mouthpiece and asked me: 'AP–Dow Jones for you, Nick?'

I shook my head and listened as she explained that I was on the other line and would call straight back. She even took down the number. That was one call I'd never make – save Barings that cost at least. Everyone in the market was beginning to guess that my position was largely unhedged. Japanese brokers employ people to work out what exposure the other houses have, by standing around the trading pit and trying to quantify what certain people are doing, and Yamaichi were very close to the truth. I'd built up a massive exposure in Singapore. I was the only buyer in the market. Everyone knew that this was ridiculous – everyone, that is, apart from the Barings management, and they just didn't know anything. They could have found out in half an hour, if they'd done the most obvious check: looking at the positions I reported to SIMEX (which included the 88888 account) compared with the positions I reported back to London (which made no mention of it).

Then Simon Jones came into the office. This was rare. Jones was Regional Operations Manager of Barings

South Asia, and never left his office to come down to see me – the arrogant bastard usually just buzzed me on the phone.

'Nick,' he said easily, 'we're looking again at the balance sheet and we're confused. Bloody Tony Hawes is coming at the weekend and we'd better have our story straight by Saturday.'

'Sure,' I smiled broadly, 'no problem. In fact, the other Tony's just asked me for a 4:30 meeting this afternoon. Why don't we all go through it then?'

'Make sure you do!' Simon said before turning to chat to Tony Railton.

I swivelled back to my desk. I now had just a few minutes to play with. I had to get out. I switched off my mobile phone and put it in my pocket. Then I shuffled the 88888 papers around and wondered about shredding them – but that was too obvious with Simon and Tony standing right there. What about taking them with me? What's the point, I thought, I knew the damage. And I was going to go on holiday – one hell of a holiday. In the end I just put them back in my drawer and locked it. They'd find them. If they hadn't found the 88888 account by mid-morning tomorrow, they'd break open the drawer and find it then. And they *would* find it tomorrow because SIMEX'd be on the phone asking for another $40-odd million of margin payments and nobody would authorise it. Time to go. I pushed back my chair.

'See you later,' I called out to nobody in particular. 'I'll be back in a while.'

I went out the door and got into the lift. Once the mirrored doors had slid shut, I pulled out my phone and called Lisa.

'Hey! You OK?' she asked, all bright and breezy.

Jesus, I winced, she knew nothing. Not even the first thing. Not even the first tiny, tiny error of £20,000 that stupid cow Kim had made back in 1992, starting it all off. And certainly not the millions and millions which had gone up in smoke today.

'I'm going to come and pick you up.' I tried to relax my throat as I spoke. 'I've got something I need to discuss with you.'

'Are you all right?'

'Sure, I'm fine. But can I pick you up in five minutes? Will you be downstairs?'

'I'll be there.'

I put the phone back in my pocket, and it rang immediately. The lift hadn't even reached the basement car park yet. I pulled the phone out, looked at it, and then switched it off.

Downstairs I walked over to the car and opened the door. As soon as I started the engine, the car phone rang. I leaned over and turned that off as well. Then I headed for the exit, pushed my card into the barrier and swung out into Collyer Quay.

The traffic was light, so I was home in ten minutes. I saw Lisa standing uncertainly at the bottom of the steps, looking at the traffic. I pulled over and she climbed in.

'Is this a kidnap?' she joked.

I pulled out into moving traffic and felt safer. So long as I was moving, nobody could creep up behind me. And that 88888 account was just waiting there. Poor old Tony Railton.

'Look, Lisa, you'll never believe this,' I faltered. 'I've

made some awful mistakes at work. I've got to get out of here.'

'What do you mean?'

'I've lost a lot of money and I need to leave. I need to resign. I've broken the law. Christ, the Singaporeans are probably going to go crazy and put me in prison. I can't tell you how bad it is.'

'Come on, Nick,' she turned to me, her eyes narrowed behind her sunglasses, 'what is this? We're getting your bonus next month and you're saying you have to leave. What's the hurry?'

'I have to leave. I have to leave today. I have to get out of Singapore. Once they've found the position I'll be able to talk to them – I just can't stand here and let them find it. And you need a break too. Come on,' I added weakly, 'you need a break too.'

I felt my voice cracking. I hated myself.

'It can't be that bad,' Lisa comforted me. 'You've been under pressure recently. Why don't you talk to Danny about it?'

I looked at the road ahead, mechanically feeding it through the windscreen as I followed the traffic. Here I was – or there I had been – a great success. I'd done well, my family were proud of me, my wife loved me. I'd been overwhelmed by this problem every day for two years, and now my wife didn't understand why I'd done it. 'It was for you,' I almost said. 'I did it to make you happy, because I could win that way.' But then I knew it was also for me: I'd had to win that way so I could run my own team, be my own boss, tower over the trading floor, earn my bonus. The pity of it was that I now realised Lisa would have loved me if I'd just joined my dad as a plasterer.

'OK,' I said. 'Look, I'll drop you at home and you pack a couple of suitcases. Whatever you do, don't answer the phone. I'll go see Danny.'

'Hang on,' Lisa said, looking around to see where we were. 'There's Blockbuster Video. Let's pick up our cash deposit – that's 200 dollars.'

I pulled over while Lisa went into the store and spoke with the management. She came out beaming.

'They wouldn't give me 200 dollars, but I stood my ground and got 180.'

'Well done!'

I dropped her off at the flat and then switched on the phone. Danny – a friend of mine who traded JGBs for First Continental – was out, but I caught him on his mobile.

'Danny? It's Nick. Can I drop round for a minute? I've got a problem.'

'Sure, mate. Come on by. I'm having my hair cut at Takashimaya at the moment, but I'll meet you at Far East Plaza in five minutes.'

I parked at the plaza and found him scratching the back of his neck.

'Flash haircut!' I greeted him.

'Scalped,' Danny said. We went upstairs into his flat above the plaza. 'So what is it? Work or women?' he asked.

He gave his girlfriend some money and firmly told her to go to the shops for a while. He must have seen the stress on my face. We sat out on his balcony and watched the traffic. Danny produced a tray with a pot of tea and some chocolate biscuits.

'I've got an unauthorised position,' I blurted out,

11

'and it's quite big. It's going to be found any minute now.'

'How big is it?'

'Big enough to be a problem.'

'The authorities won't like it,' Danny said, shaking his head.

'No, nor will Barings.'

'Well, what can Barings do? Chuck you out? So what? That's a bummer, but not the end of the world. You've got your health and your freedom.'

'I need to get out of here.'

'Well, take a short break and see how it looks when the shit hits the fan,' Danny advised. 'But it might not be as bad as you think.'

'I need to get out of here,' I said again. 'I don't want them to catch me. They'll bang me in jail as soon as look at me.'

'The right thing to do is come clean,' Danny said, 'but I can't really say that with any conviction. Look at me: when I wrote off Mark's Ferrari, I took the first plane to Athens until he'd calmed down and wouldn't beat the shit out of me!'

We argued a little more but I just couldn't bring myself to mention the size of the problem. Millions of pounds were screaming inside me, but I just helped myself to more biscuits.

'OK,' I made my decision, 'I have to get out. Right. We'll go to the airport and fly to Phuket. We'll meet you and Ches there tomorrow and see what happens. I'll be sacked then, and we can take it from there.'

We trooped downstairs and got into the car. Danny drove as we went back to the flat and picked up Lisa.

'I unplugged the phone,' she said. 'Clearly some people would like to talk to you.'

The drive to the airport was a funny, elated half-hour. None of us could quite grasp that I was running away. I almost believed them when they talked about going out for dinner next week. Danny was having some friends to stay, and we agreed to have dinner on Tuesday. Lisa and Danny argued about where to go, and finally agreed on Keyaki, a Japanese restaurant. I stared out of the window and counted the cars we passed, each car another hurdle crossed, another step closer to getting out.

'You're doing a Reggie Perrin!' Lisa suddenly exclaimed.

'Who's he?' I had no idea.

Both Lisa and Danny laughed and told me about the TV character Reggie Perrin's fake suicide. I laughed too. It wasn't such a bad idea.

We bought tickets for the next shuttle to Kuala Lumpur, and by late evening were checked into the Regent Hotel. At lunchtime the next day, Friday 24 February, I faxed my resignation to James Bax and Simon Jones. I asked the lady at reception to delay sending it for an hour, which gave us time to catch the flight to Kota Kinabalu. We had tried to get to Phuket, an island off Thailand, but all flights were booked. Kota Kinabalu is in east Malaysia, just next door to Borneo and Brunei. It looked great, but most importantly it wasn't Singapore, and we didn't want to stay in KL for the whole weekend.

It was a two-hour flight, and Lisa and I were picked up by the hotel minibus. By the time we arrived, the sun was setting. We walked out to the pool and stared out over the sea.

'Oi, sweetness! Birthday boy! Wake up. Want a cup of tea?'

It was Lisa. She smiled at me over the top of her Ray-Bans and I loved her all over again. I looked around at the pool, and at first I couldn't work out what was wrong. Then I realised that it was totally quiet: there was nobody screaming at me, no telephones, no Barings nobs, no Tony Railton or Simon Jones, no Mary Walz or Tony Hawes. Nobody here wanted anything from me.

'Do you reckon they've got any burgers?'

My fetish for hamburgers was becoming a joke. Wherever you go in the Far East there are McDonald's. With the salt and gherkins and something spicy which they must pick up from the air, these burgers taste even better than the ones back home. I reckon I could excel at a blind tasting of Big Macs around the world.

'They could do. But if you have one, we'll have to work out at the gym.'

'You're obsessed! Give me a break.'

Lisa stood up and leant down to kiss me.

'I'm going to get you back into shape. That belly is driving me nuts.'

'It's a deal,' I laughed. 'Room service!'

Later we took a stroll around the resort, hand in hand. As we walked past the newspaper stand I glanced at the headlines. Yesterday, Friday, the Nikkei had dropped 300 points.

'They chose a good day to get out,' I said. 'The market's stood up to it.'

'You think it's all OK, then?' Lisa asked me as we went back to our room.

'It looks like it,' I nodded, forcing myself to believe it. 'They'd have got my fax on Friday, found the position and unwound everything. The market's held up well.'

'But you're still out of a job?' she persisted.

'I'm definitely out of a job, believe me. I've lost them money.'

'It wasn't just you.'

'I was in charge of them. But don't stress me, wench.'

'What are we doing after this weekend?' she asked.

I looked past Lisa out of the window. In the Shangri-la Tanjung Aru Hotel, with its sky-blue swimming pool and smart umbrellas, its instant room service, starched red and green napkins, hot sun, cold beer, and white-water rafting – if the train was back on the rails – nothing seemed to matter. For the first time in God knows how long I was feeling relaxed. I could feel some muscles loosening down my back which had been clenched tight for months.

'It's going to be fine,' I heard myself say in a rather dreamy way. 'Let's go to that Italian restaurant tonight, go white-water rafting tomorrow, have another great day, and then we'll see. I'm out of Barings, but what the hell? We'll travel up to Thailand, go to Australia, get back home next month and look around. Now come on: where are my birthday presents? What's in that bag you've been hiding from me?'

Lisa pulled a bag out of the cupboard and began handing over the cards and presents which the family had sent out. I loved seeing their handwriting on the cards more than anything – I loved thinking that they'd sat down and written out those cards at home, and the cards had then found their way out to Singapore and into Lisa's bag even as we flew off to Kuala Lumpur. I caught sight of the Queen's head on the stamps – now she was a favourite Barings client. All the big cheeses at Barings talked about her account. She was meant to have £40 million invested with Barings. Forty million? That was peanuts. God, if I'd had an exposure of only £40 million I'd have been laughing. I'd be out in the pool doing somersaults off the diving board.

'Here's your present,' Lisa said with a grin.

I opened it – it was an old print of Singapore, drawn from Stamford Hill. We both laughed.

'I'm never going to see that place again!' There was a knock at the door. Fuck! Who was that? I looked around to hide, but Lisa had already bounded over to the door and flung it open.

'Room service,' said a waiter in a starched white jacket, pushing a trolley.

'And here's your burger,' Lisa laughed. 'Just look at those french fries!'

THAT night the hotel told us the doddery old train was back on the tracks, so we set off early on Sunday morning to go white-water rafting. Given that the Nikkei had only dropped 300 points on Friday, I didn't bother to switch on CNN. We left too early to catch any of the papers in the hotel lobby, but who cared? We were on holiday. I had no worries. I made myself believe that it was all over. I'd resigned, I would put it down to experience, we'd have a holiday and go home next month.

We took the train up the river with five or six other holiday-makers, smiling Hong Kong Chinese and a couple of Koreans. We carried the inflatable dinghy to the river bank, pulled on life-jackets and helmets and lurched out on to the water.

The river started off slowly, quietly, flowing between sheer banks where vines climbed over the tops of the trees. I sat at the front of the raft with a paddle and trailed one hand in the water. It was clear and cool and I felt like toppling over and drifting downstream.

Soon we hit the first gorge. The raft dashed about, doubling up and bouncing into the white foaming water. I held on and looked across at Lisa. She was laughing as the spray flew into her face. Her blonde hair was stuck across her forehead and hung down in rats' tails around the back of her head. She looked so gorgeous, so happy. She flashed me a radiant smile and held up the waterproof camera she had brought with her. I was just beginning to wish there was nobody else there, so I could have dived across the boat at her, when someone shouted *'Hold on!'*

It was too late. The raft bucketed into a wall of water, buckled underneath me and tipped me overboard. I shut my eyes, threw my hands up around my head, and felt the squashy bottom of the raft push down on me. I hadn't had a chance to take a deep breath, so I just kept my eyes and mouth shut and let the current take me downstream. In those few seconds I suddenly thought: 'Why not let it go? Why kick back up to the surface?' What a great way to go. Verdict: Accidental Death. I'd never even know what happened to Tony Railton, what he thought when he opened the 88888 account, whether his jaw hit the desk or fell all the way to the floor, what happened to Barings, what the Nikkei did. I'd be well out of it. But then I thought of Lisa, and I kicked my legs. I may have run away but I wasn't going to desert her. By the time I bobbed up, bright green and red stars were exploding in front of my eyes.

'Nick!'

I saw the raft and there was Lisa waving at me.

'I've got it on film! You were amazing!'

I swam over towards the raft, which was idling near the river bank. I saw one of the guides dive overboard and thought that he was coming to rescue me. I was about to wave to tell him I was fine, but he didn't even look my way – he was going after the paddle I'd dropped.

'I thought you were a goner,' Lisa yelled. 'Where's the life insurance?'

'Fuck me!' I spluttered out water and held on to the sides of the boat. 'I thought that was it!'

'We were going to launch a lifeboat!' Lisa laughed. 'You could be a stunt man any time.'

I heaved myself over the edge of the boat, and some of the Chinese contingent reached out and helped me, all laughing and drumming their chests and going 'Hoooooo!'

'Hooooooo!' I agreed, wiping the water from my face.

I looked down at my leg and saw a bright purple gash swelling up on my shin.

'Lucky there's no piranhas here.'

'Hang on!' the guide warned us. 'We're heading for the next one. It's a snorter!'

We threw ourselves back into action, all pushing with our paddles and blinking the water out of our eyes as the boat tossed around beneath us.

By the time we came out of the gorge we were exhausted. We lay back against the rubber sides and watched the green forest spin slowly past. When we saw the jetty at the other end, Lisa and I nodded at each other and somersaulted backwards into the river. Buoyed up by our life-jackets, we floated downstream on our backs, and I could hear nothing above the quiet surge of the water.

Back at the hotel we flopped down on to the bed.

'Do I deserve a burger?' I asked.

'How's that leg of yours?' Lisa rolled over to take a closer look.

'It'd heal instantly if you kissed it better.'

Lisa leant down and gently kissed it.

'Better?'

'Much better,' I nodded, 'but I really banged my elbow. It's agony.'

'Shall I kiss that better too?'

'And you know, my neck was badly cricked when I hit the boat . . .'

'And my shoulder really aches,' Lisa said, drooping her shoulder down and showing me a white bikini mark.

'So are we saying no hamburgers?' I whispered.

'Let's just postpone them,' Lisa said.

WE woke up on Monday morning feeling wonderfully calm. The weekend was over, and it was time to get back to Kuala Lumpur. We agreed that Lisa would go to

Singapore, sort out some of our things and arrange for the furniture to be moved back home. She'd give the key back to Barings, then come and join me in Phuket. We'd stay there a week, as some friends were coming up the following weekend, and then head off to Australia. We'd go home when we'd squared my father and her parents with my resignation. I knew that Dad would be desperately upset, but he'd understand that the pressure had been too much. I could help him out with his plastering, take it easy for the summer. Lisa wanted to get back home to London and help out her uncle, who ran a sandwich bar in the West End.

It was a bright day, and we lay around by the pool and whiled away the morning until it was time to pack our bags.

'Let's get some biscuits for the journey,' Lisa said. We mooched along to the hotel store and browsed among the shelves, looking at biscuits.

'There's Pringles here and Ritz,' Lisa called out from the other side of the shelves, 'or do you want these Jacob's Fruit and Nut Shortcake?'

I looked up, trying to work out which biscuits I wanted to take with us, and as I did so someone walked past me carrying a copy of the *New Straits Times*, heading towards the cash till. He had folded it in half, but out of the corner of my eye I saw the thick black headline: BRITISH MERCHANT BANK COLLAPSE.

Suddenly I couldn't care less which kind of biscuits we bought. Lisa was still chatting away, but I was too stunned to move.

'Lisa,' I whispered, 'buy that newspaper. I can't read this. Barings is bust.'

As Lisa picked up the paper and started reading the article, which mentioned a missing trader, I was looking out at the hotel. We were in the middle of nowhere, halfway along the north coast of Borneo. We were in a prison. How the hell were we going to get out?

Lisa was going to sign for the biscuits and paper.

'Pay cash,' I said. 'Don't sign anything.'

'Thank you,' smiled the sweetshop attendant, oblivious.

I

The Watford Gap:
From Watford to Barings

I TURNED AROUND FROM the bar, carrying the tin tray of beers, and started squeezing back through the crowd. I had my head down, and was concentrating on not spilling the bottles and inching sideways between the shoulders and elbows in my way, so I only looked up at the last moment. It was the sudden quiet, the space opening up around me which acted as warning. I looked up, with my hands still holding the tray, just in time to see the chair come swinging down from about seven and a half feet up. It was a solid wooden chair, brown with cracking varnish, and it was held by the back. I must have looked surprised, certainly my chin was tilted up at just the right angle. With no hands to protect me, the chair legs hit me smack in the face. My nose burst back into my skull, exploding somewhere behind my eyes. When I tried to yell, my mouth and jaw didn't work. As I collapsed I felt the tray lightening and dropping towards the floor, but I never heard the crash. Loaded with eleven bottles of Grolsch it must have made quite an impressive mess.

As for my friend Pete, he was the lucky one. Considering that he'd started it all, he was outrageously lucky. He told me what had happened as I lay in hospital with my jaw meshed together by something like chicken wire. The bouncers had moved in and formed a line across the dance floor, hurling people away from each other. I was carried along into the wrong half, and a gang of them set into me – which was when my jaw really fell open and began to flap. Pete was also on the wrong side of the line, but when he was kicked up against the wall he happened to fall against a red button which opened the emergency exit, and he fell out through the door among a whole load of dustbins. One or two of them followed him and gave him a couple of kicks, but he scrambled away and went round the front to try to get back in.

'I wanted to pull you out,' he promised me.

I tried to keep a straight face – it hurt too much to smile. Then he'd got in the club, seen me looking rather out of things on the floor, and managed to get one of the bouncers to haul me out, by which time the police had arrived and we were taken to hospital.

Pete took me home at 11 A.M. the next morning. My nose hurt more than my jaw, which was just as huge and numb as if a dentist had been let loose with a builder's drill. I could see my nose through both eyes, which made me feel cross-eyed – a feeling reinforced by both of them beginning to close. I ran a bath and lay in it until I woke up to find it had gone cold. Then I tried to shave in the mirror, which was rather like trying to shave a rotten apple – the razor kept slicing through the soft, puffy skin and the grazes started to bleed again.

Then I put on a clean shirt and suit, took a handful of aspirin and set off for work. At least the bags under my eyes from the hangover were well concealed by the bruising.

'Nick! Are you all right?' Everyone stared at me as if I'd fallen to earth from another planet.

'I'm fine,' I said. 'I was just in a car crash last night. I was in the back, and I butted my head against the front seat and broke my nose and jaw. The guys in the front were much better off; they had seat belts on.'

I WAS working at Morgan Stanley, one of the most successful American banks, where I was on a training course in the Settlements Division for Futures and Options. I was twenty years old, earning £20,000, and I'd just bought my first flat in Watford. My friends couldn't believe it: they were working as plasterers and builders, electricians or plumbers, some of them in shops but most of them out on building sites. The first day I moved into my flat I had a party. We soon realised that I had no cutlery, so we all trooped down to the local Indian restaurant, ate a vast amount of vindaloo and then pocketed handfuls of knives and forks. Lucky it wasn't a Chinese restaurant or I'd have had nothing but chopsticks in my kitchen. Then the lighting blew. Someone found some old lights in a skip outside and rigged them up straight from the mains, so they flashed on and off like a disco.

But at work I was the model employee – nobody knew where I came from or what I did at weekends. I wore my suit and tie and learned fast. The world of futures and options was expanding rapidly, and few people really understood how they worked. Morgan Stanley were one of the key players in the market, and they invested a good deal of time in training the back office staff like me who sorted all the deals out, as well as recruiting the best dealers to go on to the trading floor at LIFFE, the London International Financial Futures and Options Exchange.

I first worked in the City as a school-leaver aged eighteen, when I joined Coutts & Company, bankers to the Queen, in 1985. I worked there for two years, settling all the cheques, but never came across one signed by Charles Windsor. In fact, despite its posh name, Coutts had all the problems of any High Street bank: bounced cheques and wives running up vast overdrafts without telling their husbands. I was lucky to be there: I was told that over three hundred school-leavers had applied for the job, only two people had been asked to interview, and I'd been offered it. But the work became increasingly boring as I simply pushed piles of cheques around the large office and bundled them up to be filed in some vast warehouse.

A friend of mine told me about the job at Morgan Stanley, so I went along for the interview and was offered it immediately. That was in June 1987. I was told I could either work in Foreign Exchange, settling all the bank's foreign exchange dealings, or in the Futures and Options Division, settling rather more complicated deals. I opted for Futures and Options, thereby sealing my own future.

Every morning I took the train to Euston and then the Underground down to Oxford Circus. I left my home life behind me. I sat through the day, sorting out settlement problems, and finally left at around 6 P.M. Often I couldn't get away until 9 P.M., and I'd call home from Euston and my father would drive down to the station and pick me up. He'd go back to whatever he was doing, but I'd call around asking who was going where, and then the fun would start. After spending all day in a shirt and tie, at night I'd often get out there and behave like an animal.

Nobody at Morgan Stanley had any idea what I got up to. One night, after watching a football game, a gang of us crowded into a disco and took all our clothes off. We stood around chatting as if being stark bollock naked was the most natural thing in the world. My friend Pete had the endearing habit of going up to any girl he fancied, pulling his cock out of his trousers and gently slipping it into her hand. He'd done this to a girl who was happily chatting to her tall black boyfriend in a club at Batchwood in St Albans. 'Get out of here,' the boyfriend had warned him, 'you're out of your league.' Undeterred, Pete had stayed, and then I'd agreed to buy the next round of beers. Pete had come to give me a hand, and that was when the chair came down on me and taught us that we really were out of our league. Pete was just annoying – I'd have punched him too if he hadn't been my friend. He definitely deserved being beaten up, I just wasn't quite sure that I deserved having him as a friend.

My mother died a happy woman – she was happy because she'd just heard from the doctor that, with her kind of cancer, she had at least another ten years to live. She said to us, as we sat around her bed that evening, that it meant she'd be able to see the family all married and happily settled with their own children. She told us that the doctor had promised her she'd live to be a grandmother. Victoria was thirteen and Sarah just ten, and she was determined to be there as they grew up. We left her that night and were all so thrilled that she'd be there to look after us. She really made the house tick. She had fought for us all our lives. Even if I'd wanted a silly thing like a Pringle sweater because all my friends at school had one, she'd work some extra overtime and manage to buy it. She made me realise that I could work hard *and* have friends. At school, the class split into swots who worked hard and lads who played football; I managed to be both a swot and a lad, which was unprecedented. I was even made a prefect, which should have alienated me from the lads who hated prefects, but I was still accepted. And the confidence I had to mix with both sides of the class – who were poles apart – came from my mother, who assured me that if I put in the work, the results would look after themselves.

I was at work the next morning when a nurse called me and told me to come to the hospital. My mother had taken a serious turn for the worse.

'Can it wait until this afternoon?'

'No,' the nurse said.

From the tone of her voice I knew I had no time to lose. I dropped everything and caught the Underground to Euston and then the train to Watford. But I was too late; my mother had died. One look at my sisters' scared white faces in the waiting room told me that. She had been put into the morgue, but I wasn't brave enough to go and see her for one last time. I managed to go to the crematorium for her funeral, but I've never been back to where her ashes are buried. I was too scared. I wanted to go back and talk to her, say goodbye properly, but I was frightened that I'd never find the right words. I put it off and put it off, and in the meantime I made a promise to myself – and to my mother – that I would look after the family. I'd do anything to help the girls along.

The one legacy my mother left me was the clear understanding that I was the one person in the family who should push hard to get on in life. She'd pushed me in my exams, she'd helped me type up my application form to Coutts, and she'd always sent me out with ironed shirts and polished shoes when I was at home. As I moved on to Morgan Stanley, I had a clear sense of having to do it all myself. There was no help from my father, who never understood what I was doing or why I set off on an hour's commute to the City all dressed up in a suit and tie every day. My brother Richard left school at the same time as me and started working for my father.

My father retreated into his own little world. He was a plasterer, and I would help him out some weekends when he was busy. But I was aware that I was the eldest child, and that my two sisters were still at school. My family and friends couldn't conceive of the sums of money I was dealing with at work. When I told my friends that I was working for a bank, most of them assumed I would be handing out tenners at the Barclays on Watford High Street. I was learning to move large sums of money around, millions and millions of pounds, sometimes swapping them for dollars or Japanese yen, and making decisions about which bank to deposit them with overnight. So the sums of money I was responsible for were large – and my salary of £20,000, plus a £20,000 bonus, was equally large. It went a long way in Watford.

As I pushed through all the settlements for the futures and options deals, I began to see that the real money was being made by the dealers. I was stuck in the back office, sorting out paperwork, while the dealers who were out there on the trading floor were earning vast salaries and bonuses. My friends in Watford would have been amazed to be earning the £20,000 I was taking home, but my mother had always pushed me higher, and I began to aspire to becoming a trader. Of course, I wasn't alone in this: every self-respecting settlements clerk dreamed of becoming a trader, putting on one of those grotesquely coloured jackets and shouting their heads off in the trading pit. They knew that this was the way to earn a fortune and buy a Porsche. I didn't care about the Porsche so much, but I wanted to do better so I could make money and take care of the family, so I began to plan a route.

At that time the golden boy of the trading floor was James Henderson, who had been hired by Morgan Stanley for a big salary and was doing a lot of business. I studied his dealing slips as they came through to me, and I spoke to him on the phone a couple of times to clear up some discrepancies. I managed to have lunch with him one day, and he mentioned that things were so busy he needed a runner to do all the stuff which was too menial for him. I was earning my £20,000, but I was prepared to take a salary cut to get this job because I knew that once I was on the floor I'd soon start making myself more than useful. I asked if I could have the job, and he agreed. I was delighted. Although it only paid around £15,000, it was the first step on the ladder, and I'd be able to see how the dealers really worked. But my boss refused to let me go. He told me I'd have to stay in the Settlements Division for three months. When I said this to James, he insisted he needed someone now. My boss wouldn't budge, and the job went to someone else.

That afternoon, Friday 16 June 1989, I resigned from Morgan Stanley, called a headhunter and asked what jobs he had available. He told me that Baring Securities were looking for someone for their Settlements Division. He went on to say that Barings was a small merchant bank, the oldest in the world, highly respected and so on. He arranged an interview with Barings for that evening, so I went along past the Bank of England to their Portsoken Street offices and had a half-hour's chat with a charming, quietly-spoken man called John Guy, who offered me the job.

After a weekend with Pete, in which he excelled himself by walking up behind a girl who was sitting down and calmly placing his cock on top of her head, I worked out my month's notice at Morgan Stanley and reported for my first day's work at Barings on Monday 10 July 1989.

2

Barings Bank

BARINGS BANK WAS FOUNDED in the City of London by Sir Francis Baring in 1763. It was the world's first 'merchant bank', a bank which provides both finance and advice for its clients, but will also trade on its own account as a 'merchant' – taking risks by buying or selling stock or land or coffee like any other trader. Flexible and innovative in their ideas for financing trade, Barings soon became internationally successful. It would look at any proposal, whether it was for extracting copper from the Congo, trading wool from Australia, or funding the construction of the Panama Canal. Since it was not a High Street bank, where thousands of people deposited their funds, Barings had just a small capital base, so it had to live and thrive on its wits.

When I arrived in 1989, Barings still operated in exactly the same way. Staff were now issued with security passes, and there were some green flickering Reuters screens giving instant share prices on every stock market across the world, but Barings' principles seemed to have stayed pretty much the same.

The head office was decorated with old share certificates of previous ventures, framed on the walls. They were large, engraved documents of maroon and green, with pictures of steam trains and men in top hats, and had wavy watermarks down one side. I was told how, in 1803, Barings had financed the purchase from France by the fledgling United States of America of the southern State of Louisiana, among others. The cash-flow calculations were all based on cotton prices and the impact of the abolition of slavery. Alongside its great Jewish rival, Rothschilds, Barings was first choice as financial adviser and banker for governments, large companies and wealthy clients. In 1886 Barings floated Guinness on the London Stock Exchange, an issue which proved so popular that mounted police had to be summoned to stop the crowds from invading Barings with their application forms. It must have been a scene rather like the offer for sale of British Telecom in the 1980s, when the same kind of people queued up for hours to buy a few shares and 'stag' the issue – sell them the next day for double the price.

By the turn of the century Barings had become banker to the royal family, and in their time members of the Baring family have received five separate hereditary peerages as rewards for their services to banking. I was told that this is a record for any family. It certainly beat mine. Although I wasn't that interested in who or what Barings was – it was just the next job for me – I did find out some of its history. It was hard not to when it was drummed into you every time you walked along any corridor to the Gents.

When I joined Barings the senior peer of the family

was Lord Ashburton, who was just about to retire as Chairman. He was a great friend of Margaret Thatcher, and left Barings to become Chairman of BP, Britain's largest company and one of the twenty largest companies in the world. The other Barings peers who have married across the length and breadth of Debrett's include Lord Northbrook, whose ancestor, the first Earl of Northbrook, was Governor of India and First Lord of the Admiralty under Gladstone; Lord Revelstoke; Lord Cromer, whose grandfather was Consul of Egypt and whose father was Governor of the Bank of England and British ambassador to Washington during the Nixon years; and finally Lord Howick, whose father was the last colonial Governor of Kenya and who established the great Baring Charitable Foundation, which ultimately controlled Barings and gave vast sums of money to charity.

I would walk up the stairs and see all these family portraits staring serenely into space above my head. They had the faraway look of men who had seen the world, bought what they wished of it, and were content to rule their far-flung empires from a calm distance. They needn't muddy their hands any more. They had people like me, Nick Leeson, twenty-two years old and up from Watford, to do it for them. That was fine by me – I was prepared to get stuck in and earn myself a good living from them.

I started off in the same department I'd been in at Morgan Stanley, working in the Settlements Division for Futures and Options. I'd only been there nine months before I realised my prospects in London were limited. I was tucked away in the division, reporting to a boss who was very senior, and I could see that I would have to wait for ten years to inherit his job. I rapidly became completely bored and asked for a transfer.

One of Barings' most spectacular successes in the 1980s was the operation set up by Christopher Heath to trade stocks and shares in Japan. Barings had carved out a wonderful position there just as the Japanese Stock Market started to boom. Throughout the 1980s Heath was celebrated as the highest-paid banker in Britain, with a salary of something like £3 million. Nobody knew exactly how much he was earning, but we all knew that it was a huge amount – and it all came from the dealing he was doing in the Far East. Japan had been where he'd started, but there was also amazing business going on in Hong Kong, Singapore, Indonesia and all the other Asian countries. People described them as the 'tiger' economies, and we all looked across to the Far East as an exotic place to work; a fast, racy place to make a fortune, where the bars offered cheap cold beer and James Bond women.

So I jumped at the chance to go and work in Indonesia, but when I arrived in Jakarta I found that the realities of Barings' overseas operations were very different from their appearance. While I had read in Barings' glossy literature all about their innovative approach to doing business in the Far East, and how they had unique experience and a valuable customer base, I found that actually it was in a complete mess. The bank didn't even have an office in Jakarta: we were working out of a room in the Hotel Borubudur. Barings were sitting on £100 million worth of share certificates, which they couldn't pass on to the customers and claim the money because the certificates were in chaos. Nobody at Barings knew how to sort them out. They were stacked up any which way in a basement strong room in the vaults of the Standard Chartered and Hong Kong and Shanghai banks. I took my first look at this mountain of bearer bonds – which could be cashed immediately if anyone walked off with them – and realised there was one hell of a job to be done.

Christopher Heath may have been earning his £3 million, and Barings may have won all the accolades for breaking into the Asian market, but beneath this impressive veneer the reality of Barings was shoddy and inefficient: the bank was sitting on a £100 million hole in their balance sheet. If the auditors had been strict, they would have classified this shortfall as a liability – and possibly one which should be written off as unrecoverable. This would have been a disaster for Barings' balance sheet. It would have thrown all their ratios awry and severely limited their ability to lend money – effectively limiting their ability to act as bankers.

I worked in that airless, windowless dungeon for ten months, sorting out the chaos of Barings' unclaimed share certificates. It was the toughest job I've ever done. The problem Barings had was that they'd sold shares to customers, bought in equal numbers to balance the trade, but then accepted share certificates which didn't match. Since the stock market had fallen in 1989, the people who had bought the shares weren't particularly keen to pay for them – and they were using all sorts of excuses not to hand over any cash. Their main excuse was that the share certificates were either in the wrong denomination, unacceptably tatty or not properly documented: all of which was true.

Each day I made tiny inroads into the vast mountain of paper. I worked out which trades each bank had done with Barings, found the right certificates, worked out what documentation was needed to go with them, and then walked round to the banks and demanded payment. I carried the share certificates in a kit bag, and if anyone had mugged me they would have picked up several million pounds' worth of eminently cashable certificates. The Indonesian certificates are all bearer bonds – the equivalent of a blank cheque – so they are of value to whoever happens to have them in their hands. If I'd felt so inclined, I could have slipped off to South America with a bundle and need never have worked again.

I had spent a month in Hong Kong on my way out to Jakarta, and although everyone had told me that Hong Kong was a great city, I hated it in comparison with Jakarta. I found myself in the Jockey Bar, where everyone in Hong Kong goes, and saw a whole bunch of brokers and bankers who thought they were God's gift to the world. They stood around giving their opinions on everything as if they owned the place. They all had incredible egos, with little justification. But Jakarta was wonderful: there were no pompous ex-colonials who assumed they'd been born to rule the world; just a bunch of Indonesians in bars, who played pool and drank beer and got on with life.

At first Barings warned me about leaving my hotel, and insisted that their driver pick me up in the air-conditioned car so my feet hardly touched the ground. But then I realised I wasn't going to be murdered if I stepped outside, and wandered off on my own until I found all sorts of places which were just like Watford. We played 'Winner Stays On' on the pool table, and I'd be there until three in the morning trying to hold off a couple of the locals, who had clearly played as much pool as me and were determined not to be beaten by a fresh white face.

I'd been in Jakarta for about three months when Barings sent some people to help me out. I didn't think much about this, but when I next walked into the basement strong room I found a beautiful blonde girl staring at the piles of share certificates with wide-eyed astonishment.

'What the hell are we meant to do with these?' she asked. 'Build a bonfire?'

'I'm halfway through them,' I told her. 'You should have seen them when I arrived.'

Her name was Lisa Sims. She was from Kent, and this was her first posting overseas. I've always prided myself on being able to hide my feelings, but Lisa took me completely by surprise.

By Christmas 1990 we had reduced Barings' exposure in Jakarta to £10 million, and when the auditors came round they agreed that Barings need not make any provision in its balance sheet for this liability. The £100 million hole which had been stuck in the bank vaults could now be wiped off the computer. No doubt Christopher Heath was paid another million for doing so well, but Lisa and I didn't care. We had done a good job, and we were in love.

I returned to London in March 1991, and from then on was seen as the settlements expert in futures and options. I had patience and stamina, I applied painstaking logic, and I knew that in the end I could sort out any problem. I got my head down and stuck to it, and I wasn't afraid of asking the most stupid questions. People at the London end of Barings were all so know-all that nobody dared ask a stupid question in case they looked silly in front of everyone else. I always found that the most basic, obvious questions are the ones which are most difficult to answer, and which normally bring out the crucial piece of missing knowledge.

Throughout 1991 I travelled on Barings' expense account looking at their fledgling operations in Europe and the Far East. I accompanied the Development Officer, Tony Dickel, around the world as Barings looked to exploit new opportunities. We visited Frankfurt, where we suggested that Barings should expand their office to plug into the growing European business; then Hong Kong and Manila, and late in the year we went to have a look at the Singapore operation.

Barings had acquired a seat on the Singapore International Monetary Exchange – SIMEX – but had not activated it. The Barings subsidiary had an office staff of around seventy, and they did all the usual things like buying and selling Singaporean shares, researching the local markets and offering fund management and banking facilities, but they had no ability to deal in futures. Any requests which came to them to buy or sell futures or options had to be brokered through another trader, so Barings lost the opportunity to charge that commission. Tony Dickel and I advised Barings that they should activate the trading seat and staff up in order to take advantage of the growing business there. After my success in Jakarta, I'd been promised that I could look out for a post that suited me. Tony Dickel and I discussed the Singapore operation throughout January and February 1992, and I mentioned that I'd like to be involved. He spoke to James Bax, Regional Manager of Barings South Asia, who had heard of my success in Jakarta. In March, Tony Dickel finally came back and said that not only did the powers-that-be really want me, but they probably wouldn't go ahead without me. They wanted me to set the operation up and run it. I was to be the General Manager: recruit traders and back office staff and make money. Lisa and I were thrilled. The news of our transfer to Singapore came through in March, ten days before our wedding.

I DIDN'T know what to expect. Everyone was sitting down chatting behind me until the hubbub abruptly fell to that absolute silence which heralded her arrival. Then my cousin John took a signal from someone at the door and bent down over the organ. I hardly heard the music, I just stood up with the congregation and waited. Before she'd reached halfway I couldn't bear it any longer: I looked over my shoulder and saw Lisa coming up the aisle with her father Alec. She hardly seemed to be walking, she was just gently drifting towards me, leaning on Alec's arm and staring straight ahead. I almost fainted – she looked gorgeous. I couldn't take in the details of her dress, but it was a vast ivory-coloured silk number, which floated around her, pushing forward with each pace. As she came closer I felt as if a force-field was approaching me, pushing me back. I stopped breathing completely, and then had to remember to take a deep breath as the blood drained from my head.

Lisa stood beside me, and I looked through her veil into her eyes. We must both have been frightened. I loved her so much I hardly dared smile at her. She looked beautiful and pale and fragile, like a porcelain figure. Then the bright white March sun shone through the high windows behind me, and a broad shaft fell straight on to Lisa and lit up her face. She smiled, and I saw the blood in her cheeks. I noticed that among all the folds of ivory silk she was holding a bouquet of strong colours, red and yellow freesias, and she had more freesias in her hair. That was so typical of Lisa, I thought, to combine the soft ethereal colour of her wedding dress with some strong, real colours. Behind her I could see her bridesmaids, her sister Nadene, my sister Sarah, and the two little ones, Rachel and Nina, wearing bottle-green velvet tops with white lace ruffs and tartan skirts.

We turned to the vicar. I was so intensely aware of Lisa beside me that I hardly heard him as he welcomed us and started the first hymn. Since it was Lent, we had been unable to decorate the church with flowers and the choir stalls were empty. But the early spring sun shone down on Lisa, and the scent of her bouquet and the flowers in her hair filled the tiny whitewashed church.

Afterwards we stood outside, with the wind blowing at the ladies' hats and almost making off with Alec's topper. Everyone was laughing, simultaneously trying to hold on to their hats or keep their skirts from billowing up. Our cousin opened up his stainless steel camera case, which was fitted with built-in holes for lenses, and offered it to us: instead of lenses it held little orange jellies made with vodka.

Confetti flew in our faces in clouds, and I could see Lisa's mum Patsy dishing out handfuls to everyone from her handbag, giggling and crying at the same time. Finally we made our way down the gravel path outside the church, past the graveyard and under the tall chestnut tree which was just coming into bloom, with white flowers like ice-cream cones dancing in the wind among its lime-green leaves. We stopped for more pictures and then climbed into the old Rolls-Royce. It was a magnificent car, with a deep leather seat, and Lisa and I sat facing back out of the window as everyone waved and cheered and·held on to their hats, and lit cigarettes and whistled, and stuffed the wedding sheet into their handbags and took pictures and ran alongside for a few steps, until finally we drove out into the road and left them behind.

The chauffeur was a huge man with a snowy white beard and the turn of phrase of Ernest Hemingway. 'Congratulations,' was all he said.

Lisa and I looked at each other, and held up our left hands so our brand-new gold wedding rings shone together.

'Hello, Mrs Leeson.'

'Hello there. Enjoying yourself?'

'Not a bad way to spend the day, nice little drive around the countryside.'

And then I leaned over to kiss her, afraid to touch her

hair because it was so beautifully piled up, but her lips met mine and I smelled the freesias in her hair and I knew that nothing could ever beat this feeling. And nothing would ever take it away from us.

'First pint's on Alec!' Uncle John roared as we stood for the photographs. Lisa was smiling and laughing and looked utterly at home in her dress. How do women do it? A morning suit's one thing, because men wear them to weddings all the time; but brides wear their dress only once, a huge great dress like a ball gown, and they're completely at home in it.

We walked up the lawn to the hotel, a red-brick Georgian place near Brands Hatch, and went into the ballroom. While I had expected to remember only the wedding reception, in fact the whole afternoon and evening became a blur and I found it was the church service which stuck in my mind. Even as I chatted to everyone, I was aware that Lisa and I had stood beside each other in the church and passed the most intense moment of our lives together, and while I loved everyone at the reception, I adored Lisa. By making our vows public, we had now forged a secret private relationship which nobody would ever break or understand.

Alec and Patsy are the best hosts in the world, and at our wedding they excelled themselves.

'I've mixed feelings about losing my daughter,' admitted Alec in his speech, 'but at least she's found her prince.' He went on to announce that we would be leaving to live in Singapore for 'between six months and two years', and everyone was silent for a moment. I looked around at all our family and friends. We would miss them. We'd be back, but I knew our lives were going to be separate for a long time.

When I stood up, all I had to say was the opening words of my speech – 'My wife and I' – and everyone burst out clapping and cheering. Lisa had that effect on people.

After the speeches, Alec's friend John got on to the keyboards and started singing 'I Just Called To Say I Love You', and as Lisa and I stepped out on to the dance floor, everyone joined in singing: 'We just called to say we love you!' After two choruses the dance floor was packed, and it stayed that way until well after midnight.

The only casualty was the husband of one of our friends from Barings.

'How are you enjoying yourself?' Lisa asked him.

'Better than *my* wedding,' he said, in full earshot of his wife, a larger-than-life lady who steamed towards him and pretended to punch him. Unfortunately she misjudged the distance and hit him smack in the face. He fell like an ox, and two men had to carry him out to a bedroom to recover.

The next day we drove up to Victoria and caught the Orient Express to Venice, where we spent three days at the Cipriani. We wandered around Venice and got wonderfully lost in the tiny jumbled back streets, coming out unexpectedly into massive paved squares with pink houses and towering churches, where we put coins into the picture lights to illuminate the dark Tintorettos and Bellinis and reveal their stunning reds and blues. We drank cappuccinos in St Mark's Square and then cuddled up to each other out of the chilly March wind as the hotel vaporetto took us back across the water.

A week later we left our winter coats behind and flew to Singapore.

3

Singapore

WHEN I FIRST STEPPED out on to the trading floor, I could smell and see the money. Throughout my time at Barings I had been inching closer and closer to it, and in Singapore I was suddenly there. I'd been working in various back offices for almost six years, pushing paper money around, sorting out other people's problems. Now, out on the trading floor, I could work with instant money – it was hanging in the air right in front of me, invisible but highly charged, just waiting to be earthed. As I watched the traders all screaming at each other in their red jackets, I imagined an electrical thunderstorm. There was lightning in the air, and all I had to do was give the right signals and it would charge through me as if I were a copper conductor.

'Anything happening?' I asked Fernando, the Californian whizzkid who dealt in Nikkei futures in Tokyo. He spoke so fast that none of my Singaporean team could understand a word he said.

'Nothing.'

'It's dead here as well. Nobody's playing.'

We waited and watched. In front of me the screens were still. Luminous green figures, pulsing slightly, but unchanging. The market could lurch any which way at any time. I was learning to look three seconds ahead at best. George Seow, the first trader I had recruited, was signalling a price of 18,590. I had to watch his hands carefully. We were a new team, and I was just picking up on the crazy hand signals traders use, like bookies at the racecourse indicating betting prices. We were watching the September futures contracts on the Nikkei 225 index, which is calculated from the fluctuating value of an underlying 'basket' of shares – rather like the Dow-Jones index or the 'Footsie' 100.

Futures contracts enable you – for the cost of a small 'margin' payment up front – to buy or sell this basket of shares at a given price in the future, typically anchored around four dates: the ends of March, June, September and December. Given the uncertainty of future prices, the value can move around wildly as people take different views about how the Nikkei share index itself might trade. The futures contracts and the index move in broadly similar lines, but the time gap and the leverage in the futures market means that the futures are far more volatile than the share index itself.

'Five-ninety and trading small,' I told Fernando. This meant 18,590, but we didn't have time to stand on ceremony so we never bothered saying how many thousands it was.

'Six hundred and thin too.'

We had just set up shop in SIMEX, and I had no authority to trade myself – I was just there to fill Fernando's orders from Tokyo. I would take his orders

46

down the phone, signal them to George, and tell
Fernando whether we'd completed them. The deals were
very simple. We were doing something called 'arbitraging': Fernando would watch the futures contract in
Osaka, centre for Nikkei futures trading, and I would
tell him every two seconds what was going on in
Singapore. Sometimes a local trader would be buying in
one market without the ability to trade in the other, and
he might have to fill an order which pushed up the
whole market price in SIMEX. For a few seconds a difference would open up between the Osaka and
Singapore prices, and that's when we went into action.

'Where's Daiwa? Aren't they long?'

'Daiwa's long, I'm sure. They've been trying to ramp
it all day to get out.' Your position is called 'long' if
you've bought in the hope that prices will rise, enabling
you to sell at a profit later on. Similarly, being 'short'
usually means that you've sold in the expectation of a
price fall, which will enable you to buy back at a cheaper
price.

George signalled 18,580 from the pit, which con-
trasted with the Osaka screen price of 18,600 for a
couple of seconds.

'Five-eighty here,' I told Fernando. 'There's a seller
out there and he wants to deal in size. He's coming.
Shall I low-tick him?'

Many traders have set limits on the profit or loss they
can take during a day. If the market moves a certain
distance from their entry price – say for example they'd
bought at 18,700 and the market fell to 18,600 – then
they might reach this limit and be forced to sell to cut
their losses. This is called a 'stop loss'. By 'low-ticking'

someone, I was going to give a new price to the market and push it in a new direction – in this case downwards. I was trying to flush out the market to see if there was a stop-loss seller, since as soon as my offer was made in the pit and put up on the screen, the market would see it and it might trigger just such a sale.

'Yeah, flush him out,' Fernando said. 'Squeeze the fucker. Get ready to pick up the pieces.'

'How many?'

'Two hundred. And at best. Buy them . . . *now!*'

I signalled the price of 18,580 to George and then moved two fingers to the side of my body, signalling 200, the quantity, with my palm facing towards me to indicate a buy. I flicked my ear to tell George that he had a tick discretion on the price.

George spun round and spreadeagled his arms, shouting into the pit. I heard him shout once, then the red jackets were straight on to him, screaming and yelling and tearing him to pieces. Sure enough he'd forced a seller's hand. He was in and out and then spun round and nodded to me, scribbling down the deal on a trading card and then waiting again.

'OK,' I told Fernando. 'Bought 200 at 580.'

'Cheers, Nick, I've sold at 590.'

We had sold in Osaka and bought the same contracts in Singapore for a £16,000 profit. And the risk? Two and a half seconds before, the market would have seen us coming like a big red London bus and moved up. Even as I looked back to George, he was signalling 590.

SIMEX is a much smaller market than Osaka, so sometimes a local dealer who only has authority to trade in SIMEX will push the Nikkei index around the

SIMEX pit, and the same contracts might have different prices in SIMEX from those quoted on the Osaka exchange in Japan. SIMEX is also a proper market, in the sense that everything is 'open outcry' – there are only real buyers and real sellers. In Osaka, bids and offers are put on screens and the market moves in a different way. You can put all sorts of bids and offers on the screen which change the way dealers think the market might move – and this could be different from the underlying direction as represented by the 'real' deals in SIMEX. The dealers in SIMEX could see the latest prices in Osaka, but they couldn't see the size of the orders. But I could put up prices in Osaka, which made it look as if the market was moving in one direction, and then do the opposite in SIMEX, where there was a real market operating in real time with real buyers and sellers. So if the market was trading at, say, 560 in SIMEX, and I put in 500 contracts offered at 570, 500 at 580 and 500 at 590, nobody would buy them. I'd effectively be telling the market that it wasn't going up because it was top-heavy with all those sell orders sitting above it in Japan. So people would sell, and I'd wait until the market had traded down a while, start to buy and then remove my previous sell orders from the screen. The market would start to trade higher now that the pressure was removed, and I'd sell at the higher price and make a profit. It was a game of muscle, and if Barings did big volume we'd be able to move the markets, and by sitting on the fence looking into both markets we could dive in and out at will – so long as we were fast. Very fast. But we'd done it. And it was only 8:55 A.M.

* * *

ARBITRAGING futures and options is, technically, a low-risk business. The only real risk is in the split seconds it takes for Fernando to tell me what he wants to do, and for me to tell George and for George to do it. This is a real risk, however, since somebody else might be doing exactly the same and get there first. If this happened, then the price would move against us and we'd be 'hung'; we'd have to accept a worse price and make a smaller profit – or even a loss.

It was frantic work, and the profit margins were small. You only make a fortune by taking a long-term view on something – perhaps for a morning or a whole day. Generally not overnight because so many things can go wrong for you overnight: presidents can be assassinated; crops ruined by hailstorms; earthquakes can erupt. Very few traders have the authority to hold a position overnight, since the profits can be huge, but so can the losses. When the market moves up or down 1,000 points a day, the downside can wipe you out. Of course, a big investor like Warren Buffet makes all his money on long-term investments, and any fund manager will always point to ten-year performance charts, but then a lot of other big investors, like George Soros, make most of their money on a two- or three-day punt: and the beauty of it is that it's instant profit. Plus – if you're a dealer – it all goes into the pot for your bonus.

When you make your own decisions about when to buy and sell, it's called 'proprietary trading'. I wanted to move into proprietary trading, but for the first year I was content to be an order-filler for Fernando in Tokyo and our Singapore clients. It is a stressful job, since you have to balance all the trades and ensure that you do not take any risk on to your own book, but you do not have the stress of running a large position, of taking a gamble. That can give you sleepless nights and burn you out. I wanted to build up to doing that.

I'd hired two traders, George Seow and Maslan Tuladi, to operate on the floor; Eric Chang to help me on the telephone; and Risselle Sng and Norhaslinda (Linda) Hassan to handle the settlements in the back office. Since I hadn't taken the exams at that time, I had no authority to trade on the SIMEX floor itself. But I was in charge of the entire team, and I was determined that we were going to be the best.

Throughout 1992 the customers rolled in. When I first arrived in Singapore, SIMEX was only doing a daily total of some 4,000 trades. It was a tiny exchange. Most of the big dealers dealt the Nikkei in Osaka because they could buy and sell in size. Then, during the summer of 1992, just as I was getting going, an amazing surge in business happened. Osaka imposed various stringent regulations on the futures and options dealers: they had to pay much higher deposits when they dealt, and there was no interest earned on these deposits – the interest was just pocketed by the Osaka authorities. A minimum commission was also stipulated.

The Osaka authorities made a bad misjudgement: within weeks the trade started to move to Singapore, and soon my telephone was flashing non-stop from 8:00 in the morning until 2:15 in the afternoon, when the bell rang for the close of trading. In between these times the number of contracts traded rose from 4,000 a day to over 20,000 a day, and I was taking my share of the orders without stopping, flashing them to George or Maslan, and then picking up the next call almost before they'd gone into the pit. After 2:15 the chaos had to be sorted out. I'd walk the two hundred yards from SIMEX across the plaza to the Barings offices and start working through all the dealing slips to reconcile every trade. Everyone else would leave me, and I'd be there until well past midnight checking the trades. It was as chaotic as the mess in Jakarta, but I knew that I could get through it. It was just a case of keeping your head down and sorting it out. After my training at Morgan Stanley, I was one of the very few people who understood how futures and options should be settled, and how much money would have to be paid across to the exchange as our clients' positions either moved with or against the market.

In any dealing system there are errors: someone misunderstands a hand signal and buys the wrong amount, or buys at the wrong price, or thinks they have discretion when they don't, or buys the March contract rather than the September one, or even buys rather than sells. If this happens, the bank has to take the loss. The customer has bought or sold in good faith, and will have gone on to trade on the back of that first deal. If it was our mistake, we had to try and rectify it. If there was nothing to be done, the error was booked into a separate computer account known as the 'Error Account', the position closed off and the resulting loss – or sometimes gain – written off against the firm's profit.

When we started dealing we had an Error Account numbered 99905, into which we dumped all the errors before they were transferred over to London. Then I got a telephone call from Gordon Bowser, who was in charge of all Barings' derivatives settlements.

'Can you set up another Error Account and keep them all in Singapore? We don't want to be bothered with all these tiny errors you're clocking up. There's over fifty a day, and so there are a hundred entries needed to reverse them. The auditors will start asking questions.'

I put the phone down and turned to Risselle.

'Can you create another file?' I asked her. 'We need another Error Account.'

'Sure,' she said, clearing her screen and tapping keys. 'It's all ready. What number do you want to give it?'

'What's your lucky number?' I asked.

'Eight,' she said. 'Eight is a very lucky Chinese number.'

'How many numbers does it have to be?'

'Five.'

'There you are then,' I said. 'Let's give it all the luck it can handle. Let's call it 88888.'

And so Error Account 88888 was born – the 'Five Eights' account.

After a few weeks London called again.

'We'd better go back to where we were,' Gordon said. 'Book all your errors straight through to us. We have a new computer system which can handle it. And by the way, why do you make so many errors?'

'If you saw the floor here, you'd understand,' I told him. 'It's utter chaos, but the business is good.'

Error Account 88888 became dormant almost as soon as it had been created. But it was still lodged in the computer, it had still been created as a bona fide error account, and not much later I dug it out of my memory and out of the computer.

* * *

It was a Friday, 17 July, and everyone wanted to leave the office. We'd all been invited to a meal at the Hard Rock Café by the United Overseas Bank, and we were dying for some cold beer. The air conditioning in SIMEX had been broken all afternoon, and we'd been working with our ties halfway down our necks. Everyone was sweaty and the telephones were ringing non-stop. I was particularly bothered because I'd been trying to keep my eye on Kim Wong, whom I'd just recruited to work alongside me and Eric on the phones. I was so busy signalling to George or Maslan that I could hardly see her. But she seemed to be coping well.

When the bell rang at 2:15, there was a huge cheer. The market had soared by 400 points, we'd all done good business, we'd all made good commissions. And now we could get the hell off the trading floor. Back at the office, I was confronted by piles and piles of trading slips. By six o'clock I was halfway through them, but then I got stuck. I couldn't work it out: there was one slip – a sale note for twenty contracts – and I couldn't see the balancing purchase. If this was a mistake, we were miles off beam. I looked at the initials on the slip: it was Kim Wong.

I re-counted all the slips. By eight o'clock it had dawned on me that Kim had made a big mistake. In direct contravention of the customer's orders, she had *sold* rather than bought the twenty contracts. The client would expect to have bought these contracts, and we would have to make them good to him. Since the market had risen throughout the afternoon, Barings had sold well below the market level. In fact, I calculated, if we had to make the client good and also reverse the wrong deal which Kim had done on the exchange, we'd have to buy back forty contracts – and lose £20,000 doing so.

I buried my head in my hands for a minute. Shit, shit, shit, I swore, the bloody stupid fucking cow. How could she have done it? But then I slumped back in my chair and looked around the empty office and all the empty black swivel chairs and thought back over the day: it had been a madhouse. Nobody could have known what they were doing. It was all Simon Jones' fault, I swore, and Mike Killian's in Tokyo: the mean tight-fisted bastards wouldn't let me employ anyone. They wanted to keep our costs down to the bone; Simon Jones had hired this girl on a salary of £4,000 a year. It was disgusting, and all so he could look after the bottom line. Everyone else I'd wanted to employ had been turned down, either because they cost too much or because the sales people didn't think the surge in volume would continue.

I pushed myself away from my desk and took the contract note up to Simon Jones' office. He was just on his way out.

'Simon,' I said, leaning against his door frame, 'we've been hung in a big way today. The new girl's left us forty contracts out. It's too big and too late to ring around.'

'What's the damage?' Simon shuffled some papers into his briefcase and made to go.

'Twenty thousand at the close of business.'

'Sack the cow.' He slammed his briefcase shut. 'She'll never work on SIMEX again.'

'It was hell out there,' I said savagely, hoping my tone of voice would make him back off Kim.

'It's busy, I know,' Simon replied, changing tack. 'Look, I've got to fly. Why don't you write to Bayliss about it?' Andrew Bayliss was Deputy Chairman of Baring Securities Limited (BSL).

'OK.' I turned on my heel and left him.

I was in a blind fury when I arrived at the Hard Rock Café. It was an impossible situation: I was meant to be carrying out all this business, with a tiny team who had no experience, because Barings were too mean to pay the going rate to employ decent people. All for the sake of a £4,000 salary rather than £4,500, or even £5,000, we had a £20,000 loss. And this could double in seconds if the market opened higher on Monday morning. I wasn't authorised to hold even an overnight position – and this was now a *weekend* position.

I walked into the restaurant set upon bawling Kim out and telling her to fuck off out of there so I could get drunk. But as I stormed across the floor I almost collided with a tiny girl hurrying across towards me in tears. Kim had her head down and could barely see where she was going because she was crying so much. I hardly recognised her.

'Nick, I'm so sorry about that trade,' she said. 'I just lost my head and got confused by everything.'

'It's fine,' I told her, feeling wretchedly guilty that I'd even been thinking of shouting at her. 'We've all made mistakes, and much worse than that. I'll just book it into an error account and nobody will mind. They won't even see it.'

'I'm so sorry,' she blurted out in hoarse tears again. 'I've been waiting for you while everyone else has been having a good time. I'm going home now.'

She shot out of the door. I looked across the restaurant to where the Barings crowd were indeed having a good time. Five or six of them were dancing on the tables, and everyone was singing along to the Stones' 'Get Off Of My Cloud'.

'I said hey, hey, you, you, get offa my cloud!'

Lisa was sitting with George. I loosened my tie and walked over to the table.

'Have a beer, shithead!' George shouted. I picked up an icy Tiger beer and gratefully swigged it back.

'Did you see Kim?' George asked. 'She was looking for you.'

'She found me.'

'Hi, darling,' Lisa said as she came over to kiss me. 'Everything all right?'

'Fine.' I reached for another beer. 'Everything's just fine.'

The music changed.

'Hi, ho, silver lining!' roared the crowd on the tables. There was a splintering crash of broken glass and howls of laughter.

I ordered a hamburger and thought of Kim Wong sitting on the bus on her way home. She lived with her parents on the far side of the city. It wouldn't be easy for her to find another job on SIMEX with just one week at Barings on her CV. And if she lived with her parents, she'd be bringing in money which they needed – even on £4,000 a year. She certainly wouldn't blow £50 on an evening at the Hard Rock Café.

THE next Monday Kim Wong didn't show up for work.

The phones started ringing, and I hadn't a moment to write to Andrew Bayliss. Barings were still out by forty contracts. The Nikkei didn't move much either way; the loss was still £20,000. I had the ticket in my pocket, and at the end of the day I went up to Risselle.

'I need to put this error into the Five Eights account. Can you do it for me?'

'Sure.' She cleared her screen and pulled up Account 88888. 'What's the deal?'

'Twenty March contracts on the Nikkei.'

'There it is,' Risselle smiled at me. 'No problem.'

So I booked a fictitious trade to the customer, Fuji Bank, for the twenty contracts they'd bought. To do this I made a notation on the daily trade sheet that Fuji needed to be made good for the twenty Nikkei contracts at the price they'd specified. From the daily trade sheet this trade would be booked into the computer in the normal course of business, so when Risselle keyed in the trade it would reconcile with the daily trade sheet. However, if it was left at that, it would obviously cause a problem since we hadn't actually *done* the trade in question, so I also had to book the opposite, reconciling part of that trade: I asked Risselle to enter a *sale* of twenty contracts into the computer as well, booked to Error Account 88888.

The position after Kim's mistake was that Fuji had sold twenty Nikkei contracts. The position after my entries to the daily trade sheet was that history had been rewritten – Fuji had now fictitiously *bought* twenty contracts at the original price they wanted; Error Account 88888 had sold the same twenty contracts at the same price to balance that, and the real sale of the contracts, which Kim had done, was booked to 88888 as well. Thus Fuji's twenty-contract sale had switched to a twenty-contract buy, and the error account had absorbed the discrepancy, making it short of forty lots. This rewriting of the trades was invisible to SIMEX because the original sale was now in the 88888 account, so that tallied with their records. There was also no price difference on the fictitious buy and sell trades since they were done at the same price and cancelled each other out. I had had to put forty contracts into 88888 in order to crystallise the initial loss.

It was a neat solution, and bought me a little breathing-space to think how best to deal with the problem. I was desperately short of time, and even more so when Kim told me that she couldn't cope with SIMEX and left Barings at the end of the week.

'Great,' I cursed her again. 'I need never have hidden those forty contracts. She could have been sacked and that would have been that.'

'You can't keep staff any longer than me,' Simon Jones joked when he heard about Kim's departure. 'They just can't stand the pace here.'

He couldn't care less. He'd lost about half a dozen secretaries in the last year.

'Have you made that customer good?'

'Yes.' I left it at that.

Simon Jones didn't want to know specifics. I've never dealt in equities, but friends of mine have pointed out that you can't make the customer good by simply admitting your mistake, giving him the stock at a higher price and reimbursing him with the cash, because he puts the contract note straight into his computer and starts running his tax calculations from that price. Also the track record of his portfolio is reviewed as performing from that price. If you supply a contract at a *different* price, it throws all these calculations off beam, and also messes up his calculations about how to hedge (effectively, bet the other way to protect his exposure) – which he would have done on the back of the original price he told us to deal at. And then of course it is also thoroughly unprofessional to go back to the client, cap in hand, and admit to some crass mistake. So, for all these reasons, it was widespread practice to conjure up fictitious deals if an error took place, and then solve the problem internally. It happens every day in the broking world.

I turned my mind to solving this problem. It was too big for me to put into the London error account, and I'd been too slow to take responsibility for it. It was horrible. Kim's mistake had suddenly blown up in my face to become my problem. If I'd only discovered it at 5 P.M. on Friday, I could have discussed it more rationally with Simon Jones, or called Japan to see if they could help me, or just come clean and told London about it. But I'd told nobody. I'd hidden it.

WHEN you're working in futures, you have to make daily cash payments to SIMEX if your trades go against you. These cash payments are called 'variation margin payments' or 'mark-to-market payments'. Each day SIMEX makes a running calculation on the value of the futures you've bought or sold, and if the current price has moved away from your traded price, you have to pay up, and the cash you pay is passed on by SIMEX to the clearing houses that have made money. Conversely, if the price goes with you, you receive a cash payment via SIMEX. SIMEX thus works as a transparent financial house, which matches all the buyers and sellers and passes the money back and forth each day.

The reason for these payments is to avoid problems being caused to the market or to other users by anyone defaulting on their contractual obligations. Futures and options are so volatile that if no payments were made until they expired, the loser could face an enormous liability and end up collapsing without being able to pay. This in turn could lead to a domino sequence where all the brokers collapsed. By demanding payment each day SIMEX ensures that everybody in the market knows exactly what their position is, and if the mark-to-market payments become too much, they are then forced to cut their position.

In order to ensure that Barings had sufficient cash to make these daily payments, and because – if the market was particularly volatile – SIMEX might demand a midday payment, we always had funds on deposit from our clients.

Kim's £20,000 loss on the twenty March contracts was relatively small. Three days later the market had risen another 200 points, and it was now a £60,000 loss. I had to cut the loss.

But £60,000 was far too big a figure to tell Simon Jones. And now I also had the problem of explaining why I hadn't told anyone all week. So I pushed that £60,000 under the carpet and into the 88888 account. If

I told Simon Jones, he'd give everyone on the trading floor a hard time, and might even stop me from going on the floor. I was just beginning to see that my own operation running Futures and Options might become a success when I'd been hit by Kim's loss. I couldn't bear it if Jones then used this loss – which was nothing to do with me – to slam me back down into Settlements.

I hardly had time to wonder whether it was a crime or a convenient solution when the phone rang. It was Dave Mousseau at First Continental Trading.

'I've got ten contracts here which don't balance,' he said. 'George swore that I'd told him to buy, but I know I said sell.'

'Let's look through the tapes,' I said.

'The video cameras don't show anything,' he said. 'I've already done that.'

'Shall we go fifty-fifty?' This was always the first offer to resolve a problem.

'Fifty-fifty, fine,' he agreed.

Now I had another five contracts to balance somewhere else. I called George and asked him to phone around to see if anyone was short of five contracts. Strictly speaking we weren't allowed to deal after SIMEX had closed, but everyone called around trying to balance their books in the late afternoon. My trouble with Kim's contracts was that they were just too big to hide, and everyone had gone home by the time I'd found them.

My dabble in Error Account 88888 had been a useful way to buy time. But my main preoccupation then was not the forty contracts, but how best to help Su Khoo, a Malaysian trader who was the options dealer and Head of Proprietary Trading for Baring Securities in Tokyo. The crucial significance of this was that Su Khoo was a proprietary trader: she bought and sold large numbers of Nikkei contracts. The deals I did were all booked to her account in Tokyo, and she would check them – and if they looked out of balance she would cut the position.

Over the next few months, up to the end of 1992, I put over thirty errors into the 88888 account. This was bad, but not catastrophic. There were other errors in the London account, but I put into 88888 the particularly large discrepancies which I thought would get my newly recruited traders into trouble. There was no hard and fast rule – an error's an error – but the traders knew that if they'd made a bad mistake they could refer it to me, and then it would find its way into the 88888 account. It wasn't our money; it wasn't our clients' money; it was Barings' money, and every bank has an error account. Barings just had two of them. At the month-end, when the print-outs were reviewed (which Barings' accounts department would scrutinise), I closed down all the open positions I'd been running and passed a journal entry to the 88888 account to bring the balance back to zero. I passed the other side of the entry by deducting the loss from my only other source of income, my commission earned. This wasn't a foolproof method, and it relied on the losses being small and the income being large, and I knew that if the internal auditors asked me to explain it, or if the losses grew, then I'd have to find another way of hiding them.

I WAS awake the moment before the alarm clock went

off. I instinctively reached out and smacked the top down so that it wouldn't wake up Lisa, and then dragged myself out of bed to run a bath. I'm addicted to baths, and I was just lying full-length with my toes turning the hot water on and off when Lisa barged in and told me it was time to get going. Dawn and dusk come swiftly in Singapore, and while it was pitch dark when I awoke, it was broad daylight by the time I got out of the bathroom. I found it rather odd that I never saw the dawn – I went into my windowless bathroom in the night and emerged in the day.

We left the flat, with the sofa still rumpled from where we'd sat and watched a video, and I put the rubbish bag outside with the cardboard pizza boxes stained with tomato sauce.

Lisa dropped me off at the Delifrance café at the bottom of the Overseas Union Bank (OUB) building, where all the traders gathered to have a coffee before heading into SIMEX. They were standing around in their shirt sleeves. Their trousers were the bottom halves of suits, but nobody wore a full suit in Singapore. By the time you left for home, you'd have six pristine suit jackets and six worn-out pairs of trousers. I saw my friend Danny and bought him a coffee.

'So what's it going to be?'

'It's gotta stay strong. Look at the US figures yesterday and the Dow overnight.'

'And the yen's down too.'

'What about inflation though?'

We always indulged in this kind of bullshit patter, as if either knew what was going to happen in the market, or even that we had any kind of strategy. We both knew that you went into the market and screamed your head off and just traded two seconds ahead and changed your mind every third minute about what you were doing.

'Sod that.' Danny transferred his coffee to his left hand and proffered his right. 'Bet you a hundred it keeps its gains.'

'Done!' I slapped it hard. 'You'll lose in the last half-hour,' I promised him.

I gulped down my orange juice and coffee and we took the lift up to the trading floor. Our $100 bet was more in our minds than any of the millions of dollars we'd be buying and selling during the day. My yellow and blue striped trading jacket was hanging on the back of my chair, and I clipped the security pass to the lapel. My initials were Lisa's initials: LJS. Everyone had three initials on their badge, and the dealers generally worked out all possible acronyms. One girl had worn the initials BJS, but after a few months she realised everyone was calling her 'Blow Job Specialist'. She couldn't live up to that so she changed her badge. A few months back I had finally got George drunk enough to divulge what everyone was calling me.

'It's obvious,' he'd wheezed. 'LJS stands for small dick. *Lan chiau* is Chinese for dick.'

I mulled this over.

'Where's the J and the S?'

'The J? The S?' George looked confused.

'There's a J in the middle and an S at the end: LJS.'

'Oh, we haven't bothered about that!' George laughed. 'It's too good as it is: *lan chiau* small dick.'

'But there are three initials and you're just taking the first, that's hardly a nickname.'

'Stop being so pedantic,' he said. 'It's your nickname, and the more you argue, the more it'll stick.'

So there I was: *lan chiau* small dick.

George himself flaunted GEE and Maslan ADI, and they'd clearly chosen carefully – they didn't get any shit since none of us could conjure up a good nickname. Danny was VIZ, after the comic, but he was commonly known either as Bubble (since he was Greek – Bubble and Squeak: Greek), or Triple D, standing for 'Danny Don't Drink', which happened to be true. Another of my traders, Din, had some long name, Sharifudin Bin Rakiman, and his security pass had DIN because he thought he created such a noise around him. But we just called him 'Fat Boy', and he lived up to all our expectations – when he joined SIMEX at the beginning of 1992 he weighed just forty-three kilos, but a year later clocked in at over seventy.

I got to our booth and stood by the phones. For a few seconds it was quiet. I looked out over the trading pits at the order-fillers, all wearing their red jackets: red is a lucky colour for the Chinese, so almost every jacket was red. Only the large white foreigners, pasty Americans and Brits, dared wear any other colour. Then the first panel lit up, and I picked up the phone.

Mid-morning I was in the middle of signalling a sell to Fat Boy when the outside line buzzed. This was rather unusual. Even more unusual was the introduction.

'This is Ang Swee Tian. I was wondering whether you could help me.'

Ang Swee Tian was the President of SIMEX. When he asked you for help, you helped.

'I'd be delighted to,' I said, trying to sound as calm as I could, while catching sight across the trading floor of Fat Boy gesticulating wildly and apparently threatening to punch another dealer. For an awful second I wondered whether the President had found out about my illicit dealing with the 88888 account.

'There is a valued customer of SIMEX who wishes to speak with you. I am going to give him your telephone number, and when he calls I should be grateful if you could try your hardest to accommodate him.'

I couldn't begin to see what he was driving at.

'Of course,' I promised.

'His name is Philippe Bonnefoy. He is staying at the Raffles Hotel.'

And that was that.

Ten minutes later the outside phone rang again.

'Mr Leeson? I wonder if you could help me. My name is Philippe Bonnefoy.'

'What can I do for you?'

'Perhaps you could come for tea? Shall we say four o'clock?'

And with that he rang off.

I stood still and wondered what was going on. The outside line rang again. I hesitated and then reached out for it. I'd had enough outside calls to keep me going for a while.

'Oi, shithead!' It was Lisa. 'What are we doing tonight?'

After we agreed to go out for dinner, I left the dealing floor and caught a taxi over to Raffles. I called up from reception and was asked to go to the second floor. I knocked at the heavy lacquered door. Philippe

Bonnefoy was younger than I expected, a neat, well-groomed man in a blue suit, Oxford brogues and a Hermès tie. The hotel room looked unoccupied, with just an open briefcase over on a side table. Bonnefoy was talking on a mobile phone, and he motioned me across into a seat, waved at the tray of biscuits and then listened. After thirty seconds he merely said 'Fine,' and then clicked off the phone.

'Mr Leeson,' he shook my hand, 'I have been advised that you would be able to help me.'

'I hope so.'

'You see, I do a lot of business on SIMEX, a considerable amount of business. With the exception of George Soros, I probably trade more than anyone else in the Nikkei. Sometimes I trade over 5,000 contracts a day.'

Five thousand a day! That was huge! That would generate commission of around $100,000 a month.

'Could Barings handle that amount of business?'

'Would you want to settle through us?'

'No, I'd settle through FIMAT.'

FIMAT was the Singapore brokerage arm of the French bank Société Générale. I stirred my cup of tea and wondered what else to ask.

'What is your business?'

'I work for the European Trust and Banking Company. It's a bank based in the Bahamas.'

And that was all I got out of him.

'I'll call you,' Philippe said as he ushered me to the door.

When the hotel door closed behind me with a heavy clunk, I realised I hadn't touched my cup of tea. I wondered whether Philippe Bonnefoy would pick it up and pour it down the sink, or leave it to get cold and be cleared up by room service.

I called Mike Killian, Head of Barings' Global Equity Futures and Options Sales in Tokyo, and told him that we might be picking up a heavyweight client.

'Excellent,' he said, sounding a bit peeved that the call hadn't come through to him. 'Roll on those bonuses.'

Killian sounded rather miserable. I imagined his gaunt face, with the chunks taken out of his cheeks where he'd had a biking accident, brooding over the phone. I'd never trusted Mike Killian – he gave the impression that he was out to champion everyone's cause, but in fact was a great back-stabber. I was learning to handle him with kid gloves, particularly since I knew that he was out to keep the costs of my operation to the minimum.

'It's something called European Trust and Banking,' I said neutrally. 'Based in the Bahamas.'

'Great place,' Mike said wistfully. 'Ever been there?'

'No.'

'Superb scuba diving.'

We talked briefly about credit checks, but since they weren't going to be clearing through Barings we agreed it wasn't a problem. Two weeks later European Trust and Banking was declared fit to be a Barings client.

I was busy buying for Fuji Bank one morning when the phone rang.

'Philippe here,' announced the quiet voice. 'I'd like to buy 4,000 June contracts at best.'

Four thousand! The total number of contracts which

went through SIMEX in an average day was 20,000. Four thousand was a massive order.

'Fine,' I agreed. 'I'll do some of it in Osaka, some here. The price is 350 at the moment, but this will move it.'

'Try not to pay more than 400 for them and see how you go.'

I signalled to George to come over and see me.

'We've got to buy 4,000 June.'

'Four thousand! Outrageous!'

'What's the liquidity today?'

'Tight as a flea's arse. You'll get away with 500 and then the market will move.'

'Eric, do we have any other sellers?'

'A couple of hundred.'

I thought for a second and the market ticked up.

'Right, let's use the sellers to try to keep a lid on it. Just knock the market back and then buy back up. I'll put 1,000 through Osaka, and you try to get 1,000 here. Then some of the early buyers will come back out to sell and close off their positions. If we do it early enough, they'll ride their positions until the end of the day and then we can pick those up, maybe another 1,000 in both markets.'

George walked back into the pit and waited for a while. Then he opened his arms wide and dramatically offered 200 contracts. It took him a long time, with lots of drama and shouting. God, he looked as if he saw the end of the world coming. The red jackets around him bought reluctantly, and the market fell more and more. He looked as if he was doing shit-loads of selling, but really he was doing nothing, just kidding the dealers. The market had to decide whether he was a genuine seller or not, and after ignoring him for a while, a few dealers began to believe that he had a large selling programme to push through. More of them turned tail and began to sell in front of George, and the outcry increased. George acted well, and the market fell away from him. He looked desperate and kept signalling the price back to me. It had fallen from 400 down to 300. I nodded at Maslan, who went and stood a few yards away from him. Maslan started buying and George was still apparently selling. But George couldn't seem to sell enough, and Maslan had already bought 500 when George turned and bought 500 from a couple of dealers who had followed his selling. They bought in another 500 and the price started tracking back up to 350. I spotted a few more purchases, and then the din rose and he was buying more. Then he cut out and came swaggering back to me. I'd bought in Osaka, and the price there was firm.

'We've bought 1,500 already. Nobody saw us coming. We hopped in on 500 like a stealth bomber. Then it started getting ridiculous.'

We'd bought 3,500 by lunchtime, and everyone knew we were buyers. The SIMEX liquidity is low because lots of local traders are trading on their own account, and their limit is very low. They trade in fives and tens, and they're a complete pain in the arse. If George spent too much time dealing with them, it'd alert the market to what he was doing. However, this had worked well today, since he'd laboriously sold through them and everyone had spotted him as a seller, and then he and Maslan had bought a couple of big tickets from Morgan Stanley.

I called Philippe, trying not to sound too pleased with myself.

'We've bought 4,000, average price 370.' Philippe was happy: the average price was good, but also all the sell orders we'd had from clients had been filled at the top of the market. Everybody was happy.

'Very good,' he said.

I put the phone down and punched the air.

'Fuck me! That's $8,000 commission coming our way!'

Philippe kept us busy all right. He was certainly the largest trader on SIMEX, and he pushed through an astonishing amount of business. But the only odd thing about him was that he never seemed particularly concerned whether he made or lost money. After that first trade I could never detect any satisfaction if he was up, or anger and disappointment if he was down. With every other client I knew what hurt them or pleased them. But Bonnefoy was completely unreadable.

George Seow was in a bad way. He was sitting back behind a full ashtray and a row of empty Tiger beer bottles, his shirt and tie stained, his eyes out of focus. A slim Malaysian prostitute in a red halterneck and black hotpants was slipping her hand encouragingly along his thigh.

'You're wasting your time,' I told her. 'He's too far gone.'

She moved off sullenly back to the bar.

'George, what's up?'

'We've split up. I'm a free man. I've told her to fuck off.'

I knew that George and his wife had been splitting up

for some time, since he'd been going out with one of the girls on the trading floor, but this seemed final. It was nearly Christmas, and the bar decorations of Santa Claus and reindeers in the snow looked grotesquely out of place.

'I'm going to have the time of my life,' he assured me with owlish solemnity. 'I've got a lot of lost time to make up.'

George was thrown out of his house and spent Christmas at our flat. He was remarkably good company, under the circumstances, and we had a few other friends round to try to help George drown his sorrows. It was a strange Christmas, but a good one nevertheless.

We settled back to work in January, but George began to lose his grip. He'd be out drinking every night, and he'd arrive on the trading floor still half-pissed from the night before, smelling of stale beer and cheap perfume. Once he wore the same shirt for three days in a row. I didn't feel that I could do much about it, because he was one of my best friends. He reminded me of some of my Watford friends in that he didn't care what people thought of him.

Singapore is a very strict place, and most of the people tend to behave themselves. It is also a very small place, so anything you do is always reported to everyone. But I liked George's attitude. He knew that he was one of the best traders, and his policy was to do whatever he wanted outside work.

But he became a problem to me because he started making mistakes.

'What the fuck is this?' I towered over George and held out a dealing slip he'd scrawled across.

'I bought 100 September,' he said.

'You bought? Fuck me, I said *sell*.'

'You said buy.'

'This is ridiculous, you're miles away. What else have you done?'

George gave me his sheaf of trading cards. I looked down them and noticed he'd scarcely filled them out. He'd jotted down a couple of shorthand notes. I tried to think how we could get around this problem. It was another version of Kim Wong's mistake: we were hung with an overnight position.

'OK,' I said, turning away and putting his slips on my desk, 'I'll sort this one out.'

I worked through the slips. George had done a lot of trading, but there were a lot of errors. I was left with 420 contracts on Barings' books which we'd failed to sell for our customers. We had told the customer we'd sold, so I couldn't do anything about that. We'd have to make it good. But I was stuck with this position. I stood up and walked over to Risselle.

'I need to put another trade into the Five Eights account,' I told her.

4

1993 to the 1994
Internal Audit

> 'The recovery in profitability has been amazing . . .
> leaving Barings to conclude that it was not actually
> terribly difficult to make money in the securities
> business.'
>
> Peter Baring, Chairman of Barings

I SAT AND STARED at George's errors. Most people would
have seen just a few pieces of paper with a slanting
scrawl across them and a few round numbers. They'd
have taken them for scrap paper and chucked them in
the bin. But for me they represented a watershed:
George had been hung for £150,000. He had bought
rather than sold 100 contracts, worth around £8 million, and we were in trouble.

All the money we dealt with was unreal: abstract
numbers which flashed across screens or jumped across
the trading pit with a flurry of hands. Our clients made
or lost thousands of pounds, we just made a commission. Some dealers in Japan did proprietary trading and

risked Barings' own money, but not us in Singapore. We just arbitraged back to back with no risk or filled other people's orders. The real money was our salaries and our bonuses, but even that was a bit artificial: it was all paid by telegraphic transfer, and since we lived off expense accounts, the numbers in our bank balances just rolled up. The real, real money was the $100 I bet Danny each day about where the market would close, or the cash we spent buying chocolate Kinder eggs to muck around with the plastic toys we found inside them.

George's mistake was enough for us to wave goodbye to our salaries and bonuses – and even to the cash for our chocolate eggs. It would knock the stuffing out of us. He'd be sacked on the spot and I would have my operation taken away from me. I was building up an amazing business, with Philippe Bonnefoy as my main client, and a team made up of traders and the girls in the back office. They all reported to me, and although Simon Jones was meant to be running the show, everyone knew that I was the boss. Most of the girls refused to talk to Simon, they dealt only with me. I'd been more than fair to them, and had always invited them along to meals and made sure they'd come along to the office parties. They would do anything for me.

If I let George's mistakes go through I could kiss goodbye to my whole lifestyle, and the girls' and the traders' careers. Two girls in the back office depended upon me – Risselle and Norhaslinda; three order-fillers – George, Maslan and the Fat Boy; and Eric Chang, who answered the phones with me. Six people whose careers would vanish. Of course nobody in SIMEX would miss us. They'd remember us for about half an hour on the morning after we'd all been fired, then they'd be back to the market. Our places on the trading floor would be superstitiously avoided for a moment, in case the bad luck was contagious, but then they'd be swallowed up.

IT was easy putting George's trades into the 88888 account. After all, it was a bona fide account in the computer, which had been set up in order to accept such mistakes, and I had used it last year. But this was such a big error that I could not possibly cover it up as a foreign exchange mistake, a glitch of some kind, or pass the entry against the profit line of commission income. It gave me three serious problems.

The first problem was how to get the duff trades out. Normally they're cut the next morning: the numbers are small, the loss is crystallised, and the loss becomes the final balancing item on the profit and loss account. You declare your gross profit, deduct the losses in the error account, and that's your bottom-line profit. But George's errors were too big to simply sell and take the loss on the chin: they'd knock our heads off. I had to hide them, and there was no easy way out – unless of course the market leapt a long way upwards.

The second problem was more difficult: I could hold the contracts in the 88888 account, and nobody would be any the wiser until they came to the month-end, when the Barings internal accounts division added up all the assets and liabilities, reconciled them and declared Barings' net assets. I knew that this only happened at the month-end. But if they then saw the true balance of the 88888 account – which was automatically part of their system – and subsequently saw the open position as 100 contracts, they would immediately question what this liability was. Then they'd find out that not only was it an unauthorised position, it was larger than most of the authorised ones. I'd be marched off the trading floor and leave my stripy jacket behind.

The third problem was the most ominous of all. Each day SIMEX makes a margin call and requests funds. In a highly complicated calculation, SIMEX demands margin payments to take into account not only any money you'd lost today but also the money you *might* lose, under normal market conditions, the next day. The contracts in Account 88888 would show up on their screens as a Barings client account, and they would send through a request for a small percentage of the liability, depending upon the market's volatility. I had no cash in the 88888 account, so I had no means to make this payment. When Kim Wong had made the first mistake, I had used clients' floating funds to bail us out and make the SIMEX payments – which were comparatively small – and then cut the position and booked the loss. This system had worked all through 1992, and I could vary it by deducting the loss from the profits from my commission income as well. While I could still use some of this cash for part of the deficit, George's and my own mistakes in running positions were now simply too large for the clients' excess cash to fund them all.

I sat at my desk long after everyone had gone home, and doodled a few lines and boxes and arrows across my notepaper. I put Singapore in one box, London in another, and drew the cash flow between them. Barings Singapore held very little cash on deposit, it was all cleared back to London. Each day we put a request over to London for a cash transfer to meet our clients' daily margin payments and any proprietary positions held. We didn't officially do proprietary trading, since Mike Killian thought it might scare some clients away (specifically, clients who suspected we might put ourselves in front of their orders and gain from the subsequent market move, a practice known as 'front running'). However, Barings had been very active in proprietary trading from the day that I arrived in 1989. Most of this trading was booked through Fernando's books in Japan, but we kept it quiet, and in fact there never was any front running.

The cash flow which funded our customers' dealing came from London. Brenda Granger, in the Settlements department at the London head office, transferred Japanese yen over to us, or Tony Hawes, Barings' Group Treasurer, authorised lines of credit at Citibank for us to draw on. These yen were then passed on to SIMEX. As the positions were increasing, so was the margin that I needed. I needed yen to pay for the losses and I also needed money to cover the margin payments. I had to solve the problem and convince London to send me money, lots of money.

I drew a large yen sign (¥), and then speared a dollar through it. I needed both dollars and yen, and I needed them totally at my discretion. I could probably bluff London into sending some more dollars over and say it was for some sort of client funding. They might fall for that. But I was sitting on a loss at the month-end – a yen loss which could only be concealed by a yen credit.

Futures and options work in funny ways in Singapore – they can be funded by a combination of US dollars and Japanese yen. The initial margins are payable in either dollars or yen, but the daily variation margins calls are due in yen. As I scribbled around the boxes, it dawned on me that if I sold options, I would actually receive a premium, a payment from whoever bought them – this would be in yen, and I would be able to use it to balance the yen deficit in the 88888 account.

I drew up two columns, a profit and loss column and a balance sheet. The profit and loss account is prepared along with the balance sheet, but I knew that people in Barings were more interested in the bottom line than they were in how it had been reached. They just looked at the balance sheet to satisfy themselves that they were in control of the operation and left it at that. They focused rather more on the profit and loss account, since this spelled out the profits which drove their salaries and bonuses: Barings' policy was to give the staff bonuses of almost half the pre-tax profits. The average ratio for bonuses compared with salaries for directors was 75:25, and when many directors were earning over £500,000, they certainly pushed the profit and loss account for all it was worth.

If I could reduce the 88888 account to zero, and transfer the debt to the balance sheet, I would be halfway there. And then if I could get Barings to fund the balance sheet debit on a daily basis, I could roll forward all the 88888 account's positions and losses.

This would leave a balance sheet entry which would indicate a payable to Barings and a receivable from SIMEX. Barings London would be happy that their money had been parked in SIMEX and was theoretically owed back to them – it was an asset. And I would postpone the need to register the losses in the 88888 account.

This was my solution:

	Profit & Loss	Balance Sheet
Futures		
Initial Margin		
Payment to SIMEX		debit $
Variation Margin		
Payment to SIMEX	debit ¥	
Options		
Receive premium		
selling options	credit ¥	
Initial Margin		
Payment to SIMEX		debit $
	zero ¥	debit $
Ask for US dollars		
from London		credit $
Month-end Balance	zero ¥	zero $

In order to balance the books, I had to do two things: first I had to sell exactly the right amount of options at the month-end, to bring in the same amount of premiums in yen as the loss sitting in the 88888 account. The profit and loss account would then show a balance of zero, and everyone would assume that the 88888 account was still dormant.

Secondly I had to ask Barings London to transfer a dollar payment which would fund both the margin on the futures I bought, and the margin on the options if they moved against me. Depending on how the market went, this would be a daily request which would balance the dollar side of the balance sheet.

By selling options I was exposing Barings to a capital risk in that the value of the options I held could rise or fall – I was effectively taking on an illicit proprietary position.

I looked at the two columns and drew a large question mark around the cash coming from London. The plan would only work if London agreed to transfer sufficient funds to meet the extra daily margin requests – which would include the requests for the unauthorised position in Account 88888. This would be unthinkable in any other bank, certainly unthinkable at Morgan Stanley, but my lines of communication with London were so vague that nobody knew who I reported to, and they tended to let me get on with my job.

But then I thought again: they would surely justify any cash transfer. After all, the whole point of buying options or futures rather than the underlying shares is that it saves putting cash up front. It's a gamble, but it's a gamble which shouldn't absorb too much cash. If I were to conceal these losses, I had to pull down more money from London; I had to rely on their sloppy approach to my funding requests. If the market went against me I'd have to ask for funding every day. Explaining that away should be impossible; there was no logical reason for it, however hard I tried to think of one.

I decided to cross that bridge when I came to it, so I put the diagram into my desk drawer and left for home. It was past midnight and the streets were quiet. I wondered where George was – probably getting plastered at Zouk's disco. I drove home, my mind relaxing. I had worked out a solution to protect us all. The main thing was to trade out of the losses, and I would try to trade futures to do so, but at least I had a safety net in the prospect of options if I couldn't trade out of the futures by the month-end. It was 18 March – I had two weeks.

THE next fortnight was the busiest we'd ever had. I arrived at the desk at 8:00 A.M. to find the telephones ringing incessantly. Philippe Bonnefoy started putting through enormous amounts of business. I stood shoulder to shoulder with Eric and two new girls I'd recruited, Carol and Eve, and we grabbed the phones all day. After two days I asked Risselle to come over from the back office and help us out. I put Maslan on the edge of the pit with his back to George, and he would net off all the trades as we signalled them to him. He'd then spin round and give George the net position. I kept George sober for a week. But, on 26 March, I added up our position and saw that we had yet more errors. As well as these errors, the market had moved against me. I had lost another £70,000.

I calculated how many options I needed to sell, worked it out as a 'straddle' of 50 contracts, sold them and booked the deal into the 88888 account.

A straddle is a deal where you sell both a 'put' and a 'call' option together, at the same strike price. Put and call options are contracts which give you the right, but not the obligation, to buy from (call) or sell to (put) the writer of the contract. You pick a level in the market, say 18,000, and you effectively bet that the market will be at or near this level when your option expires. The closer the market is to this level when that happens, the more of the up-front premium you will retain. If the market moves down from 18,000, the call option that you sold will become worthless, but the put option moves into the money.

The person to whom you sold a put option at 18,000, whereby you agreed to buy from him at 18,000, will obviously exercise his right and make you buy at that price if the market drops. He has thus pre-sold to you at 18,000 and can then buy at, say, 17,500 in the market and make 500 points profit. When you sell a straddle, your profit is limited to the first premium you receive for the put and call options. If you do not hedge the position your potential loss is unlimited: the market can move against you in either direction. If the market stays at 18,000, you receive a premium from the sale of both the put and the call options, and since the market doesn't move, neither of these options is worth anything so you keep the full premium.

I needed premium, yen, to hide the loss. I decided that the market was going to stay stable, and I was attracted to the large premiums from straddles, so I sold straddles, took in the premium and made the balance on the 88888 account appear to be zero. If the market moved against me, then I'd have to pay more margin calls to SIMEX – and I'd have to ask London to provide them. I didn't hedge the position to protect my exposure, since that would mean doing more futures trades and I needed all the premium I could get to cover the losses already accrued. It was a gamble, and a messy one at that.

Risselle calculated the daily margin payments for all Barings' positions and our client positions and waited for the SIMEX request to come through. She then faxed a demand to Brenda Granger in London for $750,000. She made a notional split between the figures, saying that $350,000 was for our clients and $400,000 for Barings itself. The $750,000 was transferred into our account at Citibank that afternoon.

I felt no elation at this success. I was determined to win back the losses. And as the spring wore on, I traded harder and harder, risking more and more. I was well down, but increasingly sure that my doubling up and doubling up would pay off. I was long of futures and short of call options. As the market traded through the strike price of the options, I redoubled my exposure by buying futures which hedged the short calls. This worked – the market kept going up. The risk was that the market could crumple down, but on this occasion it carried on upwards and turned out to be the perfect hedge: the profit on the futures was exactly equal and opposite to the loss on the options in the 88888 account. As the market soared in July, my position translated from a £6 million loss back into glorious profit.

Lisa and I had a barbecue with some friends that Saturday night, and I went out on to the balcony with a bottle of beer and stared out over the city.

'You look happy,' Lisa said as she came out to stand beside me.

'I've pulled something off,' I said. 'I've been sailing a bit close to the wind to protect George, but it's all come right.'

'What do you mean?'

I suddenly realised that if I mentioned the £6 million loss which had cropped up and then cleared, Lisa would be scared to death. I had been surprisingly unmoved by how the numbers had added up – for me it was the principle which mattered. The numbers were just a load of zeros.

'I ran up a £1 million loss at one stage,' I said, trying to make it sound sufficiently small to be of little significance.

'A million! Christ! And this was all for protecting George?'

'Well, each of the traders had their problems. We're just under the cosh the whole time. They don't know what's going on.'

'Don't do that again,' Lisa said. 'It won't help you in the long run.'

'It's not a problem. I can handle it.'

'But don't lose a million again. You'll scare the life out of me.'

I was so happy that night that I didn't think I'd ever go through that kind of tension again. I'd pulled back a large position simply by holding my nerve. I was back in profit, and we could get on with making more money. I was earning £50,000 a year, and my bonus was going to top £100,000. We were talking about buying a flat in London as an investment.

* * *

But first thing on Monday morning I found that I had to use the 88888 account again. I was in a bizarre situation, in that I had one foot on the dealing floor and could authorise the sale of options to bring in the yen; but I was also in charge of the girls in the back office, who would carry out any of my requests. I could see the whole picture, and it was so easy. I was probably the only person in the world to be able to operate on both sides of the balance sheet. It became an addiction.

As well as the astonishing behaviour of the London staff, who transferred this money to Singapore without questioning what it was for, my concealment was helped because I was supposed to report to four different people. My direct supervisor was Simon Jones in Singapore, but he wasn't interested in the futures and options side of the business. He was Regional Operations Manager of Barings South Asia, the Chief Operating Officer of Baring Securities Singapore, and a Director of Baring Futures Singapore (BFS), which was my operation. But his office was on the 24th floor of Ocean Towers, while I and Baring Futures were on the 14th. I'd go up to see him in the afternoon, but we mainly talked about football. He was a highly aggressive man, whom most of us feared – he was notorious for sacking secretaries and had been through eleven in two years. We had a little in common because he used me as a link-man to place all his football bets. As for business – we scarcely talked about it.

Another notional boss was Mike Killian, Head of Global Equity Futures and Options Sales. I had worked directly for him when I was first taking orders, and we still spoke several times on the telephone each day, but he was based in Tokyo. Although he wanted the profit that was attributed to me, I was having less and less to do with him.

Then, lastly, I had two more bosses in London – Mary Walz, and her boss Ron Baker, in the Financial Products Group. In due course Baker began to be excited by the size of the profits I was reporting, and he took direct responsibility for me. Ron and Mary had both been at Bankers Trust together, and they formed an awesome duo. Both prided themselves on being tough and gutsy, and it was a brave man who dared to contradict them or stop them when they had the bit between their teeth.

My reporting lines were as hazy and inbred as the Baring family tree itself. Apart from these four bosses, I also asked Brenda Granger in Settlements for the daily transfers of cash. It was a bizarre structure, and one which allowed me to run my own show without anyone interfering. It was only later that I came across a memo from James Bax, Regional Manager of Barings South Asia, to Andrew Fraser, Head of Equity Broking and Trading in London. It was dated 25 March 1992 – just a week before I arrived in Singapore:

My concern is that once again we are in danger of setting up a structure which will subsequently prove disastrous and with which we will succeed in losing either a lot of money or client goodwill or probably both . . . In my view it is critical that we should keep clear reporting lines, and if this office is involved in

SIMEX at all, then Nick Leeson should report to Simon Jones and then be responsible for the operations side.

If this memo had been taken seriously I would have been installed in Singapore with a clear mandate just to manage the settlements side of the business. I would have had no access to the traders, and thus could never have asked them to sell options for a secret account. I would not have talked to Mary Walz or Ron Baker or Mike Killian and been able to play them off against each other. If the traders had made mistakes, I would have found them and made them their problem not mine – I would never have had the mechanism to hide them. And of course James Bax was right – although I was fighting hard against it, Barings were set to lose both a lot of money and a lot of client goodwill. But for the time being, it looked as if I was proving James Bax wrong: I won considerable amounts of client goodwill, and we made a lot of money.

As my losses in Error Account 88888 began to creep up again from the zero balance I had managed to achieve in July, I found myself growing increasingly angry that I hadn't shut the whole thing down and never used it again. I began to trade aggressively to make the money back, and these trades never turned out the right way for me. I was celebrated as the top dealer on SIMEX on the back of Philippe Bonnefoy, and everyone envied the business I was doing for him. Yet this was also a double-edged sword, as I was out of my depth. I was beginning to drown under the numbers he was throwing at me, but I couldn't show them to any-one.

'Nɪᴄᴋ! Nick!' Carol was pushing my arm to wake me up. 'Come on! Philippe's been on the phone and he wants you to call him straight back. He's got some urgent trading.'

'God!' I opened my eyes and peered up at her. 'How did you find me?'

'George said you'd come up here to crash out.'

I rubbed my eyes. They felt as if someone had pulled them apart and poured a phial of fine sand into each one. I could feel the Tiger beer oozing back out through my skin. I could smell my bad breath. I stood up and pulled some mints out of my pocket. I chewed them around, but they stuck to my teeth and I couldn't dis-lodge them. I shoved another one into my mouth, sucked it hard and then swallowed it whole.

Last night I'd matched the boys beer for beer, with whisky chasers thrown in for good measure. Then I'd shown them the drink where you pour a shot of Drambuie into a glass of beer. You wait for it to sink to the bottom, drink the cold beer, and then hit the warm Drambuie, which promptly explodes in your head like a depth charge. They'd loved that one.

I'd arrived at the Barings booth at 8 ᴀ.ᴍ. and looked at the market for a bit, but had then had enough and gone to the lounge upstairs. The traders' lounge was full of armchairs where traders crashed out, farting and burping and nursing their hangovers. The lavatories were always full of puke, blocked up and with footprints on the seats where everyone squatted rather than sat to have their crap. I had an upset stomach, but by the time I'd found a half-presentable lavatory my bowels had miraculously shrivelled up. All the same I'd thrown up at the smell of the rest of the puke and then crashed out in an armchair.

I followed Carol down on to the dealing floor and tried to close my ears to the roar around me. The market was trading in a tight range, and the dealers were just trying to find out its limits, pushing and shoving at the spread to see where it was weakest. I dialled Philippe in the Bahamas. The phone went through several exchanges, growing fainter and fainter with each one, until it made the final connection and Philippe picked it up.

'Philippe, it's Nick.'

'I want to do a cash deal,' he said, 'selling the 220 calls and buying the 200 calls in December.'

'OK,' I said, playing for time. 'Anybody showing you anything at the moment?'

'I have an offer of .138 for size.'

I waited for him to add another sentence – anything which might help me understand what the fuck he was talking about. He didn't.

'OK,' I said again. 'I'll see what I can do.'

Philippe put the phone down before I could say anything else. I stared across at the dealers all yelling their heads off and wondered what the hell I was supposed to be doing. What did .138 mean? I knew that Philippe had bought a lot of the 220 calls a couple of months ago, and that the market had fallen so much that he was probably looking to cut his losses on those and buy something a little closer to the market, but I had no idea what the .138 signified or how I could match it. I keyed in the relevant Reuters page and checked the options prices trading in Osaka. The 220 calls were trading at 200 and the 220 calls were trading at 1400. I played around with the numbers on my calculator and saw that .138 was a ratio: but the equivalent ratio off the screen was .143, 200 divided by 1400. I rubbed my face to try to clear the grogginess. What did Philippe's ratio of .138 mean? It must mean that someone else was offering a bigger discount on one side of the transaction in order to get the business. With the large size of option trading Philippe did, there was a discount somewhere. I called Adrian, a trader in Tokyo.

'I've got Philippe wanting some options. He wants to roll over the 220 September calls into 200 calls in December. He's been offered a spread of .138. Can you do anything?'

'I'll get back to you.'

I held on while Adrian made a couple of calls, and then he was back on the line.

'Point one three eight is a good offer,' he said. 'I can match it but anything higher is a bit risky. I could just do .139, but not many and not easily. The market needs to move down a touch.'

'How many can you do at .139?' I insisted, feeling impatient. 'Or even .140?' I didn't understand these ratios, but I knew that I had to keep Philippe's business.

'No more than 1,000 at .139.'

'OK, mate, thanks.' I rang off.

I should have heard the warning bells, but my head was too fuddled and all I was thinking about was the need to keep the business. I called some other people in Tokyo, Merrill Lynch, Banque Nationale de Paris and

Paribas. The upshot of it all was that they would all come in at .138, but nobody wanted to come in at .140. They all said it was too risky.

I put the phone down feeling more aggrieved. I was going to lose this business.

'Nick!' Risselle held up a phone. 'Philippe.'

I hadn't got my thoughts together at all.

'Hi, Philippe.'

'What can you do?'

'I've got people interested at .138, but whoever you've spoken to has already put the word around the market, and they're not interested at .139 or .140.'

'I can't give it to you at .138,' Philippe said neutrally. 'My other broker will get crabby.'

I felt like slamming the phone down: that was the market price, and if he'd come to me first, as he should have done since I worked my balls off for him, we'd have done the business and gone home happy. The wanker was pulling one over me.

'How many have you got to do?' I asked.

'About six thousand. And they're yours if you can get them away at .139.'

'Give me two minutes.'

I put the phone down and looked at the prices again. They hadn't moved. My head was throbbing with a hangover and a growing sense of anger that Philippe was dumping me into this. I couldn't stop and ask whether I should just wave goodbye to this business – I began to want to do this deal at all costs. I had a hunch that it was Société Générale who had offered him .138, and I was determined to nick the business off them. I put my hand in my pocket for a tube of fruit pastilles, but it was empty. I reached for a trading card, slowly bit the corner off it and began to chew.

What I was planning is called 'legging'. Throughout my childhood I'd spent a lot of time legging it from policemen or my father, and legging it meant running away – doing something wrong, running away and getting away with it. 'Legging it' in the market has more serious implications. It means that you promise a client that you can do a deal at a given price – which at the time is impossible – then you gamble that the market will move in your direction and you can fulfil the deal at a price which doesn't make you a loss. It's basically the same as taking a proprietary position, except that you're working against yourself in the sense that your client's order – if it is big – will move the market in its own right. I had no authorisation to do this, but the commission I'd earn on 6,000 option contracts would be impressive, and best of all I'd be seen to be the big player in the market. Société Générale would be left out again – and Philippe should come to me first for the next business.

I called Philippe back. 'I can do it at .139.'

'Good,' he said.

'What's the exact size?'

'At .139,' he mused for a second, '6,500.'

I had the job. It was almost 11 A.M., and Philippe would be going to bed in the Bahamas knowing that he'd done the deal. I called Fernando and told him that the best I could do was .139. He took 1,000, and Banque Nationale de Paris and Paribas each took 500. So far so good. I'd done 2,000. Then Merrill Lynch pulled out from the 1,000 they'd been talking about.

'No can do,' said the trader.

'OK, catch you later.'

I walked over to the Nikkei pit and pulled Maslan over, so that I could cross the 2,000 options with him and bring the purchases from Osaka on to the SIMEX books. Other people can come in when you cross a trade, and you have to take their orders as well. I knew that people respected me when I did a cross, since I was fair and always acknowledged their trading – unlike some other houses who refused to spread the trade around. That wasn't a problem; I was happy if everybody joined in. There was some interest at .139, but not too much. I crossed the 2,000 options which I'd arranged over the phone, sold another 1,000 with CRT and 1,500 with SBC, and then couldn't get rid of more than 100 to the other minnows in the market. I was 1,900 option contracts short. If I carried on standing in the pit, I'd flag my intentions to everyone. I decided to back off and walked back to the Barings booth. I was now legging 1,900 option contracts, and things weren't looking good. I sat at the booth and pulled out some more trading cards. I nibbled at the corner and enjoyed the clean bleached taste of the paper. My forehead was beaded with sweat, which I wiped with the cuff of my jacket. A horrible feeling of loss began to creep inside my stomach. I wasn't just legging it, I was out on a limb here. Most traders only have authority to take a proprietary position of 100 option contracts. I was sitting on 1,900 with no authority whatsoever.

I looked at the screens and listened to the noise of the market, trying to see where it was heading. But of course it was impossible to see where the market was heading: by its very nature it was like trying to drive using only the rear-view mirror. I felt paralysed. Then I decided to separate the order, the basis of legging, and sell the 220 calls now, and try to buy back the 200 calls as the market continued falling. The difference between the bid and the offer on the options meant that I was going to need quite a big market movement to bring me home safe and dry, but I couldn't see any other way. I signalled to Maslan in the pit, and over the next half-hour I managed to sell 1,900 of the 220 calls at 190 – some way short of the 200 they'd been earlier, but not disastrous, I thought.

When I keyed the figures into my calculator I saw that the small price difference on the 220 calls (190 rather than 200) had a huge impact on the ratio – my calculator kept flashing .1357 at me, taunting me as if it was saying: 'OK, fuckwit, what are you going to do now?' I re-checked the market. Everyone now knew what I was trying to do, and they were still offering the 200 December calls at 1,400 and bidding 1,370. I couldn't even put my bid on to the screen, since it was way too low.

The market traded a little lower at the end of the day, but at nothing like the amount it needed to be to bring me back into a halfway decent position. Fernando and the others had all been right – it had been too risky to do it at .139 – utter madness to stretch it any wider. By the last five minutes of the market I still needed to buy 264 of the December 200 calls to make Philippe good at the ratio of .139. Since Philippe kept all his positions with FIMAT rather than Barings, I was unable to simply pass a book entry in the back office and put the loss in the 88888 account. I had to physically transfer the position to FIMAT.

The bell rang to signal the last minute of trading. I signalled to Maslan to bid 1,365 for 264 contracts in the December 200 call, and hurried over to the trading pit. I was hoping to take advantage of some other activity in the trading pit to hide it, but there was nothing. My trade at well below market was jumped on by a number of players – both Swiss Bank and CRT joined my bid, so I had to sell to them as well.

I went back to the booth. My trade with Philippe had been a disaster. He was fast asleep in the Bahamas, unaware of the trouble I'd made for myself. His position was all square, and the options would be transferred to FIMAT and all would be well. But I had been unable to leg the trade and had been forced to take another 500 December calls into my 88888 account as an open, unhedged position. With the spread between the bid and offer for these options, I was already looking at a loss of US $125,000. And what was more, I had the headache of an open position which could swing even further into loss. Not only did I now have to worry about the bid and offers spread, but the position would be dragged around and increase with any adverse movements in the market. I was in deep shit.

ON 13 September 1993 Peter Baring, the Chairman of Barings, had a meeting with Brian Quinn, the director of the Bank of England in charge of all banking supervision. An extract of the minutes of the meeting was released in which Peter Baring laconically commented: 'The recovery in profitability has been amazing following the reorganisation, leaving Barings to conclude that it was not actually terribly difficult to make money in the securities business.'

He went on to tell Brian Quinn that the Baring Securities Limited sub-group (BSL) would be the biggest contributor to the Baring Group's profits in what was likely to be a record first half, and he confirmed that the bulk of this sub-group's business was agency business rather than proprietary trading.

As I stood in the box and grabbed phones, signalled to George or Fat Boy, bought and sold, watched the market lurch about, gobbled sweets and even chewed the trading cards themselves, I imagined Peter Baring's quiet voice in some splendid lofty office in the Bank of England as he sat back on a leather sofa and stirred his Earl Grey tea and admired his brightly polished toe caps.

'. . . not actually terribly difficult.'

I could never say that with the right intonation. The 'actually' needed to be drawn out, the 'terribly' be accompanied with a raise of the eyebrow and a wry smile to signify surprise. This was a conversation between two experienced bankers who were smugly congratulating themselves on this secret way of making money. And they would have shaken hands in farewell and gone their separate ways, each thinking what a super chap the other was.

They should have known better. Certainly Peter Baring should have known better. Making money is never easy – his ancestors, who built up the bank and took risks and went out to visit canals and railways, would never have said that making money was 'not actually terribly difficult'. Nobody in the real world thinks that making money is not actually terribly difficult. My father knows that you have to work hard and that you get paid £20 a square yard for plastering and that you've got to keep the customer happy to get referred on. The laundry on the corner, the boy who delivers newspapers, the lawyer working above the estate agency just at the wrong end of the High Street – they all know that making money is never easy. And if it's easy, then it's a gamble. And even the toughest gambler knows that he's fighting against improbable odds – otherwise why are casinos such plush places?

If Peter Baring had ever come out on to the trading floor in SIMEX, when we were thrashing ourselves to work harder and trying to match 2,000 trades after midnight when everyone else had gone home, he'd never have said that making money was 'not actually terribly difficult'.

I was trying my hardest to make money. I was trying to protect the bank from some of the crass errors which crept in because the traders were too overworked and stressed out to make rational decisions. I was trying to keep Philippe Bonnefoy, the largest punter in the Nikkei, as sweet as possible. But I wasn't making money. In fact, I was losing money. I had hidden some losses, and rather than staying in control of them, they were taking on a life of their own.

Fridays couldn't come quickly enough. The Osaka market was all jammed up with the volume of business and the dealing screens had blocked. Since they couldn't deal without screens, all the business from Osaka had diverted to SIMEX, which was an open outcry market and didn't need dealing screens to post the prices. We just shouted louder and dealt when there was a matched buyer and seller. But the volume of business was vast. When the bell rang on Friday for the close of business, I knew that I had two days over the weekend to try to match all the trades before Monday. Lisa was pissed off that all our weekend trips were being cancelled and she had to stay in Singapore, but there was nothing I could do about it, and I could see that this weekend would be no different.

Each day this week the market had soared by over 1,000 points after lunch. I had never seen anything like it, and nor had SIMEX. That much was clear since the settlement screens kept blacking out and we couldn't enter the trades as soon as they were done. We had a terrible back-log of trades to account for; I'd been trying to reconcile them every night and hadn't left the office before 3 A.M. so far this week. I looked around at the other booths and saw everyone looking shattered. It wasn't just Barings who were having these problems, it was across the whole of SIMEX. The only difference was that we were doing ten times the volume of anyone else, and without any back-up staff to handle it. I was doing most of it myself. We'd had to leave last night with another fifteen trades unresolved – and Risselle was back in the office already trying to work them out. The SIMEX records were all wrong, and ours were not much better. I called Risselle.

'Any luck with those fifteen trades?'

'Not yet, and the SIMEX figures disagree by 500 futures contracts,' she said.

'OK, keep going.'

I put the phone down and bit my lip. Five hundred contracts was a massive discrepancy. I knew that the dealers had been all over the place, trying to use a completely manual system when the screens were all down and SIMEX's own systems weren't working, but I couldn't believe we were that many out. I didn't have time to go back to the office, since dealing was about to start and the panels on the booth were already lighting up as Carol took down opening orders.

We were short-staffed. The root of the problem was that I had nobody around me who could do the work. Mike Killian refused to employ anybody at a salary of $15,000 because it would eat into his bottom line. He maintained that the bottom line was sacred, and that the fewer costs above it, the more money for all of us. But I was desperate for people to help sort out these trades. SIMEX were saying that we were 500 contracts short of our declared position. I had to decide whether they were right, in which case I should immediately buy 500 contracts, crystallise the loss as an error and square it that way; or perhaps SIMEX were wrong, and they'd send through a statement in mid-afternoon saying they were wrong and leaving the position as we calculated it. It was a complete gamble on my part. I didn't think we could be so far wrong, so I decided to leave things as they were, and assume that SIMEX would correct the mistake later on.

The bell rang for the start of trading, and the lights started flashing on the panels. I put the 500 futures contracts to the back of my mind, and started picking up the phones and signalling across to George in the pit. We traded without pause all morning, and when the bell rang for the end of the morning session I thought of running back to the office, but then realised that I really ought to sort out all the trading cards I'd scribbled on and reconcile them with the clients' tickets. I started to write out the tickets while someone ran to get some sandwiches. Sandwiches hadn't become a hit in Singapore: there was no concept of a Bacon, Lettuce & Tomato, or avocado, or even wholemeal bread. A Singapore sandwich consisted of two triangles of damp white bread on either side of another triangle of processed yellow cheese, stuck together with sticky margarine. Every half an hour I'd be calling Risselle, frantically hoping for good news, but never getting any.

I could smell sweet and sour Chinese food around me. Normally no food was allowed into SIMEX, but these were exceptional circumstances and the officials didn't mind. Nobody wanted to leave their booths with the market in this kind of mood. A smell of rank sweat wafted past me, easily overwhelming the smell of sweet and sour pork. It was George, his shirt sticking to him.

'Bloody air conditioning is down as well as the screens, it's a total brown-out.'

'Where are you off to?'

'I need a cigarette.'

'Get back in ten minutes,' I said. 'We need the morning trades agreed before we start this afternoon.'

'Not much chance of that, Nick,' he said. 'I can't find

any of the fucking locals. They've all gone out to eat somewhere.'

'Well, grab them as soon as they're back, we need to get on top of this.'

'Yes, sir!' he said, with heavy irony.

George just wasn't taking this seriously. It was fine for the dealers – they could complain about the screens and the air conditioning but they went home at the end of the day with no responsibilities. When I left the dealing floor I then had the whole extra job of running the back office. And I had to try to get the numbers to add up, and when they didn't – which they didn't – I needed to trade out of the loss. I was in too deep to own up to losing this money. It had become my own private nightmare.

I let George go upstairs to have his cigarette, and I started scribbling out the details of the morning's trading on the respective tickets, so the girls could call the customers and confirm their trades.

That afternoon was a replica of the previous week. The market soared by 1,000 points. Orders came in thick and fast, Chuo Trust and Banking bought 3,000 contracts and all of them at market. I couldn't work out what they were doing, but they were pushing the market to the moon. The orders were great, and everyone in Tokyo was patting themselves on the back for winning the business, but in Singapore we just couldn't handle it.

When the bell rang for the close of trading, we all collapsed in our chairs. Friday was just around the corner. Another day was over. We could all get out and hit the cold beers. Everyone except me: my problems were just starting. I would have to go back to the office and sort out all the mess, starting with today but also clearing the rest of the week's trading.

'Nick, I've got a problem.' It was Dave from First Continental Trading.

'What is it?'

'It's with George.'

'So? Speak to him about it.'

I wasn't normally so rude, but I'd been telling Mike Killian for weeks that we couldn't handle Dave's trading as well. We'd always had a lot of complaints from Dave, but Mike always came down on his side and insisted that we made them good so that we'd keep the commission income stream as a profit. Income was all that mattered to Mike Killian. He never gave a thought to the problems generating such a tiny amount of income caused and he just couldn't see that this little worm was giving him the run-around.

'George won't talk to me.'

'I don't blame him.'

'I reckon I traded June, George says it was March and there's a 200-point differential.'

'How many contracts?' I asked.

'A hundred.'

'Since when did you start trading a hundred contracts?' I mocked him. 'You've only ever done ten.'

'It was a sure thing,' Dave whined. 'Check the tapes.'

I didn't know what the truth was, but I knew he'd only call Mike Killian and threaten to take his business away from Barings. Then Mike would be on the phone to me for an hour, I'd have to stay later by another hour to sort out the whole week's back office shambles, and I'd have to accept Dave's word in any event.

104

'OK, Dave, I'll make you good. Now just get off my case.'

I just wanted to get back to the office and sort out all the problems.

I'd left the trading floor at 6 P.M. and it was now 10 P.M. I was no nearer getting the numbers to balance. All the trades had to be done in sequence, and I was working through Monday, Tuesday and Wednesday to try to get a balanced figure for the start of business on Thursday.

By three in the morning I saw that I'd almost finished the reconciliation. I didn't like what I saw. I sat all alone on the 14th floor of Ocean Towers with the wrong figures staring up at me from my calculator. Dave's problem today had cost us $75,000. But the worst thing was that the 500 contracts – which I thought were a discrepancy which would be ironed out by midday – turned out to be a real number. I tapped the figures back into my calculator: the index had soared by 1,000 points that afternoon. I stared at the numbers in complete disbelief; a feeling which then rose up from the pit of my stomach into my throat and almost made me sick. I'd lost about US $1.7 million by not closing out the 500 contracts first thing that morning. The volumes of business were so huge that any mistake was going to be a big number, but this was the biggest single mistake I'd made.

I hunched in my chair in a panic. Then the moment passed and I realised that I was all by myself: nobody would ask me to explain that figure right now. I had all night to hide it. I looked up, out of the window and over the Singapore skyline. I could see the bright lights of Singapore harbour winking in the distance. I was all alone in the office; I was exhausted; I'd get home to find Lisa asleep; I'd have to leave home early tomorrow morning when she was still asleep to get back in here; and then I'd be trading on SIMEX again at 8:15 and handling another twelve phone calls all at the same time. For the only time in the day, I was alone and in silence. I was in charge of my own world up here. I knew what went on on the trading floor, and I knew what happened in the back office. If I was to keep this job, I had to hide the losses. I'd then do my best to get out of them, but I couldn't admit them to anyone.

I stood up and went to the window. It wouldn't open. I was living in a hermetically-sealed world where I breathed no fresh air and handled no real money. I stared out through the thick plate glass. I knew that when light was passed through thick glass, it bent, and if it was passed through a prism it bent into a spectrum, since the thickest part of the glass slowed the light down more. Rather like the spear fisherman who makes an allowance for the distorting effect of the water, which means that the fish is not quite where they see it, I tried to imagine where the lights really were as I watched them through the window. I leaned my head against the cool glass and admitted to myself that I was going to hide that US $1.7 million just as surely as I'd hidden the previous losses. Like the light bending in the strange world of the plate glass, my morals had bent in the unreal world of the trading I was doing. I had become crooked. I'd allowed myself to bend under the pressure to perform, and I was now a step removed from myself.

I stared at the glass and saw my reflection, a distorted white face looming back at me from the blackness of the night sky. I hardly recognised myself – I'd become a disgusting caricature. The bright, charming man who'd married Lisa Sims and had been promoted to run Baring Futures Singapore had become a crook – a man whose face was now staring back like a rotting melon. I couldn't meet my own eyes. I was ashamed of myself and what I'd become. It had started off so small, but had rapidly seized hold and was now all across me like a cancer. Thinking of cancer reminded me of my mother – thank God she'd died before she'd seen me turn into this person, this creature who inhabited a remote world on the 14th floor of Ocean Towers at three in the morning and decided to hide almost $2 million of losses by sleight of hand. It was not what she had brought me up to do.

'NINETEEN ninety-three was a good year for investment banking,' Peter Baring announced as he released Barings' results in February 1994. Barings made profits before tax of £200 million and deducted £100 million for staff bonuses, which gave a net pre-tax profit of £100 million.

I had concealed a loss of £23 million in Account 88888. My official profits were not declared separately, since they were all in Fernando's or Ben Hoffman's trading accounts in Japan, and I didn't have an exact idea how much they credited me with, but it was over £10 million. In the context of the Group's profitability my hidden losses were large, but I simply sold more options, asked for more funding from London and rolled the entire position forward.

I was beginning to grow rather numb at the size of the rising losses. At first I had been terrified of the £60,000 losses I made, but as they rose, I had to accommodate increasingly large figures. Some days I made £5 million profit simply because the size of the position led me to large swings; other days I lost £5 million, and I was back towards £20 million, then £30 million, and soon in 1994 up to £50 million.

The reason why the losses grew was that I had to sell unhedged positions to bring in a decent premium. Obviously, despite what Peter Baring said, making money is actually terribly difficult, and I had to take unprotected risks to try to win back the lost money. And although I was winning sometimes, more often I was losing. I had started off long of the market, waiting for prices to rise, and as the market fell I doubled and redoubled my position to try to take advantage of any bounce. A bounce had to come soon.

Sometimes I flipped the whole position over, liquidating the entire portfolio in the 88888 account and taking the opposite view. I realised that the position was beginning to dominate the way I looked at the market. I no longer had a clear idea of where the market was heading, I only had a clear idea of where I wanted it to head in the light of my hidden position. The first time you buy or sell anything you do it because you need to. But then you take on a position. The second time you make a trade, you do it with your position at the back of your mind. If that goes against you, you might double up the stakes. This is gambling at its simplest. If you double up, you halve the amount the market needs to turn for you to make your money back. But you double the risk. Everyone knows that you shouldn't do it, yet everyone does it. If you go into any casino in the world you will see rather grimly determined people sitting at a roulette table and doubling up and redoubling when the black goes against them. But you've got to have deep pockets to pay for it: if the black goes against a £1 bet sixteen times, you'll end up needing to stake nearly £33,000 to stay in the game. Everyone's got £1 to bet, but not so many have £33,000. I was trying to keep on top of the 88888 losses, but I had an unhedged position, and an unhedged position is the most dangerous gamble.

JUST after my twenty-seventh birthday in February 1994, Barings staff received their bonuses for 1993. I was given £135,000. Everyone in the office had done well. I had given the girls in the back office a twelve-month bonus, and the traders on the floor an eighteen-month bonus. I'd given George Seow £50,000. This was the largest amount of money he or his family had received in their lives. George went out and bought himself a car. Lisa and I bought a flat in Blackheath.

'It's an insurance policy,' Lisa joked, 'for when you get sacked and we have to go and work back in London as a plasterer and a waitress.'

The flat needed a lot of work done on it, but Lisa's grandfather and father worked hard to put it right.

My operation, Baring Futures Singapore, had done well, and the business was still soaring upwards. I'd recruited three more girls to help sort out the settlements in the back office, and four more traders to handle the business on the dealing floor. My one problem was that the 88888 account was still in loss. I'd grown used to the size of the figures – it had a paper loss of over £30 million – but I couldn't get it to go away.

I took the bonus. I felt I had no choice but to take it – because if I didn't, then my whole deceit would be discovered and we'd all collapse. I partially justified it to myself on account of the £90 million I had saved Barings in Jakarta, and the profits I had booked across to the accounts in Tokyo, but I knew that I was hiding a dangerous loss. I'd got it down to zero before, I'd just have to do it again. And then I'd never touch the 88888 account again. I'd leave Singapore and do something else.

When I saw the Barings Report and Accounts for 1993, which were published in March, I realised that I was beginning to be relied upon as an important profit centre for the whole bank. Barings as a whole had made pre-tax profits of £100 million. There were a number of expenses deducted before that figure, but the dealing profits from Asia totalled £35 million, and my profits from Singapore were apparently in excess of £10 million. I saw that the entire Asset Management side only made £32 million profit before tax, and the investment banking about £72 million. In his glossy pages of genial congratulation to the whole group, Peter Baring commented: 'It was particularly gratifying that Baring Securities recovered strongly following the reorganisation completed early in the year and produced an outstanding result.'

He also made an interesting comment about the balance sheet:

> The new format includes the disclosure of significantly greater detail, particularly in relation to the Group's balance sheet whose composition can, of course, change significantly within short periods. For this reason it would be naïve to suppose that greater disclosure of balance sheet data will necessarily give users of accounts a better understanding of the Group; indeed, the extra data will, in many cases, serve only to divert attention from the fundamentals of the business, much of which is conducted without using significant balance sheet space.

As I wondered at the use of the word 'naïve', I flicked through the glossy report, in its navy-blue binding with the gold embossed star and eagles' wings, and saw tucked away on page 56 the three-line mention of Baring Futures (Singapore) Pte Limited. It was there among all the other rag-bag of Barings offices across the world, in a list including Jakarta, Buenos Aires, Mexico City, Paris, Lima and Bogotá. I wondered whether any of the other offices listed in the back pages were also hiding things in their balance sheets. Peter Baring was making a serious mistake about the balance sheet: it wasn't just the outside investors who were fumbling to get to grips with Barings' balance sheet – it was Peter Baring and all his team. I was creating a hole which they weren't checking.

Peter Baring's picture was right in there on page 3. He was the Page 3 pin-up. On page 29 it revealed that he was earning £212,000 a year and had been awarded a profit share of £1,000,000 for 1993. He'd also been given £30,000 towards his pension, to bring his total income for 1993 to £1,242,000. And that was before taking into account any car or health insurance or mortgage assistance or free personal telephone calls. I looked again at his picture – he looked a nice enough man, but it was hard to believe that if he applied for a job at Goldman's or Morgan Stanley he'd be pulling in £1.2 million as his starting salary. And particularly for a man who took such a relaxed view of the balance sheet.

At the beginning of 1994 Ron Baker, Head of the Financial Products Group, became my immediate boss, and the pressure rose on the profit and loss account. We were all driven to make profits, profits and more profits. For the first seven months of 1994, my Singapore arbitraging and trading operation generated profits of about £25 million, out of a group total of £50 million. I was the rising star of the group.

'Your figures are so high they're going to check up on you,' Simon Jones said as we chatted about the World Cup.

'Oh yeah?' I smiled as my stomach seized up, rose in my mouth and seemed to flip over my heart.

'Yeah, they're sending out Ash Lewis for the audit.'

'Ash Lewis?' This was bad. She had a reputation for absolute thoroughness. She was a director of Baring

Brothers. I felt as if I was going to be strapped down in a dentist's chair and have my teeth picked over. I was trying to hide one massive hole which she'd spot and dig her metal spike into: 'Aha,' she'd say, 'cavity in G3.' Bile rose sour on my tongue and I licked my lips.

'So what about Italy?' I changed the subject. Football was always safe.

'Bunch of wankers,' Simon dismissed them.

'There's going to be a lot of money on Argentina,' I nodded.

'Really? Without Maradona?'

'So the locals say.'

'Sounds interesting.'

'OK,' I said, detaching myself from the door frame of his office. 'Better get back downstairs.'

'Fuck!' I cursed as the lift doors closed behind me. 'Ash Lewis!'

'CAN Nick Leeson from Barings please report to reception, Nick Leeson from Barings to reception, please,' the SIMEX tannoy announced.

I straightened my jacket and tie and wiped my hands on my trousers.

Ron Baker and Ash Lewis were waiting by the barrier. They made an incongruous couple – Ron was short, dark and bearded, with a bit of a belly pushing out in front of him. He was wearing a shabby suit with a bad tie; Ash Lewis was tall and graceful in a grey suit, a no-nonsense woman who looked as if she could smell a bad debt a hundred miles away. She didn't smile. I felt transparent in front of her, like an X-rayed skeleton.

'Hi,' I introduced myself to her.

'Hello,' she said as we shook hands.

'Hi, Nick,' Ron said. 'Let's see the action then.'

I led them into SIMEX. Looking at the Nikkei pit through the eyes of Ash Lewis, I realised she would hardly notice the shouting, teeming chaos, she would see it all as a simple operation to be audited: you bought or sold, you booked the trade, you made a profit or a loss when you reversed it and either sold what you'd bought or bought what you'd sold.

'This is Risselle, this is Eric Chang.' I introduced the team at the Barings booth.

'Hello.' Ron hardly looked at them, he was watching the pit. 'Now, Nick, who's doing all the business here? We're the biggest, right?'

'We do a lot of arbitrage,' I said, 'so we do have high volume.'

'Can we get closer to the pit?'

'The best view is from up here.'

I showed them around the two other pits, the options and the Japanese Government Bonds. I saw my friend Danny and he winked at me and kept out of my way.

'What's the order flow?' Ash Lewis asked.

'We get an order over the phone,' I explained, 'signal it across to George – he's that guy there with the pudding-basin Beatles haircut waving his arms – he does the deals, writes them each on a separate trading card, then gives these to us at lunchtime and the end of the day, and we put them on to the daily trade sheet and a customer order ticket and log them into the computer, both our computers and SIDEX, the SIMEX computer. At the end of the day we cross-reference all the deals, and then SIMEX calculate how much we owe them. We make the payment the next day.'

I felt that I could handle things so long as we were walking around SIMEX just talking. I was at home here; I could hide among all the silly red jackets and the shouting, swearing and dealing. I was only worried that she'd find me out in the back office when there was nothing but numbers on paper to look at. I couldn't see a way to stop her getting at the numbers. She was watching me, unsmiling. She was a tough lady, tough as granite; she hadn't even laughed at George's haircut, which was pretty funny by any standards. She was going to be difficult. I pushed the thought to the back of my mind. Something would turn up.

'Ash is going to start up at Baring Securities,' Ron said as they left SIMEX, 'spend a week there and then come down to Futures.'

'How long do you reckon it'll take?' I asked her.

'Three weeks,' she said.

I waved them off and walked back into SIMEX. I found Danny in the JGB pit.

'Bubble,' I said, 'do you want to have some lunch? I need a drink.'

'Ash Lewis has been called back to London,' Simon Jones said.

I was leaning against his door frame, as usual.

'Who's going to do the audit?' I asked, trying to keep the jubilation out of my voice.

'James Baker and Ian Manson.'

The first meeting was called in Simon Jones' office. I

was on the trading floor when they called me and asked me to come over. It was raining outside, so I pulled my jacket over my head and scurried across Raffles Square to the Barings offices. I had no idea what they would throw at me, but I felt it had to be better than Ash Lewis. Simon Jones, James Baker and Ian Manson were sitting there waiting for me.

'Sorry to drag you over,' Simon said, not sounding sorry in the slightest.

'No problem.'

'James and Ian just wanted to meet you. They're taking over the internal audit and will start with me. Then they're coming down to you in about a week. They'll review all the systems and cross-check all the paperwork. The usual stuff.'

James Baker and Ian Manson nodded in agreement and smiled at me encouragingly. I met their eyes and smiled back.

'Fine,' I said. 'I'll give you anything you want.'

'And we understand that Rachel Yong would be a good contact point too,' Baker said. Rachel was our Finance Controller.

'Yes, just speak to her, she'll put you right.'

'How much time do you spend on the floor and how much back here?' Manson asked.

'I'm in here first thing, about 7:15 or 7:30, then I go to the floor from about 8 until 10:30 and then again at 11:30. Trading closes at 2:15. And then I'm back here after that, sorting out the trades and checking them all off against the SIMEX listings.'

'When's a good time to catch you?'

'Catch me when you can!' I laughed. 'But afternoon

is best. SIMEX is a bit of an animal house, and you won't be able to hear yourself think in the mornings.'

And that was the first meeting. All Baker and Manson had to do was look at a balance sheet during the month, and they'd see that the funding I'd received from London didn't equal the funding I'd passed into SIMEX. I had a week's grace.

Early the next week I slipped up to Simon Jones to tell him about a massive World Cup bet.

'It's unbelievable,' I said. 'There's a Malaysian syndicate betting that Bulgaria won't show up for their quarter-final match against Germany. They say they're going to make some political statement. They're offering even money that the match won't take place.'

'Why wouldn't Bulgaria show up?'

'Exactly, it's madness. I think it's free money.'

'OK,' Simon said, 'I'll bet against that. And what's more I'll bet that Germany win.'

'How's the audit going?' I asked as I took Simon's cash.

'Piece of cake,' he said. 'They're not going too deep. They're just internal, you know; not like I used to be.'

I went back to my desk and put Simon's money in the drawer. Both the Malaysian bet and the internal audit looked good. But I wasn't entirely sure that Germany would win. It was turning out to be a strange World Cup, possibly because the Malaysians and Singaporeans betted on everything else as well as the result. They made vast bets on the number of corners, or throw-ins, or the number of people sent off or booked – things which had nothing to do with the result. Cameroon were always good for a liquid market in the number of bookings and sendings-off. In the event, Bulgaria did of course show up, although I wondered whether some Malaysians had paid them not to. And to cap it all, in the last ten minutes Iordan Lechkov headed a spectacular goal, so Bulgaria beat Germany and Simon Jones lost his money.

IF Baker or Manson asked for the 88888 account, the girls would call me first and ask what they should print out. I was ready for that call. I would tell them to make a journal entry which brought the balance to zero, and then bluff my way through the numbers of trades on the account. After all, it was supposedly a dormant account. But they might just ask for a print-out of all accounts, and 88888 would show up on that.

The other risk was if they asked to see our total position as reported to SIMEX – that would also show up the 88888 account, with its massive loss and open position, and their eyebrows would hit the roof just as fast as their jaws hit the ground.

But both those risks were slightly alleviated in that the girls would alert me to their request and I could then try to do something about it. The girls knew that anything to do with any of the accounts was my pet project, and they would refer it to me. They didn't know the implication of the 88888 account and the strange figures I was pushing through it, but they knew enough to realise I was sensitive about it.

The unquantifiable risk was if they asked for a balance sheet. Each day a balance sheet was produced, and it only balanced at the month-end. All through the month there was a massive black hole: the missing £50 million I'd now lost in the 88888 account. The girls had no understanding of the balance sheet. It just sat around on their desks, on my desk, and was filed away every day and replaced with the new one, and then at the month-end the figures all changed dramatically – not that they would notice – and it balanced. Since the girls weren't accountants they wouldn't understand what a balance sheet could reveal, but Baker and Manson would immediately see that, although the assets equalled the liabilities, the cash paid over from London and into SIMEX on behalf of clients and Barings' own proprietary trading didn't equal the cash we owed to those clients and on our house account. I had put around half the cash into SIMEX to fund the position in the 88888 account.

The missing ingredient on the balance sheet was cash. At the time of the audit, July 1994, I was down about £50 million, and I hid it just by writing in some false numbers. A simple balance sheet for my operation would look like this:

CUSTOMER BALANCE	£110M – DEBIT
SIMEX RECEIVABLE	£60M – CREDIT
CASH HELD AT CITIBANK	£50M – CREDIT

This would mean that the customers, including Barings itself, had deposited their money through Baring Securities Japan and Baring Securities London, and London and Tokyo in turn had passed this funding on to Barings' account at Citibank in Singapore. Of the £110 million Barings Singapore had received in our Citibank account, it appeared that we had passed £60 million through to SIMEX, and held £50 million in the Citibank deposit account.

But what I had actually done was to use the £50 million to pay for the losses in the 88888 account. The Citibank account was empty, devoid of cash. I made a simple entry into the Citibank line and made the balance work – I just wrote in a simple journal entry reducing the deficit in the 88888 account and increasing the balance at Citibank. It was a ridiculous way of hiding the missing money, since if they picked up any Citibank account they would have seen that there was no £50 million. I had normally sold options to make good this shortfall and bring in cash, but I was now rolling forward such a large position that it was increasingly hard to sell options. I was hoping that Baker and Manson wouldn't check off the Citibank account. I hoped they would just read the entry, see that £50 million was written in, acknowledge that the money deposited by Barings equalled the money we had paid to SIMEX plus the money in the Citibank account, and leave it at that.

So the real nature of the balance sheet was that the customer funds of £110 million had all been used: £60 million passed on to SIMEX, and £50 million to fund 88888's losses. The Citibank balance was utterly bogus.

I waited and waited, but the call never came. Baker and Manson spent about a month in the offices, rummaging around and looking through all kinds of files, but they completely missed what was staring me in the face every time I went back to my desk. I began to spend as much time as possible on the dealing floor, hoping they would go away. Finally I received a draft copy of the report. Sure enough, they had written that I should provide daily reconciliations of the margin calls. The report contained a background note:

> BFS [Baring Futures Singapore] must deposit both initial margin and, if appropriate, variation margin on all contracts open with SIMEX on behalf of clients, which are mainly Baring Securities offices. BFS in turn requests margin deposits from clients.
>
> Leaving aside certain timing differences and other minor exceptions, all figures should agree. If they do not it is possible that either SIMEX or BFS are calling for incorrect margin amounts . . . There is no check to ensure that the amounts called by SIMEX or BFS are the same.

The note concluded: 'At present it is theoretically possible for fictitious house trades to be booked to BFS's system and extra margin called.'

I went along to see Baker and Manson, waving a copy of the draft report.

'It's fine,' I said. 'You've really got this operation taped. The only thing is that the daily reconciliation is going to be very difficult to do, because of the timing differences which keep cropping up on the SIMEX demands for margins.'

They didn't seem to want to contradict me. If they

did I had a host of other excuses up my sleeve which were all equally meaningless, but in the face of my implacable resistance to this they meekly backed down and agreed that weekly reconciliations would be more acceptable. In fact, as the internal audit was developed through two and then three drafts, the point was gradually dropped, and at one stage they were talking about monthly reconciliations. As soon as this threat began to fade, I began to relax.

When the final report came out, I realised I'd got off scot-free.

The audit seemed primarily concerned with how long Barings Singapore could go on making such wonderful profits, rather than the nature of the profits themselves.

'The focus of our audit was to seek answers to some of the questions raised by such exceptional results,' Baker had written, and he went on to ask four key questions about the million-pound profits which had been booked to my operation:

—Have the rules been broken to make these profits?
—Have exceptional risks been taken?
—Does the business have a monopoly situation?
—Are these profits going to last?

They predictably criticised my position as head of both the trading floor and the back office:

The audit found that while the individual controls

122

over BFS's systems and operations are satisfactory, there is significant risk that the controls could be overridden by the General Manager. He is the key manager in the front and the back office and can thus initiate transactions on the Group's behalf and then ensure that they are settled and recorded according to his own instructions.

Despite coming so close to the truth, they then backed down. They recommended that another manager be appointed to the back office, but then wrote:

We have attempted to explain in the report how BFS's proprietary trading activities have grown to be such an important source of Group profits. Broadly we concluded that BFS has an almost unique capacity to arbitrage effectively between SIMEX and Japanese markets; the arbitrage activity in turn generates opportunities to run positions with limited downside risk. In the end BFS will not be able to stop new entrants to the market gradually eroding the current level of profitability, but the process can be slowed if:

—the SIMEX agency and trading operations is managed as a single business in the broadest interests of the Group and not just the narrow interests of each product; and

—BFS's General Manager, who makes the key trading decisions, is retained as long as possible.

Although there is some strength in depth in the trading team, the loss of his services to a competitor would speed the erosion of BFS's profitability greatly.

The audit also recognised that the funding shortfalls were made up by Barings' Group Treasury in London, and that the bank should consider using letters of credit or an overdraft facility.

An indication of how lightly I'd escaped was contained in the introductory statement, which I read with my heart soaring: 'The main sources of evidence were enquiries made of key managers, primarily the General Manager. Key reports and records were reviewed but no detailed testing of these records was undertaken.'

In the end their conclusion just followed a few ideas I had aired at one of the meetings I did attend:

CONCLUSION: BFS proprietary trading/arbitrage operations owe much of their success to the unique positions of Barings in the SIMEX and Japanese derivatives markets. Strong agency flows, unique execution capacity and a communications edge allow BFS to both arbitrage between markets and profit from short-term market movements with limited downside risk. Nothing we have reviewed suggests that BFS is obtaining an unfair advantage by breaking SIMEX rules nor taking on positions in excess of limits.

Given that I was in charge of both the front office and the back office, it was astonishing that nobody really pushed anyone to change the system. It ran against the one great rule of any business. The Audit Report addressed the problem with the disclaiming comment:

> Despite the significant turnover of BFS it is a relatively small company with straightforward systems. Perhaps as a consequence of this both the front and the back office operations are managed and controlled by the General Manager, Nick Leeson. This represents an excessive concentration of powers; companies commonly divide responsibility for initiating, settling and recording transactions among different areas to reduce the possibility of error and fraud.

Their conclusion to this central problem was relaxed and languid:

> In normal circumstances it would not be desirable for one individual to combine the role of dealing and trading manager with those of settlements and accounting manager. Given the lack of experienced and senior staff in the back office, we recognise that the General Manager must continue to take an active role in the detailed operations of both the front and the back office.

The audit made a number of sensible suggestions, which would have stopped me in my tracks if they'd been implemented, such as: 'The growth in size and complexity of the business make it now appropriate for BFS's trading to be subject to the scrutiny of an independent Risk and Compliance Officer.'

But the official management response from Simon Jones, also quoted in the Audit Report, crapped on the idea:

As discussed with Internal Audit, current risk and compliance issues do not warrant a full-time officer for BFS. Since Futures activities are relatively specialised, as agreed with the auditors, the current Risk Manager based in Hong Kong has been approached to perform independent reviews in Singapore as and when required. (A quarterly time-frame is anticipated.) Gordon Bowser has confirmed that he is willing and able to do this.

I couldn't suppress a smile when I read this conclusion: good old tight-fisted Simon Jones! He was obsessed with keeping staff costs down to a minimum, which was why he wouldn't allow me to hire the best people for decent salaries. And his refusal to pay for a Risk and Compliance Officer meant that I would continue to go unsupervised. The 'quarterly time-frame' in those brackets summed it all up! The idea that Gordon Bowser in Hong Kong would be able to keep up with anything I was doing was laughable. It was like asking someone in Paris to supervise the Athens office.

'Are you happy with that, Nick?' James Baker asked as we sat around and stirred our cups of coffee in Simon Jones' office.

'Yeah, it's fine. Gordon will do a good job. We're so busy we could use some extra help.'

'You're busy, but let's not go overboard,' Simon said.

'You can see how the business develops,' Baker said affably.

'When's Gordon coming over here?'

'He'll come quarterly,' Simon said.

'That's no problem,' I nodded approval. 'Now, any other points while you've got me here? I really ought to fly back to the floor.'

'No, off you go,' Simon said.

'All the best,' Baker and Manson wished me as I went out.

BURIED inside the Audit Report on page 13 was a list of the Risk Committee's limits on the maximum intra-day positions booked by Baring Futures Singapore:

—200 Nikkei 225 futures
—100 Japanese Government Bond futures
—500 Euroyen futures

No overnight positions were authorised. By the beginning of September I had some 5,000 Nikkei futures; 2,000 Japanese Government Bond futures; 1,000 Euroyen futures and a trunkful of options totalling 20,000. The numbers were beginning to escalate.

5

1994: The Losses Mount

'Yes, I did wonder why Barings' position had become so substantially profitable. Indeed, I asked questions about it periodically in briefings and things . . . I was quite keen to know how profitable it was exactly because we did not know, and some of my questions prior to that November meeting were aimed at doing that. I thought about the profitability. I was pleased with it because we were keen for Barings to make profits, given their earlier problems in Baring Securities.'

Howard Walwyn, Bank of England

EVEN AS THE BANK of England mused over this wonderful profitability, which had apparently sprung purely from the managers' 'restructuring' of the business, part of the answer was lying buried in Christopher Thompson's in-tray, in another department of the Bank of England – the department which authorises transfers of funds.

Given the millions and millions of pounds I was beginning to ask for, Barings were having liquidity problems. It is illegal for any bank to transfer more than 25 per cent of its share capital out of the country without notifying the Bank of England. This is to protect the bank's customers, who may deposit their money with the bank, and then want it back again, only to find that it's all been siphoned away offshore leaving the bank vaults empty.

Barings' directors had a number of meetings with the Bank of England, in which they discussed permission to transfer more than 25 per cent of Barings' share capital overseas, principally to my operation in SIMEX and to Japan. This permission was talked around and around but was never given. However, throughout 1993 and 1994 Barings' exposure to the SIMEX and Japanese markets exceeded £117 million, 25 per cent of its share capital, in every reporting quarter except the one between April and June 1994, when it came in just below.

On 7 September 1994 George Maclean, the Head of the Banking Group of Barings, sent a memo to Geoffrey Barnett, the Chief Operating Officer of the Baring Investment Bank. The memo was copied to Ian Hopkins, Director and Head of Group Treasury and Risk; Johnnie Russell, Director of Credit Exposure Management; Tony Hawes, Group Treasurer; Richard Katz, Head of Equity Trading; and Liz Seal, the Financial Controller of Barings. It read in part:

On 6 September 1994 we breached our internal limit of £100 million in respect of exposure to OSE and exceeded 25% of our consolidated capital base (£117 million). Our exposure amounted to £127 million. Accordingly I telephoned Christopher Thompson at the Bank of England to report this fact and to enquire where the BoE stood on exposure to the Japanese exchanges. At our last supervisory meeting in May, Thompson had said that he would be writing to us on this subject having had the views of his Policy Unit.

Christopher Thompson, the Senior Manager in charge of supervising merchant banks such as Barings, told Maclean that the matter was 'buried reasonably deep in his in-tray'. According to Maclean, he then went on to say that he was 'happy with Barings having reported the situation and that we should continue to exceed 25 per cent of our capital base from time to time'.

This granting of the Bank of England's nod and wink of approval was never documented. The Bank's internal guidelines for managers required that requests for approval for the excess of 25 per cent of the base capital should be referred to the Head of the Division before approval was given. Carol Sergeant is the Head of the Major UK Banks Supervision. Christopher Thompson should have reported the Barings situation to her, but she knew nothing about it: 'I would have preferred to have known of the excesses quite strongly,' Sergeant later said.

Life as a banker in the rarefied circles of the Bank of England was so different from my life in Singapore. In their high, vaulted offices along Cheapside, Peter Baring could talk of it being 'not actually terribly difficult to make money in securities', or Christopher Thompson could apologise that something was 'buried reasonably deep in his in-tray' as if this was perfectly acceptable. The Bank of England gave tacit approval for Barings to transfer more than 25 per cent of its share capital with little more than a nod and a wink. Perhaps this was just something I had to deal with; my mother had taught me to knuckle down and sort out any problem I had. When I was sifting through Barings' £100 million mess in Jakarta, or trying to fight my way out of the mounting losses, I was unable to just hold up my hands and give up. Perhaps I should have wandered up to Simon Jones' office and apologised that the losses were 'buried reasonably deep in my in-tray, but how about that game of golf?'

I STOOD under the shower and tried to blast away the exhaustion of another sleepless night. I had been dozing, half-awake, turning every which way like a fish in a net, but I couldn't get to sleep. Lisa looked calm and beautiful as I finally got out of bed at around 6:30. She had nothing to worry about. I'd been careful to keep it that way. She was beginning to worry about my weight and how I was biting my fingernails so much, but otherwise she thought we were having a great time. I could turn off from work when I got home, to a degree which surprised even me. She was such fun, full of energy and plans, always joking and taking the piss – it was impossible not to get caught up in her love of life. It was only at night, when she was asleep and I was awake by myself, that the numbers returned to haunt me, and I twisted about trying to find oblivion so I could forget them for an hour. My morning shower was one of the few places where I was totally by myself.

I heard the phone ring and ducked out of the shower. Shit! It could be Ron, or Mary, Mike Killian, anyone. I blinked the water out of my eyes and reached for a towel.

'It's 7:40 and it's Danny. Are you picking me up or what?'

'Fuck, I'm sorry, Bubble. I'll be right with you.'

I'd been in the shower for over half an hour. I rubbed myself frantically and pulled on a shirt. It stuck to me where I hadn't dried myself properly. So what? In this heat and out on the floor I'd be wet through by lunchtime. I lassoed a tie around my neck and knotted it with a certain amount of satisfaction. It was an especially hideous red Versace number, which the boys on the Osaka exchange had given me after I'd made the first $1 million in trading. It clashed quite spectacularly with my yellow shirt, but then it would clash with almost any shirt, certainly every suit, and probably most wallpapers. Thank God I didn't have to look at it. It would give the locals something to talk about. I couldn't find my cufflinks so I rolled up my sleeves, kissed Lisa on her closed eyelids and set off to pick up Danny.

'Bubble, you look like shit,' I told him pleasantly. I thought I knew a thing or two about looking like shit; I'd certainly cornered the market in feeling like shit. 'Good night?'

'Four A.M.,' he said as he slunk into the passenger seat. 'God knows, it was worth it though.'

'We're too late for a coffee.'

'I need to mainline some caffeine,' he said, pointing to his jugular, 'just insert a drip in here and I'll be fine.'

We drove into the Ocean Towers car park.

'There's a space,' Danny said, 'but you'll never get it in. Here, let me park it. You'll dent the bumper.'

'Better a dented bumper than no car at all,' I said as I swung the Rover in a tight circle and banged the brakes.

'Bastard!' Danny shouted as his head lurched forward. 'It was only a write-off. It could happen to anyone. It just happened to me – and it just happened to be someone else's Ferrari.'

I locked the doors and thought about write-offs. I could tell Danny about write-offs which would dwarf the cost of Mark's Ferrari. We scurried over to the OUB building and joined the crowd of dealers at the entrance to SIMEX. They were having their last drags on their cigarettes before they started really exercising their lungs. We were a motley crowd. Nobody would have thought that these were some of the fastest brains and most highly-paid people in the world. They all looked down-at-heel and hungover, as if they'd stumbled out of some homeless shelter. Dave Mousseau of First Continental wouldn't have been let into a restaurant with his sad trousers flapping around his heels and his stained shirt and tie. Another dealer walked past and stuffed a $10 bill into the coffee cup Dave was just about to throw away.

'Thanks, sir,' Dave shouted. 'I appreciate that.'

'Wife and family to support,' said an OUB dealer.

'And mistress.'

'And rent boys ...'

'Who said that?' Dave yelled. 'Hey, Nick! Nice tie! Where can I get one?'

'Cost you more than ten dollars, mate,' I told him.

'Hey, I'm due a bonus sometime.'

'Dream on.'

And so we filed into SIMEX, each of us earning perhaps £200,000 a year, wealthy beyond the dreams of most of the rest of the world, and we started buying and selling numbers. I suppose that everyone is buying and selling numbers in some form or another, whether it's the shopping in the supermarket or sitting out a year as a nightwatchman in a warehouse for £6,000. We just had to buy and sell abstract numbers for a living. They were big, but they were unreal and they changed price with astonishing speed.

It was as if you were trundling your trolley around the supermarket, reached for some milk but then thought you might go for the semi-skimmed. Then, in the split second in which you'd taken your hand off the semi-skimmed and reached back for the full-fat milk, its price had doubled from 30 pence to 60 pence a pint. If you weren't expecting it, or had weak nerves, you might get a bit jumpy. And if that was happening to all the prices up and down all the aisles, on every product, you might get into a bit of a fix. You'd be standing there in a trance, watching all the prices flickering up and down and wondering when to buy and when to wait. You'd start rushing from aisle to aisle, shouting and yelling at people to get out of your way if you heard that corn-flakes were suddenly showing a good price; then barging your trolley all the way back to the mint sauce if that was rumoured to be a bargain. You'd be a wreck by the time you staggered to the check-out point. And you'd be haunted by the feeling that if you'd only been there earlier or later, you'd have got a much better price.

The SIMEX trading floor was filling up. Traders stood huddled together in their different coloured jackets. Most of the locals wore red, lucky red, but I could see the green jackets of Tullets shoulder to shoulder in their trading booth as they argued over what looked like an early morning error. So it happens to other people too, I registered; they've got problems as well.

The small Union Jack on the Barings podium fluttered softly in the draught of air conditioning. Normally the air conditioning packed up later in the day, and the flag was still. I smiled at the team. Carol, Risselle and Eric were all waiting for me, and I waved at Maslan and Din on the far side of the trading pit, who looked as if they were chatting about football: Din was re-enacting a sliced free kick. But where was George?

'Where the fuck is George?' I shouted to the rafters.

Risselle and Eric left it to Carol to answer.

'He called to say he'd be half an hour late.'

This was too much. He was really beginning to take the piss now. He was out of control.

'Are there any orders we need to handle?'

'Just one,' Risselle said. 'Buy 250 March futures within half an hour of the market open.'

'OK,' I said. 'You and Carol handle that one. Not too much at a time; let the market settle. I'll be right back.'

I walked away from the futures booth and crossed the trading floor to the Japanese Government Bonds pit.

The bell chimed for eight o'clock, and within one and a half seconds, the time it took for everyone to fill their lungs, the noise level exploded from a loud hubbub of chatter into a deafening roar. This was always my favourite moment. It was the opening of the market – anything could happen, anything was possible. It was very dangerous. I could step forward and with just one wave of the hand buy or sell millions of pounds' worth of stuff. And it was just stuff: it wasn't milk or bread or something you could use if the world all came to an end. My products were notionally called Japanese Government Bonds, or futures, or options, but nobody cared what the hell they were. They were just numbers to be bought and sold. It was like trading ether. The market was always unpredictable, jumping around every three seconds, but the opening was especially volatile, because there could be early morning orders which had to be filled which would drag the index all over the place. And there was always the first rush of adrenaline as we got up to speed, and then we were carried off by the roller-coaster.

I passed by the Morgan Stanley desk and chatted to Connie. She used to work for Barings, and I'd desperately wanted to match the offer she'd received from Morgan Stanley but Simon Jones had balked at her salary. She was a brilliant linesman who would have made Barings a lot of money – and with no mistakes. She could have changed my life; I might never have had a hidden loss if she'd still been with us. Without me asking, she proffered a tube of fruit pastilles. My reputation on the trading floor for eating sweets was only surpassed by my reputation for eating the paper dealing slips when there were no sweets around. I'd started scoffing sweets in earnest this year, and now I sent an order-filler out every morning to buy a barrel of them. I was eating ten pounds of sweets a day – that was almost a stone! No wonder I was getting fat. My belly was driving Lisa mad. I may have looked completely calm to everyone on the floor, but I felt that my obsession for sweets was a giveaway. At least they kept me off my nails. I didn't like the look of my nails any more – they were chewed and beginning to go red at the rims. The flesh at the tips of my fingers was uncomfortably exposed to the air and my fingers were growing rounded at the end, like the truncated limbs of an amputee.

I wandered back to the Barings futures booth, switched on the Bloomberg terminal and scanned the football results. I knew there was a packet riding on the West Ham–Arsenal derby. The markets could wait. I saw Arsenal had won, 2–0. Ches, one of my traders, was going to suffer for that. I support Manchester City – perennial losers. Well, someone has to support them, and the good days are on the way. I flicked back to the Bloomberg market indices and started to watch the Nikkei 225. I pushed the voicebox to Tokyo and asked for Fernando.

'How's life?'

'Fine,' he said, his American accent cutting through the phone buzz like a meat cleaver. 'Cash is getting a little tight though.'

'Speak to you later.' I clicked him off.

I turned around and scowled at Sean, the American arsehole who listened to everything I said and repeated my orders back to his bosses in Tokyo. I decided to work from the JGB booth. I wasn't arbitraging any more – at least not at the moment. I was trying to do something about my 88888 position. The year was drawing on, and I knew that the year-end audit would be tougher than the month-end ones. At least it couldn't be any softer. I now had an £80 million loss, which I could either trade out of – or hide.

I walked back through the traders to the JGB pit and picked up the handset. I dialled back to Risselle.

'Hi, it's me. I'm over in the JGB pit. What's the March contract?'

'Two-fifty bid for 100 lots, 25 offered at 260.'

'Anyone doing anything?'

'Morgan Stanley have been buying all morning, but they're the only ones.'

'Speak to you later.' I hung up the phone.

I stared at the blur of jackets and flashing hands around the JGB pit in front of me. They were like a shoal of fish – they all turned this way and that, all desperate to keep in the shoal and not be the loser who gets mauled by the shark, yet all trying to get to the food first. We were all part of the same organism, yet all deadly competitors who were trying to rip each other's throats out. I was now well outside the shoal, and beginning to panic.

They call it 'balls in the mouth'. I had built up a large position and needed to trade out of it. Most traders never get to such a large position because their overnight limits are smaller than their intra-day limits, so they can't roll positions forward. And even if they could, they'd never be allowed to accumulate an £80 million loss position. 'Balls in the mouth' usually described just

£3 million or perhaps £5 million at most. I was so far past this I'd almost lost touch with the reality of it all. I didn't need to be in and out of the market, nibbling away like fish feeding off coral, I needed a big move. And the only way I could make money was if the market went up. Then my balls would miraculously fly out of the market's mouth and I'd be free. If it went down, the teeth would clamp shut.

After the frenzy of the first ten minutes, the market settled down. Now if Morgan Stanley were buying in size it could mean either that they were generally bullish and buying an upward trend, or that they had sold higher and were buying back to close off their position and net the profit. Indeed, they could have sold lower and be stemming their losses. But either the market would go nicely higher or it was a short-term squeeze.

I had two options: I could either sell into the squeeze and buy back when the price had fallen, as Morgan Stanley stopped buying; or I could join forces with Morgan Stanley and bid alongside them to force the market higher. They would see me buying, and they might take the same attitude. Or they might sell into the market strength which I had created and leave me hung. If they did that, the market would fall and the teeth would chomp down a little harder on my balls.

'Carol, get me the Osaka market.' I was still deciding which way to play when she said: 'Still 250 bid for 100; 240 for 250.'

'What's above it?'

'Hang on, it's pretty thin. There are 60 lots at 270, 100 at 280 and then the screen gets pretty patchy.'

I swallowed a wine gum and wavered for the length of

time it took for the sweet to slide down my throat. Then my mind was clear. I would ramp the market.

'Enter the following orders for me below the market,' I shouted, forgetting I was on the phone for a moment. 'I want 250 bid for 200; 240 bid for 100; 230 bid for 200; 220 bid for 300; 210 bid for 500 and 200 bid for 500. That's it.'

Carol quickly repeated the orders and confirmed that Mike had put them on to the screen in Osaka. This was a big gamble. No question about it, I was going to change the market prices and catch a lot of people napping. These orders totalled 1,800 Osaka contracts and 3,600 SIMEX contracts – which are themselves only half the face value of the Osaka ones. When I first started dealing on SIMEX the whole market only traded 5,000 contracts in a day. Now it traded 20,000, so this single order was equivalent to almost a fifth of the whole day's dealing. From among all the hundreds of dealers all doing their business throughout the day, I – sitting at the JGB booth sucking wine gums – was putting through a fifth of the business. I didn't even stop to think about why Mary Walz didn't query whether I was busting my intra-day limits. If she'd stopped to think about it she'd have known that I couldn't have sold that number in SIMEX in order to arbitrage and buy back in Osaka. But she never said anything to me, and had clearly not told Ron Baker that I was totally out of control.

I shut my mind to the money I might lose. I was now beginning to be long of the market, and the position was so big I doubted I could change it all over again; it was forcing my hand. I was no longer free to think about where the market might go, I was caught in my own trap and had to rely on the market moving in one direction. If these purchases didn't push up the market to bring my options back into the money, and so reduce my 88888 losses, I didn't know what would. I knew that if the market fell, I wouldn't have a chance to cut my losses. I wouldn't be able to sell that amount either in Osaka or SIMEX. I was in it up to my neck. The market had to rise.

I realised that Carol had rung off and I was still holding the handset. I put it back in its cradle and watched the screens to see how they would react to me. The yellow print began to flicker as the prices all changed. It was like watching a virus break out: one second there was a healthy price, then they'd all been infected and all changed. There was a chance that the market would never again see those prices – or that they'd flash back to them immediately. I opened another pack of fruit pastilles and started eating: yellow, purple, red and green together, yellow, black (my favourite), purple . . .

'Sixty seconds,' said a voice behind me. It was Danny. 'Not your best, but right up there.'

'Fuck off, Bubble,' I waved him away, and started on the next pack.

The market moved up, first fifty points, then a hundred, then it hit 19,350 and stuck. The Bloomberg terminal kept repeating the 19,350 price, time and time again like a scratched record.

'Come on,' I said. 'It's got to go higher.'

I picked up the phone and dialled 808 for our futures booth.

'Risselle, it's me. Give me the market now and then the size above and below.'

'Three-fifty bid for 20; 200 offered at 360 and then 300 at all levels to 450. Three-forty bid for 200; 330 bid for 150 and 320 bid for 300.'

This sounded ominous. It looked as if we were meeting some resistance. I didn't like the look of it at all.

'OK, stay there.'

I glanced across at the screen and found the chart I was looking for. I decided that I should try to sell a little and close off my position. I had to tread carefully. It looked to me as if 19,350 should be a pretty heavy resistance point. I decided to sell cautiously, a little at a time.

I clicked the button on the phone so that Risselle could hear me.

'Risselle, can you sell 100 at 350?'

This was larger than the 20 bid, but God knows I had more where they were coming from. There was a maddening delay as the order went through to Osaka and they put it on the screen. I felt sure that the exchange had slowed down our screens, so everyone could see what we were doing.

'Any takers?' I asked.

'Nothing yet, Nick, I'm sorry.'

'Nothing done, Nick.' I heard Mike come on the line. 'An order for 50 came through just in front of you – seconds – and took that price straight off the screen. Now there's 150 offered at 340. They've eaten your lunch, man.'

'No trouble.' I tried to sound relaxed, but my stomach was knotting tighter and tighter. 'I'll be back.'

I put the phone down neatly, so that nobody would

see that I was remotely worried. I smiled to myself and looked pleased. I took another packet of fruit pastilles and snapped it in half since I couldn't wait to unwrap the silver foil at the end.

I'd lost count of the times we'd been beaten to a trade. There was always somebody just in front of us who pushed the price away from us. We weren't just being jinxed, we were being fucking well caned. We'd been joking when I was last in Osaka that somebody had bugged our phones: now the joke wasn't quite so funny. The guys in Osaka were sure. I was beginning to believe them now.

Ches came up alongside me and slumped into a chair. He rested his head on the desk muttering incoherently about the money he'd lost on the West Ham game. Christ! That was just how I felt. I wanted to lay my head down and give up. I wanted to fall down in the middle of the trading pit and lie there spreadeagled until someone wafted me away to a deck chair and a swimming pool and a cold beer. And a hamburger. Why did I always have to be the one who had to appear strong? I was about to say hello to Ches, when the screens flickered again. Fuck me! It was going down. Three-twenty was flashing. I grabbed the phone and punched 808.

'Eve? Get me Carol.' I'd have to apologise for my abruptness later. 'What's the market?'

'Three-ten bid for 100; 200 offered at 320,' she said.

'Fucking hell!' I squeezed the bridge of my nose with my left hand to try to stop the blood and adrenaline from pounding around my head. 'What's the size of the bid?'

'It's 400 bid at 300.'

'OK, sell 500 at 300. Hit it quickly!'

I waited, and waited.

'Nothing doing, Nick.'

I saw the screen change down to 290. *Come on, come on, come on, sell the fuckers* ran around inside my head, mocking me like a ticker tape.

'Nothing done,' Carol relayed back from Japan. 'Someone beat you to it and now the whole market's on top of you. There's now 1,000 offered at 300, and the last trade was 270 and it's trading small.' I shut my eyes and saw bright red and black dots dancing across my eyelids.

'OK.' This time it was impossible to keep the strain out of my voice. I was gutted.

'I'm sorry, Nick.'

I smashed the phone down. I didn't care who saw me – everyone else did it, so why not me for once? I hunched over the screen, watching and waiting. Ches's head was lolling on the desk. I was in two minds: I could either join him and let my head collapse on to the desk, in which case I doubted I'd ever have the energy to pick it up again, or I could stand up, lift up my right hand and execute him with a vicious karate chop down on to the back of his exposed neck. In the event the phone rang with the news I didn't want to hear.

'Nick, you've bought 200 at 250; 100 at 240; 200 at 230 and 300 at 220.'

'Fine,' I said, feeling anything but.

I waited for the next call. This would be the worst. Sure enough it was Risselle.

'Nick, you've bought 500 at 210 and 500 at 200.'

'And the market?' I managed to ask.

'It's 19,190 and looking weak. Osaka are asking me if everything's OK.'

'Tell them it's fine,' I rallied myself, 'and tell them to get ready to buy some more.'

I chewed my lower lip as I calculated my position. I had bought another 1,800 Osaka contracts, worth 3,600 SIMEX contracts, at an average price of 19,220. And the market was falling down past 19,190 and looking weaker. It was ridiculous. It was absurd. If I'd been able to articulate my feelings a little more, I might even have said it was tragic. I was distinctly under the moon. More than that, I was in the deepest darkest shit I'd ever been in.

If the market continued to fall, it would soon approach 19,000: one of the price levels which would trigger another round of my options, since suddenly everyone would be exercising their puts on to me. They'd throw all their put options at me and I'd have to take them. These options would add to the futures positions and push on all the losses. Rationally I knew that I should now sell. I should now sell everything in the 88888 account, hold up my hands and be escorted off the trading floor into a police van or a padded cell. I had committed unauthorised trading and racked up losses of well over £100 million. I wasn't sure whether I'd committed an actual crime, but I did know that I'd lost a mountain of money. But I couldn't sell. I knew that I'd flatten the market – take it off at the knees. I had such a large and growing position that the entire trading floor was beginning to look to me as the barometer. I had to win the situation back. But I was now firmly on one side of the market. Up until now I'd been able to sell the whole 88888 position and change it to all short, but now I doubted I could sell out. I was long, and set to stay that way.

The lunchtime break was approaching. I decided to leave the market alone until the afternoon. I'd done enough damage for one morning.

'Danny!' I shouted across to him. 'Fancy the Oriental for breakfast?'

We hadn't eaten yet, so we always called the ten o'clock break 'breakfast', even though it was lunchtime in Osaka.

We stepped out into the solid heat of Battery Road. I took a deep breath. The air was hot and dry and caught in my throat like a cigarette. Danny hailed a taxi and we went off to the Oriental. We never mentioned work or the markets, we were too flaked out. We were ushered into the calm air-conditioned luxury of the Oriental and waiters in immaculate starched jackets came to take our orders. Indistinguishable muzak played from a concealed speaker. All the noise of the dealing floor emptied from my head, and we tucked into a full English breakfast of bacon and eggs and toast and marmalade. I was a long way from Watford, but breakfast always reminded me of home in a way no other meal did. I realised when we stood up and paid that I was still wearing my garish striped dealing jacket. All the other guests were wearing discreet grey suits, so I must have looked a proper eyesore.

'You might have told me, Bubble,' I complained.

'I imagined that you knew,' Danny said. 'Most people know if they're wearing a jacket or a pair of trousers. Anyway, it covers up that nasty tie you're sporting.'

It had started to rain, and we had to wait with a line of hotel guests at the taxi rank. We got back to SIMEX just after it opened. We took the lift up to the third floor, and as I walked out I registered that the noise was much louder than usual. Something was happening. Danny and I split and I dived towards the nearest screen.

The market had fallen 190 points. I nearly fainted. It was down to 19,000. My options would be thrown at me; the futures I'd bought this morning were showing a vast loss – £3 million and growing. I walked blindly to the Nikkei desk and couldn't control my nerves.

'What the fuck's been going on?'

'The locals are trying to squeeze us out. Osaka isn't even open yet. It's a big push here. They know there's a long position in the market.'

I knew there was too.

I left the booth and marched across to the pit where Din and another trader, Spy, made room for me. Osaka would be open in ten minutes. I looked over to Risselle and signalled for the size and price showing in Osaka.

'Two hundred sellers at the open,' came the answering signal, 'not much below.'

People around me were cutting positions like wildfire. All I could hear was the scream of sell, sell, sell, as hands pushed and pushed at thin air as they tried to sell to anyone. Everyone knew that I was long, and they were looking for me to sell my position and cane the market. The locals were scared of me: they were on to a good selling run, but I could single-handedly turn the market and push it back way above their selling. They had small intra-day limits, and they'd have to cut their positions and take a loss if I pushed the market back over their heads. They were also caught in something of a fix because if they spooked Osaka, then Osaka could turn seller – and that would plunge a lot of other positions, including mine, further underwater. All this passed through my mind as I stood silently and watched the screaming horde of red jackets. What I really focused on was that if the market fell below 19,000, then all my sold put option positions would unwind horribly. My futures exposure would at least double, and I couldn't quantify the losses. I just knew that it would be horrendous – it would be like a plane crash.

I leaned across to Din and told him I was a buyer at 19,000. There was no need to whisper, I could hardly hear myself shout. He looked at me and queried: 'What size, Nick?'

'Any size, Fat Boy!'

Din went into action. He took a deep breath, swelled his chest out like Pavarotti, and then yelled across the floor: 'Nineteen thousand bid for two hundred!'

He opened his arms wide, beckoning in sellers, and they all swivelled in their tracks and started to come for him. I could practically see the dorsal fins on their backs.

I was looking across to the local traders and the Japanese houses, and picked them off as soon as they met my eyes.

'Bought 200,' Din shouted at me.

'I've bought 300,' and I confirmed another purchase from Nomura. I noticed the Nomura trader spin round and ask for instructions, and I counted under my breath while Nomura deliberated. The longer Nomura took, the more I had changed the market. He ducked back and looked at me, and he flashed another sale of 50. I snapped them up. Din looked over the edge of the pit and saw the price of 18,995 on the screens.

'Get that fucking price off!' he yelled. 'We're bidding 19,000!'

The price disappeared, but then ticked slowly up to 19,050. Nomura stopped selling. I watched the Nomura trader. Yes! He bought the 50 back at 19,050. He was covering his arse. I watched the locals. They were looking nervous. All traders always look nervous, and an outsider will find it impossible to distinguish between different types of nervousness, and impossible to know whether someone's winning or losing. But these guys were nervous, and I could tell because they were trying not to buy from me. They were looking for other offers.

I whispered into Din's ear and he went into action again: 'Sixty bid for five hundred!' Din roared, his chest puffed up with all the mock-outraged indignation a trader feels when he's forcing the market into a squeeze.

The market was moving up with us. It ticked up to 19,100. Then the Osaka market opened, and the roar grew louder again. It was a roar of pain and confusion. Osaka opened at 19,200 – the same level it had been over lunch. The locals were maddened – they had sold down to 19,000 and now the scramble was on to cover their positions. They started buying. One local was pleading to buy at 19,150 as the market ran away from him. He was signalling to me, a mad dance of courtship, his arms open, his hands holding his dealing cards. He was going to commit hara-kiri if I didn't sell to him, he was going to top himself there and then and spill his guts right across the middle of the pit. He had nothing else to live for in the next few seconds. I watched him, smiling at his histrionics. Let the bastard suffer. I waited and waited, knowing that really he couldn't give a damn. None of his wealth was riding on this. Then the price hit 19,200, and I sold to him. Without batting an eyelid he was on to the next trader, trying to buy more. This was interesting. The market was up to 19,250.

'How many did you buy?' I shouted at Din.

'Five hundred,' Din said.

'Sell them, quietly.'

Din sold 200 across to the locals at 19,250, and then four lots of 50 around the pit. I sold 200 across at 19,250. And then I shafted the one local who'd been eyeballing me for 50 at 19,250 as well. And then I got out of the rest to Morgan Stanley at 19,200. Din and I stood still for a minute.

'What's the score now?'

'I'm still long of a hundred.'

I was all square. The price held at 19,200. We waited. In fact the price steadied, and then moved back up again as Osaka moved up. It was of course still below my morning purchases, but shit, we'd held the line this afternoon. In fact we'd made a very visible profit. Din was ecstatic. He sold out the last 100 at 19,210 and we left the pit and went back to the booth. Maslan stayed there to see if we needed anything else.

I smiled when I arrived. Risselle was on the phone to Osaka. The rally was still there. I might get out of the 88888 losses yet. The locals would certainly be talking about me tonight.

'Did you see how many he bought at 19,000! Wa!'

'I'm not dealing with him again, he's bad luck! I always lose money!'

They would be drinking Tiger beer and eating chicken rice and clacking their chopsticks. If only they knew the full story. The rice would fall from their chopsticks in double-quick time.

Risselle interrupted me: 'The market's closing, do you want me to do anything?'

'Yes, we need to put a cross trade through for the 3,600 contracts from this morning. Can you and Maslan do that at a tick above?'

This was unauthorised. What this meant was that I was selling the 3,600 contracts I had bought in Osaka across to myself in SIMEX, so it looked as if the trade was arbitraged out at a back-to-back price. In the event I had actually bought these contracts at an average price of 19,200. The market had closed at 19,150. I hadn't lost a vast amount of money, but I hadn't made any either. I would buy these 3,600 contracts for the 88888 account, and then have to sell them. But I'd be lucky to get above 19,200 for them. In fact, I wouldn't be able to shift that quantity for love nor money at this time of day – or very much money, at any rate. Three thousand six hundred contracts would blow the market away in SIMEX; they'd also change the market in Osaka. Normally I didn't care whether I bought or sold – if you've shorted the market you make the same profit on the way down. But with my 88888 position I was trapped in a corner – it was much easier to buy than sell because it supported the market and pushed prices up, which delayed crystallising my loss on the options. I'd have to put them in the 88888 account and roll them forward.

By pretending to sell the 3,600 contracts at a tick above the price I'd paid for them, I was also avoiding Barings' internal risk controllers. It wasn't their job to check the trades, they only scanned the bottom line of the putative profit or loss and picked out any extraordinary profit or loss. I was doing a vast volume of trades with prices ranging all over the place, but if the bottom-line figures looked relatively normal, a small profit or a small loss, they ignored it and went on to look at other things. And, most crucially, I was bringing them back into Singapore where I could hide them. I couldn't hide them in Osaka. I needed them on my books here to be able to do anything with them.

The market closed, the noise faded. Across the trading pits there were just discarded scraps of paper and sweet wrappers. People vanished off the floor as quickly as they arrived. They left their trading jackets on the backs of chairs and soon the place was empty. I wondered where they all went: cafés, bars, brothels, Chinese restaurants. They'd go off and drink, eat dumplings and chicken rice, and that was another day. They were making money. Most of them were on commission, so however nervous they looked while trading, they were still immune to the market rising or falling. They just wanted some action. They had no responsibility. A few of them took positions, and that was a different ball game. But most of them pocketed their commission and then enjoyed spending it in the evening.

Rob shouted out that they were all going to Il Fiore to eat. Did I want to come? I went along with them for twenty minutes or so, to pack in some coffee and tiramisu, and then went back to the office. This was the start of the second half of the day.

I ARRIVED back at the office at about 4 P.M. The girls were there, polite and smiling as usual. It was so quiet compared with the trading floor that it always took me a couple of minutes to adjust my voice. I was used to bellowing to make myself heard. I looked through the list of messages and called my friend Steve back first, the easiest call. Most evenings we went boxing together to work out our aggression, and tonight he asked me to pick him up.

'Can you get away?'

'Yeah, I'll be out of here by six.'

'See you then.'

Then I looked at the other messages. Mary Walz in London was next.

'How are you doing?'

'Fine. What're your funding requirements?'

'We'll fax them through. Busy day though, good commission and some good opportunities too.'

'So Fernando told me,' she said. She always gave the impression that she knew what I was doing. She was a no-nonsense kind of woman, who just believed you should get on and do your job, balls to the wall and stuff the consequences. I liked this, but she had no idea what she was talking about.

'Catch you later,' I said. 'I've got to go and see someone at SIMEX.'

'OK, Nick.'

I didn't go and see someone at SIMEX. I had no

intention of seeing anyone at SIMEX. I took the lift up
to the 24th floor to see Simon Jones. I felt sick as I went
up to see him, and my stomach was screwed so tight
that I had to swallow a mouthful of bile as I walked out
of the lift. I passed by the large gold plaque on the wall
with BARING SECURITIES emblazoned on it, and then the
sequence of Queen's Awards for Exports, swiped my
card through the security slot and entered the offices.
The settlements area was an unholy mess, with piles of
paper everywhere. They never seemed to get larger or
smaller or indeed ever move. Perhaps they had always
been there. Perhaps they had been there when Barings
moved into the offices. They might even be nothing to
do with Barings, but belong to the previous tenant.
Whatever they were, I knew that if I'd been in charge of
this settlements area – the equity settlements – it would
look like my settlements area downstairs. It would be
immaculate. I hated shoddy mess.

'Is James around?' I asked James Bax's secretary. She
glared at me.

'Bangkok. Back tonight,' she said brusquely.

I smiled my thanks for the information. That was a
five-syllable answer. It was almost a conversation. We
were becoming good friends; I might even send her
some chocolates to thank her for going to all that trouble to enlighten me. (Actually, if I'd had to work next to
Simon Jones all day, I think I'd have become like that as
well.)

'Simon,' I turned into his office. 'Need me for anything?'

'No, we're fine,' he said. 'Good day?'

'Yeah, made some money this afternoon.'

'Any football bets?'

'Not at the moment. Ches lost a packet on West Ham.'

'Huh!' Simon snorted with pleasure. 'See you tomorrow.'

I fled back to the lifts and caught the service one, which went straight to the 14th floor, rather than stopping at the 17th and changing. It had been a typical conversation. There I was, riding this mounting wave of loss, and we carried on the banter about football.

Back at my desk, I shuffled the cards of messages and dealt myself one from the bottom. It was the *Nihon Keizei* newspaper, which monitors the Nikkei 225 index. I dealt all of them out: Bloomberg, AP–Dow Jones, Fernando, Reuters. I put quick calls back to them. They wanted my opinion about the market, as they'd all heard I'd been buying heavily.

'That's quite a position you bought there,' the reporter at AP–Dow Jones told me.

'We're fine,' I said. 'I don't know which way the client's going to play it.'

With that nonsensical comment, I rang off. I was a little concerned that they were beginning to pick up on the size of the buying.

I flicked up the screens and looked at the option prices. This was my growing problem: I'd been selling options all year, and I'd driven down their price.

Part of the price component of an option is driven by the volatility of the market. If there are lots of buyers and sellers, and prices are jumping all over the place, then options become very attractive since people don't want to tie up their money in buying the underlying security: they want the wide price movements which enable them to make good profits, or hedge their portfolio with a wide amount of margin for error. So market volatility is a part of the option price. Mathematicians have devised a way to evaluate this volatility, which they track against historical volatility and express as a percentage: on the Nikkei 225 index it was typically between 35 and 45 per cent, although in some very highly volatile markets I have seen it reported as high as 90 per cent.

When I first started selling options towards the end of 1993, the volatility had been about 40 per cent. There was a lot of buying – notably from Philippe Bonnefoy, but also George Soros, which had kept an active market going. But then I had to sell more and more. This drove down the volatility, since whenever there was a buyer, I'd hit him. Soon I was the main seller in the market and I was forcing options down the market's throat. Of course Barings assumed that it was Philippe Bonnefoy who was trading. It was a neat camouflage for me, and I always diverted attention away from my selling of options by saying how secretive Philippe liked to be and left it at that. But the price of options was falling and I had to sell ever larger numbers to bring in the cash to pull the 88888 account back to zero.

I settled back in my chair in the office and felt the sweat drying on my shirt. It had been a mad day, with George's attempt to head-butt another dealer on the floor the highlight. We were all stressed, no question, and this had been George's response when he thought the guy had crossed him. We'd had to wade into the pit and pull George away from the American. I laughed to myself when I remembered the look of complete shock on the guy's face as he realised that George was about to smash into him. I'd have to write another letter to SIMEX asking for forgiveness, which would be the third or fourth one this year. They were always threatening suspension, but so far I'd always just been able to head them off.

The phone rang in the office, and since no one else was there it rang around various extensions before I decided to pick it up.

'Barings,' I said.

'Nick?'

'Yes, who's that?'

'Aloysius from Reuters,' the voice said. 'Do you want to go and have those beers we talked about last week?'

I had forgotten the conversation, but at least today was Thursday and Lisa was out at the gym with some friends. I had time to have a few drinks.

'Why not?' I said. 'My only problem is that I've got to give one of my dealers a talking to.'

'No problem, mate, bring him along. Let's meet at Off Quay.'

'See you there at five.'

The bar was on the second floor, perched right over the Singapore river. It was a new place, full of gleaming varnished hard wood like a 1920s ocean liner. Aloysius, or Loy, as he preferred to be called, was already there, with a rather dull-looking American who also worked for Reuters. They had a bottle of Jack Daniel's between them and we had the bar to ourselves. This was going to be a boring evening.

'Jack Daniel's for you?' Loy asked.

'No, I'll stick to beer, thanks.'

George arrived. I'd expected him to arrive by himself, so we could have had a quick word in private, then part company and he'd have gone home feeling duly sobered. In fact he arrived with a whole bunch of people, most of whom were already well drunk and intent on getting drunker. Quite a few of them worked for me.

Aloysius didn't seem to mind, and even ordered drinks for everyone. He clearly had a big expense account, and people were silently calculating how much of it they could use. It was rather like feeling for the bottom of the market. The bar filled up and was soon ringing with the braying noise of drinking brokers, which is pretty much the same as the braying noise of SIMEX. The beer kept flowing and my glass was always half full, which I hate since you never know how much you've drunk.

We formed a group, all talking about George's head-butting on the floor, and while I knew that I should be reprimanding George – after all, I was going to take all the shit from SIMEX and Simon Jones in the morning – I found myself sympathising with him. The Yank had been an arsehole. As I swigged back more beer I admitted to myself that I'd have liked to smash my fist into his face too. I wanted to damage him as much as possible. Good old George, I thought fondly, he was doing the job for all of us. Fucking American arsehole, he needed a fucking fist in the face every day. As the beers kept flowing I smiled benignly at George as he re-enacted the head-butt: he was going to get off without so much as a warning – again.

There was cheering from the group next to me and I saw Loy emerge from the crowd and approach the guitarist in the corner. He took the guitar and to my amazement sang a beautiful version of 'Dock of the Bay'. I stopped drinking for a minute and just stood staring, wondering how in the middle of what was fast becoming a drunken binge he could stand up and sing something as lovely as that. Then he finished, there was boisterous applause and we all started drinking faster than ever.

A kind of no-man's-land formed around us, an exclusion zone where the other drinkers didn't walk. We were one big group and nobody wanted to mess with us. We were all shouting at each other and swearing and joking and laughing and the other drinkers stood back and looked at us and muttered under their breath. Suddenly our attention was drawn to a gang of pretty girls who were peering in through the glass door trying to decide whether to come in or not. They were all done up to the nines, and they looked like a group of Singapore Airline hostesses, supposedly the most beautiful girls in the world.

'Over here, darling!' roared one of the traders, preening himself in a make-believe mirror and slicking his hair back.

They shot a look of contempt in our direction and backed down the stairs. We turned away from the door and finished another round. Then the same group of girls peered back through the window.

'What the fuck do they want?' Aloysius yelled at me.

'They look as if they're making up their minds whether to come in or not,' I said.

'Let's give them a hand and moon them, that should make up their minds!'

'Sure,' I said, putting down my glass.

We turned our backs on the girls in unison and pulled down our trousers to reveal one dark Singaporean-Indian backside and one pasty white English one. It was just a lark, a two-second moon, and then we pulled our trousers back up. It was standard procedure in Watford, and I expected some witty riposte from them to put us in our places. All they had to do was shout out 'Fatso!' and we could all have left it at that.

But I wasn't in Watford. I was in Singapore, and worst of all I was dealing with the most pretentious breed of all – the Singapore air hostess. I drank some more and the girls backed down the stairs again. We were just joking and laughing when the door opened and they all poured in, this time with their scrawny boyfriends who came up to us and started shouting. It was all I could do to stop George from perfecting his head-butt on the leader, but I tried to calm everyone down. I was quite happy to apologise, but these guys wanted us to apologise over and over again and beg for forgiveness.

As the conversation moved into heated Chinese, I wandered off to the bar. I watched the growing tension and laughed at how self-important and macho everyone was being over such a simple thing. It was ridiculous.

'Right, that's it,' I heard one of the air hostesses say. 'I'm going to call the police!'

This was madness. All we'd done was bare our bottoms for a second and the whole thing was being blown out of proportion. I strode forward into the crowd and pulled out my mobile phone.

'Here you are,' I said, offering it to her. 'I've had enough of this nonsense. Please call the police now.'

The girl looked rather shocked and deflated. She turned and went downstairs. Her entourage followed and we were left to ourselves. We all started laughing at how absurd the situation had become, and were just drinking more when the door opened and the police walked in, followed by the air hostesses again. It looked as if the police were just going to give us a quick dressing down, but everyone was so charged up with adrenaline that they started shouting their side of the argument. The police were overwhelmed, and decided to get out of the bar and take the culprits with them. The air hostess pointed at me and Loy – although how they identified us just by our bottoms I'll never know – and we were marched off.

We were led away to a police car, and as I went outside the warm air brought on a fresh wave of drunkenness which the air conditioning had, until then, postponed. The police car took us to the central station on Beech Road, which was when I started getting scared. We had to give them all our possessions and then we were put into a holding cell. After an hour we were taken out and walked back to the reception. Then Aloysius and I were handcuffed together. My head spun as they snapped the handcuffs shut, and I realised that at four o'clock that afternoon I'd had no idea who Aloysius was or that we would be going for a drink. I should be at home by now, chatting to Lisa about her workout and getting some supper together. We were taken to hospital and jabbed to take some blood. Soon it was one in the morning, and I knew that Lisa would be demented with worry. Then we were told to strip naked so they could check our bodies for any marks. After an hour spent waiting for the results of the blood test, which I knew would be a foregone conclusion since we were well and truly plastered, we were taken back to the police station. This time we were separated, and I was put in a cell with a small Chinese man whose entire body was covered with tattoos. At least that would stop the police from finding any bruising on his body. There were two planks of wood for us to sleep on, so with my smart double-cuffed shirt and Cerruti trousers I lay on the planks and tried to sleep.

In the morning I was awake at sunrise, but nobody came to see us for hours. I paced up and down. I was mad with worry. I had to call Lisa, and I had to find out what the market was doing. Finally a policeman came by.

'Please could you tell me the time?'

'Ten o'clock.'

I sat back on my plank and tried to think. I was desperately hungover, and needed water. I felt filthy. My face felt like a rubber mask, and one which I wanted to peel off. My mind kept coming back in a tiny circle to the first thought in my head – I had a position of 3,000 futures and I needed to know what was happening. The market had already been open for three hours and anything could have happened. The bollocking I was going to get from Lisa was a secondary consideration now. At two o'clock that afternoon I was finally taken out of the cell. Aloysius and I had to give statements in a tiny white room which pressed around me like a migraine, and we were allowed to make a single call. Loy called his wife and endured an absolute bollocking. I didn't call Lisa, since only Singaporeans can give bail, I called the office instead and told them to page George or Fai – a trader who'd joined Barings – and get them down here as soon as possible.

'Where did the Nikkei close?' I asked.

'Nineteen two-fifty.'

I put the phone down. The market was 100 points lower, and I tried to work out my loss for the day. Three thousand contracts and a 100-point drop on the Nikkei meant that I'd lost over a million. And I had to carry the position over the weekend. Fai arrived and posted bail – there was a nominal $3,000 deposit – and I was away in Fai's Mercedes. I picked up the phone and called Lisa.

'Where the hell have you been?' she shouted. 'I've been phoning the office all day and they've been giving me lousy bullshit excuses for you.'

'I spent the night at the police station,' I pleaded. 'I'm in Fai's car and I'll be home in five minutes.'

'OK, but you'd better have a good explanation.'

At home I went straight to the shower and blasted away the hangover and the filth of the cell. Then I sat down with Lisa and told her all about the evening – but without mentioning the mooning incident, only saying that we'd had a loud argument. I didn't want her to worry, since indecent exposure is a big crime in Singapore. I told her that I'd have to go back in four weeks' time, when the police would have another discussion with the girls to see if they would drop the charges.

But four weeks later nothing had changed. The police took us in and said that the charges wouldn't be dropped, so Loy and I had to go through to be photographed and fingerprinted. We were put back in the cell and had to wait for six hours before being taken out again. By the time we were through, Fai and Loy's wife were asleep on the wooden chairs in reception.

'How do I get a lawyer?' I asked Fai. 'I've got to appear in court tomorrow.'

'I've spoken to my brother. He knows somebody,' Fai said.

The next day I was up at dawn. I was almost dressed when Lisa woke up, pulled on a T-shirt and came over to cuddle me. I was so scared that I almost cried, but I blinked back the tears. I wanted her to think that it was just a formality and that I'd be right back. I hadn't cried since the day of our wedding, and here I was nearly in tears because I was scared of going to court.

I drove over there and found Aloysius in his car in the car park. His answers to my questions were short, and I wondered whether he was going to change his story and push more of the blame on me. I had no idea what my lawyer looked like, but I realised that since I was the only European around he'd find me without difficulty. I waited outside Court 23, and at 8:55 a little man arrived at my side. He told me he was my lawyer, and that he would press for an adjournment, which was a formality. The judge agreed to an adjournment but asked for my passport. When I said that I'd have to send for it, I was handcuffed and bundled into a big iron cage and then thrown into the cells beneath the court – not quite the kind of formality I'd been expecting. I was the first into the cell, but it rapidly filled up, and by the time my passport arrived there was standing room only.

I spent the next eight weeks in a mood of sustained panic. I couldn't concentrate on the losses, which began to grow as I was too slow to react to the market. My lawyer appealed to the Attorney General's office for a reduction in the charges, but we heard nothing for four weeks. Then on the night before I was due to appear back in court my lawyer called me.

'I've just heard that they have increased the charge, not reduced it,' he said. 'The maximum you are facing for indecent exposure is one year in prison.'

'One year in prison!' I howled. 'For Christ's sake, I was only drunk and did a mooney. What the fuck is going on?'

'That is the letter of the law here.'

'I'm sorry,' I said, 'I didn't mean to swear. But this is ridiculous.'

'We'll ask for another adjournment in the morning,' said the lawyer.

So far I'd kept the whole episode a secret from anyone at the office, apart from the traders, who all knew. But finally I went to see Simon Jones.

'You'll need a good lawyer,' he said angrily. 'Who are you using?'

'A friend of one of the locals.'

'Ditch him and I'll instruct Jane Itogi today,' he said. 'And one more thing – if I see you down at Boat Quay or anywhere other than your apartment before this is over, I'll sort you out personally.'

'I understand,' I said, leaving his office in disgrace.

Over the next few weeks Aloysius skipped bail. The

judge lost his rag and put out a warrant for his arrest. All my friends kept offering to smuggle me across the Malaysian border under a boot-load of golf clubs so I could get back to London.

'Come on,' they said, 'a year in Changi jail! Get out of here!'

But I stayed. Lisa went back home for a week's holiday and I was by myself every night. After some weeks Jane called me.

'The good news is that they've reduced the charge, so it carries just one month in custody. But I don't want to take anything for granted.'

On SIMEX the next day John Soo, one of the local traders, came up to me. Usually I represented about 90 per cent of his trade, so since I wasn't doing anything all the locals were suffering.

'Nick,' he said, 'I want to help you. Will you come with me? I want you to meet someone.'

'Sure,' I said. 'Is he an escape artist?'

'In a funny way, he is.'

We set off in his car after work, drove to pick up his partner's wife Theresa, and then went out towards the airport and towards Tampines, where I played football. Then we turned off the main road and bumped along a dusty dirt track, which was mainly used by cement lorries pulling in and out of a huge factory in the distance. We stopped in front of a large white building.

'What's this place?' I asked.

'You'll see,' John said, clearly enjoying the suspense.

We walked up the steps and into a wide open room, which was empty save for a vast golden Buddha sitting peacefully in the centre. This was evidently a Buddhist temple. John and Theresa bowed their heads and took off their shoes. I did the same. As we looked around, I saw that there were little Buddhas everywhere, set into alcoves in the wall. John led us away to a small door; we went through and climbed up some stairs. Then we turned into another room and I caught my breath in disbelief: the walls and ceiling were encrusted with gold and jewels. I had never seen such wealth. I'd always thought that I lived in the most materialistic world in my work on SIMEX, where we just dealt in money all day, but this Buddhist temple dwarfed the kind of money I was used to. A shaven-headed monk in an orange robe came forward to greet John, who then introduced me. We bowed to each other and shook hands. When he smiled it was as though the sun had come out. He just beamed at me. I felt my shoulders relaxing, and I warmed to him immediately. I realised that the gold room was one thing, but the real wealth was in this man and his philosophy.

The monk's English was not good, so John and Theresa explained what I'd done in Chinese. At one point the monk smiled broadly at me, which I assumed was a response to the description of the mooning incident, and I shrugged my shoulders and rolled my eyes. Then he picked up a large floppy book, like a telephone directory, and asked me the time, date and place of my birth. He read for quite a while and made several cross-references before shutting the book and turning back at me. Looking me straight in the eye, he told me – through John – that I was having a very traumatic time, but that I would be all right. He warned me that there would be many highs and lows in my life, and that I needed to control my life a little better; establish a stable pattern. Having children and giving money to charity were two ways in which this could be achieved.

I thanked him and put a donation into a red envelope. We then went into a little side room, where he said some prayers. As we were leaving, the Buddhist monk pressed something into my hand and closed his hand around my fist so that I couldn't open it. Then he smiled at me once again, and I felt as if I'd been X-rayed by some powerfully benevolent force. He walked quickly away, his robes billowing behind him. After he'd left I looked down at my hand and slowly opened my fist. Inside was a tiny golden Buddha.

'It's been reduced to a misdemeanour,' Jane told me as she came out of court. 'The maximum penalty is a 200-dollar fine. I think we should plead guilty.'

She stood in front of me, formal and official.

I stood up and felt like hugging her.

My golden Buddha was less successful on the trading floor. I'd threaded it on to a piece of string and tied it around my neck, but the price of options continued to plunge. By October 1994 the volatility on the Nikkei 225 options had fallen to 10 per cent. This had triggered many dealers into selling their own positions and cutting their losses, which drove the price down further. And it also meant that the premiums receivable had crashed in price: in order to bring in the several million pounds I needed to redress my 88888 account and bring it to zero, I'd have to sell thousands and thousands of options. It wasn't a possibility.

From October 1994 I was in a hole. I couldn't sell options any more. I had to buy futures to support the market and keep it within the 19,000 range, which was the ideal strike price for my straddled options. And I could only do this with money from London. I had no more access to funds from options. I was in a corner. I was long of the market and short of cash to fuel me. I was now totally dependent upon Brenda Granger: she would have to become my golden Buddha.

6

November and December 1994

'The best-case scenario is that Nick is calling for the
right dollars but is changing the wrong figures on his
breakdown spreadsheet; worst case is that it's plain
rubbish.'

Tony Railton, 28 December 1994

THE PHONE RANG BESIDE me. I picked it up in a daze
and peered at the luminous hands of the alarm
clock: 2 A.M.

'Nick, it's Ron. I'm not disturbing you, am I?'

'It's 2 A.M.'

'Christ, I'm sorry, I had no idea. Look, the point is
this – the old farts want you to begin to unwind the
position a little. They're worried about the levels of
funding needed to keep it going. The second thing is we
need another £2 million profit before the end of the
month to secure our bonuses.'

'That's easier said than done, Ron; what planet are
you on?'

'You've got to do it, Nick. There's no room for failure. Do you understand what I'm saying?'

'I'll see what I can do.'

'Sorry to have woken you up like that, but I can't get hold of you during the day. I'll see you a week tomorrow, in Tokyo.'

Bastard! I put down the phone. I was available all day. He only had to call me. But he wanted to terrorise me, and sleep deprivation was a good way to start. Predictably I couldn't go back to sleep. I slipped out of bed and wandered into the sitting room. There was a smell of stale beer, so I threw away the old bottles and cleared up a little. Then I sat by the window and looked out at the orange lights of Singapore. Three in the morning, and nothing much happening apart from the neon lights over the street ads flooding out of the windows of the office blocks. It was like looking at a vast electronic circuit board: there were lights and buildings and fuses all over the place. I felt that if I could only plug into it in the right way, I would short-circuit the mad tailspin I was in and make that money back. I needed to find the right switch, the right sequence. I needed the market to go up. I didn't like Ron's talk of bonuses. If I hadn't made this money back, I couldn't take a bonus from Barings. I'd have to leave before the bonuses were paid.

Towards the end of the year bonuses were all anyone talked about. There were rumoured amounts and real amounts, and all my traders were confident that I would put up a strong fight for their bonuses. I would name a figure to Simon Jones and Ron Baker, and then argue it out, doing a compromise at about 75 per cent of what I proposed. All these negotiations were scheduled to take place in December.

At the end of October I couldn't sell options, so I just used a journal entry on the Citibank account to bring the 88888 account to zero. It had passed the internal audit, but the year-end was coming up, and I'd have to face external auditors who would definitely check the Citibank account balance to ensure that the money was there. My cover was getting flimsy.

Tokyo

I ALMOST made the £2 million profit Ron wanted.

'I'll get it,' I told Carol when the light for the outside line flashed. I knew it would be Fernando. Since we were now convinced that the lines were bugged, we'd stopped using the open voice line and now just dialled through on outside lines.

'Ferd, how's life?'

'It's been a bad day for us over here. People kept missing things and we've taken a beating.'

I nodded sympathetically. Fernando sounded agitated. He was so easy to read. If he'd made a fraction of the losses I was sitting on he'd have killed himself.

'I think I did OK over here,' I said slowly. 'But you know me, I haven't got a clue in terms of figures.'

'Where was the action?' he asked.

'We had a big buyer in the March futures who bought over 2,000 contracts, I think,' I told him. 'We bought the December ones against the March ones we sold to the customer. It was easy. I know our funding requirement will have increased, and Ron's going to get mad at me, but there was some good money in it.'

173

I had enjoyed the perfect arbitrage scenario. Futures contracts typically have a three-month life, so as the December contract nears expiry date, people will start trading in the March contracts. However, nearly all the business continues in the December contracts until the very last day – up until then the volume is very thin. This means that if there is a big buyer or seller in the March contracts at an early stage, he will have a dispro- portionate effect on the market. He will push it one way or another. Any market which has been distorted by bulky trading is a perfect market for arbitrageurs, since they can deal off the big player in the March contracts, and then sell in the more liquid December market. I'd been buying the December contracts in Osaka and sell- ing the March contracts in SIMEX, at better than fair market, and locking in my profit. It'd been excellent business. If only I didn't have a cupboardful of losses which had taken on a life of their own, I'd be in great shape.

I could sense Fernando's envy down the phone. I looked across at the trading pit where I'd made hay all day and smiled as I recited more of the story.

'We had quite a large slice of the action.' I left it to him to imagine how well I might have done.

'That's great,' Fernando wanly congratulated me. 'I'll catch you at the office later.'

That weekend I flew to Tokyo to join the Financial Products Group's Asian meeting. Ron Baker and Mary Walz had come over from London, and Ron was look- ing very ragged by the time I caught up with him at the Tokyo office. After a quick chat, he went off to see some of the traders, and Fernando and I sat down.

'Hey, do you want to go upstairs?' Fernando offered. 'I normally do a workout at this time of day.'

During the boom years of the 1980s, Barings had bought ten memberships of the health club on the top floor of its New Otani building. The cost was rumoured to be $1 million each. But during the recession several of the directors had been sacked, so the spare health club memberships were shared out to traders like Fernando.

'Sure,' I agreed with alacrity. 'Let's go.'

We took the chrome lift up to the 34th floor, and stepped out. The lobby to the health club was decked out in bamboo and other woods, and looked like a large log cabin. Two pretty girls in white sweatshirts stood at the entrance and gave us keys to the lockers. Inside, we changed and picked up some white fluffy towels. Fernando went off to lift weights while I wandered along to the *onsun* baths, the hot Japanese baths, where I sat on a wooden ledge with foaming bubbling water up to my neck. I sat there for an hour, feeling the tension in my back from the last week and the flight slowly dissolve away. Then I wandered around and stared out of the windows at the skyscrapers opposite, teeming with office life. I was in the middle of the world's most expensive real estate – a glass of Coke would cost £10 here – mooching around stark bollock naked and looking out at the Japanese banks, the largest money centres in the world. I wondered what my father would have made of it all. He'd have thought it a complete farce – he'd have much preferred his local pub. And I doubted he would ever have mooched around stark bollock naked.

175

The next day we took the train down to Atami. A couple of my Singapore people were with me, Rob Leaning and Fai, but otherwise it was mainly a Japanese trip. We were going to talk about reorganising ourselves, our budgets, and of course our bonuses. Ron Baker had hired a guest-house for us to stay in.

We arrived late and checked into our rooms. It was very quiet, with a minimum of furniture and colour – everything was just black or white or grey. We slept in dormitories, four to a room; our futons lay on the floor, with a wooden brick for a pillow at one end, a small stool for our clothes at the other. Despite this pristine and sparse set-up, by the time we'd finished it looked like a rugby club changing room, with clothes and shoes strewn all over the place.

We were woken up at six in the morning by an old lady, who refused to leave our room until we were all up and out of bed. We sat down for breakfast at a low lacquered table and stared at our dried fish and raw eggs.

'I'm off to McDonald's,' Ron announced. 'Any orders?'

Six of us ordered hamburgers and took the piss out of the Japanese traders who ate the dried fish while Ron was away. He came back with a crate of junk food and a life-sized cut-out of Michael Jordan, which he'd stolen from outside the McDonald's. From then on Michael Jordan came with us wherever we went. We were meant to be talking about budgets and cost-cutting, but I couldn't take it seriously: I could see that this jamboree alone was costing tens of thousands of pounds. And above all it became clear that everyone wanted to talk about bonuses, and they all clamoured around Ron and tried to talk up their case.

We spent two days at this guest-house. On the first night Ron hired a bar, where we drank *sake* until five in the morning. The next day most of the talks were cancelled as we nursed our hangovers and sat slumped in *onsun* baths. Then we had dinner at the guest-house.

A giant abalone, a kind of shellfish which is a great Japanese delicacy, had been put on a crystal platter just inside the door as a showpiece. It had been cut in half but was still alive, oozing about in its orange and creamy shell and pulsing like a vast ink-black heart. Some of the traders started squeezing lemon juice on to it and prodding it with chopsticks.

'Leave it alone,' I said, 'poor thing.'

'Well, where's it going to go now?' someone laughed. 'I mean, it's a bit late for the animal liberationists.'

'You're disgusting,' I said, and walked off to find some *sake*. It was indeed too late for the animal liberationists. The wretched mollusc – a highly expensive dish in Japan; this one would have cost £2,000 at least – was chopped into chunks and scoffed down with its reflexes still contracting.

We sat around at the long low table and started helping ourselves to the sushi and noodles in little porcelain dishes. Two geisha girls came in, both between forty and fifty, and were followed by another old geisha girl with a mandolin of some kind, who tip-toed in and sank down into the corner. She was at least eighty, with a face like a well-preserved walnut. The two geisha girls started doing a little song and dance routine, and then they crouched down and started working their way around the table. At one stage they made Ron stand up and play some game, which seemed to involve him tumbling over between their legs, and me standing up and trying to lean over backwards. We were far too drunk to care.

Then the old lady started playing her mandolin.

'Christ, what a horrible dirge!' Ron complained, picking up some pieces of sushi and throwing them at her to make her shut up. She smiled demurely, as if Ron had thrown some flowers, and kept playing. I wasn't sure if she was insulted or thought that he was tipping her in some bizarre way. The geisha girls then stood up and did a little pirouette, in which they pulled up their dresses to show that they weren't wearing any knickers.

'Two full moons!' I shouted as they simpered at us.

'Yeah!' Ron yelled, hurling more pieces of sushi at the old crone in the corner.

'Thanks for a great evening, Ron,' I said, as I eventually made my way out of the room.

'Well, thank you, mate,' he said. 'It's you who's paid for it. You get those profits coming in and we'll have sushi coming out of our ears. Can that old bat in the corner shut the fuck up?'

And he chucked another handful of sushi over at her, some of which stuck to the wall and then slowly peeled off to fall in curling orange and pink slimy chunks around her feet. When I got back to our dormitory, I lay down and my head hit the wooden brick pillow with a thump. I was dead to the world.

THE next day we all went back to Tokyo, with nothing

1 Me aged five, in 1972, when I was at junior school in Watford.

2 As a teenager at Parmiter's School, Watford. Apparently my former teachers were amazed at the later notoriety of the 'steady' pupil they made a prefect.

3 With Lisa in Jakarta in 1990, where we worked together sorting out Barings' £100 million share certificate exposure.

4 Christmas 1990: Lisa and I on a *tuk-tuk* in Bangkok, Thailand.

5 On the plane back to Jakarta, January 1991.

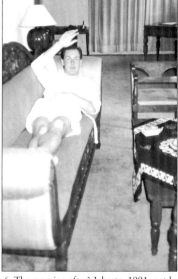

6 The morning after? Jakarta, 1991, not long before I went off on my travels with Tony Dickel, looking at Barings' operations around the world.

7 With Lisa on our wedding day, 21 March 1992, outside the church of St Edmund King and Martyr in Kent. After our honeymoon in Venice we were sent to Singapore.

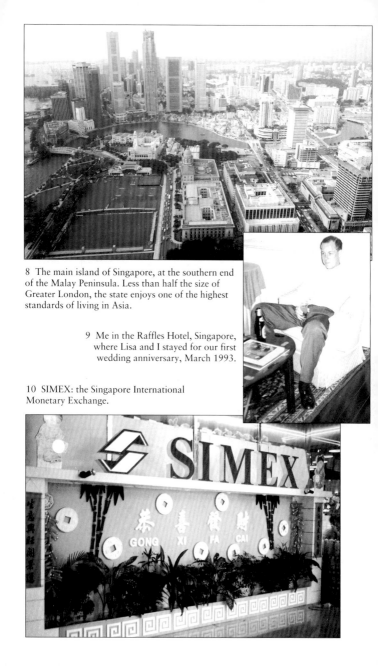

8 The main island of Singapore, at the southern end of the Malay Peninsula. Less than half the size of Greater London, the state enjoys one of the highest standards of living in Asia.

9 Me in the Raffles Hotel, Singapore, where Lisa and I stayed for our first wedding anniversary, March 1993.

10 SIMEX: the Singapore International Monetary Exchange.

11 The red jackets in full cry on the SIMEX floor.

12 The Barings crew: Ches (left), Eve (top left), Risselle (top right), and Eric Chang (right).

13 Ches with Eve (left) and Risselle.

14 Danny, a.k.a. Bubble, living up to his name.

15 In SIMEX, obviously unhappy about something.

16 The strain beginning to show. George is in the foreground, wearing his stripy blazer.

17 Rogue trader: me and Ches in SIMEX with Danny.

18 On holiday in Australia, January 1994, with Lisa and her brother Alex.

19 Australia, January 1994.

20 With friends on Lisa's birthday in August 1994, Singapore.

21 'You've been nicked' - the cake refers to my run-in with the authorities after the crazy mooning incident, but proved to be sadly prophetic.

22 At the time this photo was taken, August 1994, I was sitting on losses of around £80 million.

23 The Tokyo trip, 1994: Fernando (left) entertaining geisha girl.

24 Me in Tokyo, with souvenir. I was amazed by the Tokyo trip jamboree: it must have cost thousands, but achieved precisely nothing as far as I could see.

25 New York, December 1994: (left to right) Maslan, Ches, and Din - the Fat Boy.

26 Christmas 1994: in SIMEX with Danny ('VIZ') and Ches ('CNT').

27 Kota Kinabalu, February 1995. Lisa and I left Singapore on the Thursday, and spent the weekend on the north coast of Borneo. I am pictured here on the train which (once it got going again) took us up to the white-water rafting.

28 On the river in Borneo, Sunday 26 February 1995.

29 Arriving at Frankfurt, Thursday 2 March 1995. By the time we ran the gauntlet of photographers, I'd been allowed to change out of my T-shirt and shorts.

30 At Frankfurt, still clutching my trusty Tom Clancy thriller. I must have read the book about half a dozen times.

31 Peter Norris, former Chief Executive Officer of Baring Securities Limited. The Singaporean report refused to accept his version of events, and accused him of being 'untruthful'.

32 James Bax, former Regional Manager of Barings South Asia, also came under attack. His evidence was labelled by the Singaporeans 'false in material respects', which led to an 'adverse inference being drawn against him'.

33 Peter Baring, former Chairman of Barings. He was to find out that making money in the securities business is actually terribly difficult.

34 Ron Baker, former Head of Barings' Financial Products Group, with friend on our Tokyo trip. He was another of my bosses who resigned after the bank's collapse.

35 In Höchst prison, autumn 1995.

36 I arrived at Changi airport, Singapore, on 23 November 1995, having agreed to give up my hopes for extradition to the UK and return to face charges.

37 Changi jail, Singapore: the end of the road. On 2 December 1995 I was sentenced to spend six and a half years in the Tanah Merah part of the Changi complex.

resolved at all as far as I could see. I wasn't aware of one serious conversation in the entire two days. But Ron seemed well pleased with himself. Lisa joined me in Tokyo, and on Sunday Ron Baker, Mary Walz, Lisa and I flew to Hong Kong, to meet the Hong Kong team and discuss some internal reorganisation which Ron wanted to do to consolidate his position in Barings further. Ron wanted Mike Killian in Tokyo to report to him rather than to Peter Norris, Barings' Chief Executive Officer, and he endlessly canvassed our opinions about this idea.

The result of all this was that I was out of SIMEX for a week. We stayed at the Oriental in Hong Kong, and during one balls-aching meeting I slipped out and went downstairs to check out the prices on the Reuters screen.

I had lost money. The JGB market had risen and I was short. In contrast the Nikkei had fallen and I was long. I had lost both ways, and without needing a calculator I knew that I'd lost a fortune – at least another £20 million. My balls were dangling in the market, and the teeth had just bitten hard. I stood and stared at the screen, watching helplessly as the figures moved even as I stood there, and I had no telephone in my hand to make an order. In any event I wasn't sure whether I should sell or buy. There was nothing I could do: these were the prices and I'd lost more money. I'd taken a big punt to try to clear the account before the year-end, and it had backfired. I felt so out of the market that I began to be haunted by the odd sensation that it was nothing to do with me any more. I was trapped in an endless round of meetings in the hotel, and had no access to the real world. We spent all our time in the

Oriental, eating the chocolates and baskets of fruit which were put next to our bed every night, ordering satays on room service and then having vast buffet meals in the conference room. We wrote with the little lacquered pencils on the hotel notepaper, we saw no money change hands, we signed chits for everything from shaving gel to Hermès ties in the lobby shops, and I couldn't get a grip on my losses. I didn't know what to do about them.

I decided to wait – there was no immediate pressure, in that the month-end was still over a week away, and I'd be back in Singapore to fix the balance sheet. But the next day the markets moved against me again, and yet again on Wednesday. I stood by the same screen and watched with horror as I realised that my loss was now £50 million in three days.

'Come on, you mad trader!' It was Ron, calling me from across the foyer. 'You can get back to business soon enough. Now I need to talk to you about your bonus. You've been avoiding me.'

We sat down in the lobby with the Reuters screen flickering over his head and talked about my bonus, even as my hidden losses exploded upwards again.

'Now Nick, the budget's tight, and although you've been exceptional there's not much to go around.'

I waited until his patter dried up and he got to the punchline.

'Having said all that, I've put in a special plea with Peter Norris, and he's agreed to go up to £350,000 for you.'

I knew two things: first that this was an opening offer so I had to refuse it on principle. If I didn't refuse it,

Ron would think I was hiding something. Secondly I knew that this time around the losses were too big for me to accept it: if I couldn't control them, then I'd have to leave. I'd be caught and the game would be up.

'Ron, that's ridiculous,' I complained. 'Look, I've busted my balls for a year, I've taken us up to being the top house on SIMEX – Christ, we even won that SIMEX award for the amount of business we're putting through. You've got to come up with something better than that. I'm more than just an order-filler.'

'Of course you are, Nick,' Ron soothed, 'of course you are. As I've said, I'm pushing the boat out for you. I'm making an exception.'

I squinted over his shoulder and wished I could read the numbers flickering on the screen behind him.

'I'll see what I can do,' he said, patting my arm reassuringly. 'I'll see if it can't start with a "4".'

Ron loved having everyone hanging off his every word. He held the keys to our bonuses, and he enjoyed dangling them over our heads and making us sit up and beg for them.

London

LISA and I left Hong Kong for Singapore on 28 November, but immediately got a call from her parents: her grandfather had died. I called Ron the next day.

'Ron, Lisa's grandad's passed away.'

'I'm sorry to hear that.'

'Lisa's going back today, I'll fly out for the funeral on Friday. Is that OK?'

'What about the New York conference?'

'I'll stay for the rest of the week with Lisa's family and fly on to that at the weekend.'

'You're going to be out of the office for one hell of a long time.'

'I know, Ron, but I can't miss this funeral.'

'How are you going to make those profits come in?' Ron complained. 'Look, I'm fighting all the way for your bonus, Nick, but you need to make those profits.'

'I'll make them for you, Ron, it's just that I've got to go to this funeral.'

But he wouldn't let it lie. 'I don't want to be disappointed in you, and I know the others won't want to be either. What with this funeral and the New York conference you're going to be out of the office for nearly a fortnight.'

'I'll make the profits,' I said, through clenched teeth. 'Now is there anything else you need to say?'

'I'll call you back,' Ron said, and clicked off the phone.

I called Lisa and told her it was fine for us to go.

'Ron's hatching something, though,' I said. 'He's putting real pressure on me to make some profits.'

'Let someone else make the profits for a change,' she said. 'Anyway, I've packed.'

Ron called back. 'I've been thinking,' he said. 'You get into London on Friday morning, right? Well, I'm going to issue you with a security pass so that you can come in on Sunday evening and trade through the night.'

'What?!'

'You'll still be on Far East time anyway, so sleep

won't be a problem,' Ron went on. 'I've worked out that SIMEX will open around midnight, and you can trade through the night and not miss anything.'

'Thank you, Ron,' I said, scarcely believing my ears. 'That's so kind of you.'

'Not at all.' He waved off my heavy irony without even thinking about it. 'I'll catch you on Monday morning to see how it went. You can trade all night through the week and then we'll be in good shape by the New York conference.'

I had no time to sell options to cover the November-end balance sheet, so I made another journal entry and pretended that the funds were in the Citibank account. The numbers were large: I pretended that £65 million was sitting on deposit in Barings' Citibank account. This was getting absurd, but obviously nobody was looking at the accounting packages we were sending them. I put the matter behind me and flew to London.

I'd forgotten how cold an English December is, and when I arrived at Heathrow I was tired out from the flight and freezing. I couldn't get warm. Lisa and her parents were there to meet me off the flight, and we drove down to their house in Kent.

Sunday evening came around, and after tea we all piled into Alec's car and headed up to London. It was like going to school. Alec and Patsy, Lisa's parents, sat in the front, Lisa and I in the back. They were going to drop me off, then drive down Regent Street to see the Christmas lights and then go home. I'd stay in the Barings office and catch the train back in the morning.

We found Bishopsgate easily. The City was deserted, and Alec even jumped a few red lights since there was no traffic. It was cold and wet, and the tarmac gleamed black under the street lamps. The front doors to Number 8, the Barings head office, were shut. I got out of the car, turned up the collar of my leather jacket and peered in through the plate glass windows. The reception was empty apart from a tall Christmas tree heavily decorated in blue and gold, Barings' colours. The car waited by the kerbside as I rang the bell.

'This is madness,' Alec called from the car. 'What are you meant to be doing?'

'It's all right!' I called. 'Someone's coming.'

An elderly security guard shuffled towards the door, signalled that I should go round the back, and then mouthed: 'Are you Mr Leeson?'

'Yes,' I nodded and gave him an exaggerated thumbs-up.

I turned and waved goodbye to Lisa and her parents, and then walked up Leadenhall Street, down past the Commercial Union building where I used to work for Morgan Stanley and into the back entrance of Barings. The City was dead quiet. I thought of the vast amounts of money which all these buildings represented, and felt rather overwhelmed by their brooding silence. They just stood around me, absorbing my stare, giving no indication of what they did or who inhabited them or of any of the silly little office dramas each one hosted.

'Come in,' the security guard said. 'I really wasn't expecting you. Do you know where to go?'

I took the service lift up to the 15th floor, as the main lift was shut. I came out and made my way to Mary Walz's desk. The neon lights overhead buzzed much louder than I would have thought, and some of them came on as I walked past. Mary had left a little post-it note on her computer screen, which gave the password to get into her dealing screen.

I sat all by myself in the vast emptiness of the 15th floor and felt like a burglar. There was nothing to steal – unless I wanted to steal the packets of post-it notes, or staplers or blue Barings pencils. I picked up the phone and called Linda in Singapore.

'Hi, it's me,' I said, my voice echoing all around the office. 'I'm in the London office on Mary Walz's number. Are there are any problems?'

'We're fine, thanks,' Linda said. 'SIMEX want to see you about something, but otherwise nothing.'

'Tell them I'll be back in a fortnight.'

Then I called Risselle at the Barings booth in SIMEX.

'Any action?'

'Not much. We're OK, and we've got a couple of orders. What shall I do with them?'

'Execute them yourself. Make sure George really sees your hand signals. Then take it easy.'

I looked at Mary's little Reuters screen, built into one end of her desk, and tried to concentrate on the Nikkei. It jumped around, but without knowing what my exact position was I decided to leave things well alone. I stood up and wandered around the office a little. Then, bored, tired and jet-lagged, I found a sofa and lay down, pulled my leather jacket over my head to block out the bright neon lights and fell asleep.

I was woken at 5 A.M. by the banging of an army of cleaners. It was still dark outside, but I felt oddly awake and refreshed. I realised that the time would be mid-afternoon in Singapore, so I stood up and went to the coffee machine. A cleaner stopped her vacuuming and stared at me. We waved at each other, as if passing on a remote road. I took the scalding plastic cup back to Mary Walz's desk and sat down. The afternoon session in SIMEX would be underway. I thought maybe I should do some dealing, since Ron was expecting it.

'Risselle, how's the market?'

'It's quiet and stable.'

To buy or to sell? What was I meant to do? It didn't really matter, since I was only going to do a tiny amount anyway. The stability of the markets was helping me now. Although I'd taken a monster hit while I was in Hong Kong, this was looking a lot better. I gave Risselle a couple of rather tame orders, to buy at best around the 250 mark, sell if it hit 300. Then I read an old newspaper and waited until 7 A.M. came round, and with it a dingy grey dawn. I watched the international clocks on the wall, all digitally ticking time away in New York, London, Frankfurt, Hong Kong and Tokyo. Singapore wasn't up there, but I waited until New York showed 0200, London 0700, Frankfurt 0800, Hong Kong 1500, and Tokyo 1600 before switching off Mary's terminal, standing up, stretching like a starfish and heading for the lift.

As I walked out into Leadenhall Street, I saw that Aran's corner sandwich shop was just opening. I crossed the road and ordered a Spanish omelette sandwich. I jumped when a hand grabbed my shoulder.

'Nick, how did it go?'

It was Ron.

'All right. I did a couple of trades. Looking forward to getting home though.'

'That's great, Nick, well done.'

I hadn't told him whether I'd made or lost money; he just assumed I'd made money.

'Now I've lined up some meetings for you this week. We're seeing Peter Norris on Wednesday. Can you get in here for eleven o'clock?'

'Sure, Ron, no problem.'

'And of course you can trade every night.'

'Sure, Ron, no problem,' I repeated, rather reluctantly. And with that I took my sandwich and walked off to catch a taxi to Victoria and then the train back to Swanley.

WEDNESDAY 7 December was a fine winter's day. I noticed more Christmas decorations and the shop windows in the City were full of red and green. I went in to the Barings office, and for the first time since I'd been back I saw it during normal office hours. It was weird to see it full of people. It was even weirder when so many people kept coming up to me and congratulating me – even someone like Richard Katz, Head of Equity Trading, who'd never given me the time of day before.

'Hi, Nick,' he said, in a friendly way. 'I gather you're doing really well.'

'It's OK,' I said, playing it down.

'And you're dealing through the night here!' He shook his head in admiration.

'I'll be glad when it's over.'

'Go for it!' he said, punching me lightly on the shoulder.

I felt like whacking him full in the face. Fucking

arrogant bastard! From being too grand to talk to me, he now wanted a piece of me because he'd been fed the Ron Baker story about my success.

I was on my way to Ron's office when Brenda Granger appeared from nowhere.

'Nick! My buddy!' She was a rather matronly American lady, who liked to establish a maternal role with the people she saw as her particular 'babies'.

'Boy, do I need to talk to you,' she began. 'Now when are you going to send me some sensible numbers?'

'Give me a break, Brenda,' I said, stepping back. 'I've got a meeting with Peter Norris in three minutes' time. Can I catch you after? We can go and have a drink.'

'All right, but mind that you do come round. We need to talk. Nobody in Singapore can answer any questions without you there, and they've just asked for a heap of funding.'

'That must be for my overnight dealing.'

'I heard that you're in all night this week,' she said. 'Poor you. You must be shattered.'

I smiled and walked on to Ron Baker's office. He waved me in as he cradled the phone on one shoulder and reached for his cigars with his spare hand.

'Come in, Nick.'

I waited until he'd finished, and then he looked at his watch.

'Shit, we'd better go,' he said. 'I've asked Tarek to join us.'

We headed to the large mahogany spiral staircase which led up from the dealing floor to the senior management's office. Ron took us into a small meeting room with plush chairs around a polished table and a series of hunting prints on the walls. The one nearest me featured a red-coated huntsman taking a tumble at a hedge, and was entitled 'Heading for a Fall'.

Peter Norris breezed in. Barings' CEO was smooth and resplendent in his green double-cuffed shirt and gold cufflinks, green silk tie and double-breasted suit.

'Hello Ron, hello Tarek,' Norris said, and then, turning to me as if bestowing a special favour, he added, 'and you must be Nick.'

'I wanted to introduce you to Nick because he's playing such a big part in our restructuring,' Ron chipped in. 'And he's such a red-hot trader that I've arranged for him to come in overnight and keep trading the Nikkei.'

Norris' smile almost reached the lapels of his double-breasted suit.

'Are you really?'

'Yes,' I grinned back. This was ridiculous.

'You can't keep Nick away from the floor,' Ron went on. 'He's the key man in Singapore.'

'Sounds like you're the key man in Asia,' Peter Norris said.

'He's an animal,' Ron went on ludicrously. 'He's just insane. You should see the way he takes that market on. He's second to none.'

'Are you still enjoying yourself, Nick?' Norris asked.

This was an unexpected question. I hadn't enjoyed myself for about two years. I'd been fighting the most horrible secret and I hadn't stopped to ask myself whether it was enjoyable – in fact I knew it was horrible. It was like fighting a cancer without telling anybody. And why was enjoyment such a key part of working? I looked back at Peter Norris' openly smiling face and wondered what to tell him. I could have socked him with 'No, I've lost almost £150 million and can't see the way out,' and waited to see how long it would take for the smile to be wiped off his face. Looking at him, he'd probably laugh and tell me to go on, pull the other one – it's got bells on.

'It's all right.'

'All right!' Peter Norris and Ron laughed together at the understatement.

A waitress came in and served coffee in white porcelain cups and put a plate of biscuits on the table. None of us touched the biscuits, and we all daintily stirred our coffee. Better than the scalding plastic cup, I thought. I began to feel helpless. I felt like a prisoner tied down in the wicker basket of a hot-air balloon. I couldn't get out. Every moment more and more helium was being pumped into the balloon, and as it soared into the sky I wanted to open my mouth and shout that I was scared of heights, that I'd made a terrible mistake, that I wanted to get down – but I couldn't say a word. I could only look down and see all the happy smiling faces of the people below, like Ron Baker, Mary Walz and Peter Norris, turned up to watch me like so many sunflowers. 'Go on,' they shouted, 'our bonuses depend on you!'

'Now we need to talk about merging the Sales Area in Asia,' Ron said, 'and Tarek has some views on it as well.'

So I was being used as a pawn, I saw. If Ron could pump me up into his star trader, then say that he could replicate my success in Tokyo and Hong Kong, he would swell the size of his own empire. Mike Killian would be pushed out, another Tokyo dealer appointed who would report straight to Ron, and presumably he could claim an even bigger salary since he'd have wrapped up another host of accounts. I knew that Peter Norris didn't think much of Mike Killian, and I waited until they brought me in. After Tarek had had his say, Ron and Peter turned to me.

'What do you think, Nick?'

'It makes a lot of sense to merge the areas,' I said, knowing which way the wind was blowing. 'There needs to be control, but the trading books can be used in a way which supplements the customer requirements and increases information flow on both sides.'

I was quite pleased with this mumbo-jumbo bullshit. It didn't make much sense to me, so I couldn't think how it could possibly make much sense to them. But they beamed at me as if I'd just deciphered the Dead Sea Scrolls.

'Excellent,' Ron said, his mind still trying to get around what I'd just said, 'excellent. So you see, Peter, Nick agrees. He's been very successful with his customers. They love him.'

'Yes,' Peter nodded. 'Excellent, keep up the good work, Nick. And Ron, you sort out what you want with this merger. But do it by the end of the year.'

And with that, Peter Norris took a phone call, made his excuses and hurried out. Then, not wanting to feel inadequate, Ron also used the phone, made his excuses and hurried out. Tarek wandered off and I was left by myself. The only good thing about hiding losses from these people was that it was so easy. They were always too busy and too self-important, and were always on the telephone. They had the attention span of a gnat. They could not make the time to work through a sheet of numbers and spot that it didn't add up.

But Peter Norris had mentioned the end of the year. I walked back through the dealing floor and saw the first rash of Christmas cards. Christmas was coming; the year-end was coming. I was dreading this: the year-end didn't mean Christmas presents, seeing Lisa laughing as she opened her stocking and unwrapped all the silly things I'd given her, or even getting drunk and celebrating the New Year – the year-end meant a year-end audit.

I slipped away from the trading floor, avoiding the part of the office where I might meet Brenda Granger, took the service lift down to the basement and walked out from the car park into the street. That way I'd never see her, even if she was waiting for me at the reception. I walked along to LIFFE to meet my friend Mark for a drink, and we disappeared into a pub where nobody would find me.

New York

THAT weekend, 9 December, two hundred and fifty Barings staff from all over the world were flown into New York for a Financial Products Group conference, sales talk and Christmas party, hosted by Peter Norris and Ron Baker. George Seow, Eric Chang, Maslan, Fai and Din and the girls were flown over from Singapore. Lisa and I flew in from London.

The phone rang in our Sheraton hotel room as soon as we checked in. I thought it might be Ron, demanding another £2 million trading profit – or the call I always dreaded. It was Eric Chang.

'Hi! Eric! When did you get in?'

'Yesterday, and I wasn't part of it.'

'Part of what?'

'Haven't you heard?'

'Heard what?' My heart flipped upwards in my chest. 'I've only just this second walked into my room.'

'George and Fai spent last night in a police cell. They were bailed out by Barings. We couldn't contact you because you were in mid-air.'

'What have they done?' I said, trying to keep the relief out of my voice.

'They were caught with two hookers in a car.'

'What? In the same car?'

'Yup. They were lucky to get off with a fine and a good talking to. Fai was so loaded they thought he was their pimp, and pulled their guns on him. God knows what the police'll do to the hookers. See you at the conference. I gather you're the star of the show.'

'Hard to eclipse those two.' I rang off.

'What have they done?' Lisa asked.

'George and Fai were caught by the police canoodling with two prostitutes. Fai had so much cash on him they thought he was a pimp.'

'He's going to get you into trouble,' Lisa snorted with derision.

I couldn't face going to the presentations. I began to lose control. I couldn't sit there and listen to Ron Baker's speech and look at his slides and see the amount of money I was meant to have earned and know it was all a fake. I hadn't made them a penny – all I had to offer them was a screaming loss. I sat in our Sheraton bedroom, with its pink and grey pastel colours, and flicked up the financial pages on Teletext. I looked around the room. It was not quite as smart as the Hong Kong Oriental, but there was similar stationery over on a writing table in the corner, similar little pencils and nice baskets of fruit. There was even a bunch of flowers for Lisa from Barings FPG.

'I'm going shopping,' Lisa announced. 'I hope our credit cards are in good shape.'

'They're fine, full of life,' I said. 'Just itching for some exercise.'

The presentations started in the ballroom at 10 A.M. We filed in, slightly overwhelmed by the gigantic chandeliers and the acoustics. I sat in inscrutable silence as Ron stood up and began to talk about the money we were all making. Sure enough, he made particular reference to me.

'Nick Leeson, whom most of you know and all of you have heard of, runs our operation in Singapore, which I want you all to try to emulate. You'll hear later from Nick about how he does it, but I just want to drive home to you guys that if you could all think about Nick and perhaps come up with ideas to follow his footsteps, Barings will become one of the most successful operations in the derivatives business. We are going to make so much money. And more to the point, *you* are going to make so much money.'

We had a coffee break, and I followed the gang down to the bar. But I didn't drink coffee, I ordered a Bloody Mary. An Irish trader from some Barings branch or other came up to me.

'Good idea,' he nodded at the Bloody Mary.

'Have one too,' I suggested.

When the presentation re-started, I stayed behind with this guy, Patrick. We ordered two more Bloody Marys, and then two more. And then two more. And then we realised that we might be caught when they all split for lunch, so we wandered away from the hotel and found a sports bar at a lower level.

'I hate presentations,' Patrick confided.

'God, I hate them too,' I agreed. 'Such a waste of time when you could be out there dealing.'

'Did you say "dealing" or "drinking"?'

'I meant drinking, stuff dealing for a laugh.'

'Yeah. You're that star trader in Singapore, right?'

'Screw that,' I said, finishing my Bloody Mary.

We drank all day, watching videos of American football and baseball. I never went to the dinner that night. I was meant to be sitting next to Peter Norris, in the seat of honour, but I just couldn't live up to it. I knew I wouldn't be able to hold it together. I knew that if I opened my mouth, I'd talk about the losses and the 88888 account. At about nine o'clock I stumbled upstairs into our room and crashed out. Lisa came in at eleven.

'Nick! Where the hell have you been?'

'I've been drinking.'

'Apparently you were meant to be at some dinner and you didn't show up. Din said that Ron had told everyone you were probably on the phone, cutting some more deals and making money while they were all sitting there talking.'

I couldn't think of anything funnier than this, so I

began laughing. Lisa was mad at me. 'Have a shower and sober yourself up!'

As I stood under the shower, her hand sneaked in and twisted the tap so that the water turned freezing cold.

'Hey!' I shouted, leaping out of the shower and grabbing a towel.

'Look at you!' Lisa laughed. 'Drunk, wet and freezing. What a sight!'

The dinner I missed had been at Windows on the World, and all the pomp and pageantry of a successful operation were there for everyone to see. The location symbolised all the pride which Barings was puffing itself up with.

I had hardly sobered up by the morning. I still couldn't face the presentation, and I heard from George that Mary Walz had wrapped the proceedings up by once again looking at the Singapore operations and asking for a round of applause for the Singapore boys, who had made £28 million profit for 1994.

LISA and I flew from New York to London, where she went to stay with her parents until Christmas. Danny was also passing through London, so we met up in the British Airways First Class lounge and both flew on to Singapore. I was due to spend just one week in Singapore, then get back to London for Christmas, spend two days in Ireland, then celebrate New Year with Lisa's family, and we'd go back to Singapore in January.

But the thought was already ticking at the back of my mind that I would never come back. I would stay in

England. I would let them find the losses, sack me, and stay out of trouble. I'd been out of the sweating hell-hole of SIMEX and my 88888 account for two weeks, and I was beginning to lose touch with it.

When I arrived back in Singapore I asked Linda for the balance of the 88888 account. It was like asking for the result of a medical scan – the answer, looking as innocuous as a small print-out of figures could look – was that I had lost almost £160 million. I was in a hopeless position. I was drowning like an insect stuck in resin, clawing hopelessly but unable to pull myself out. I knew that the auditors were inching closer and closer, moving over columns and columns of figures as they approached the Barings Futures audit.

For that last week in Singapore I just let my losses sit there. I was unable to sell options, so I just rolled over the funding requirements. The market didn't go against me, but nor did it soar up and put me back on my feet. I didn't know what to do. The good thing was that everyone was throwing Christmas parties, and nobody did much business. Even the sight of Gordon Bowser didn't upset me. He came over from Hong Kong to have a look at our operation. He'd been nominated by Simon Jones to be the Risk Officer in the internal audit report – which had caused me such a scare when I thought that Ash Lewis was going to do it, but now seemed very unthreatening. I was due back in London on 22 December, and so I just trod water until I could catch the flight back home. Everyone was just cruising after the New York presentations and waiting for the money to roll in. In SIMEX, we were like kids waiting for Santa Claus.

Christmas

WE all crept downstairs wearing our dressing gowns. I remembered my primary school nativity play, when I'd worn my brown and red dressing gown, sandals, and a tea-towel over my head to make me look like a shepherd. Patsy put the kettle on, and Lisa and I pushed open the sitting-room door and stared at the presents. They spread out from the Christmas tree halfway across the room, a huge pile of glittering red and green wrapping paper. The tree's lights were on, and the walls of the room were covered with swathes of Christmas cards. We stared at the presents like a couple of kids. Patsy brought round a tray of tea and some mince pies, and then we all waded into the presents and scrabbled to find ones to give out. We didn't have stockings, so all the small stocking fillers were among the bigger presents. I'd bought Lisa a watch as her main present, but also some Ralph Lauren shirts, some 'Safari' perfume – which she'd always loved – a sweatshirt and some outrageously sexy black knickers.

'I can't wear these!' Lisa screamed with laughter, holding them up.

'Here, I'll wear them!' Patsy yelled.

'Mum! Dad! Thank you!' Lisa's sister Nadene stood up and flung her arms around Alec and Patsy and kissed them.

I opened Lisa's presents. 'Nice and smelly,' I said, holding up the 'Eau Sauvage', and then paused to open a tiny little box. Inside were the most beautiful gold and pearl cufflinks.

'Thank you, darling.' I kissed her.

'Happy Christmas,' she smiled up at me and hugged me.

Alec put his Christmas tape on, and we had Nat King Cole and Max Bygraves singing about their dream Christmases. Soon it was time to go to the hotel for lunch. My family had stayed overnight at the local Travelodge, and we all met up at the Brands Hatch Place Hotel, where Lisa and I had had our wedding reception.

Patsy sobbed as we went through the door. It was the first Christmas she'd spent without her mother and brother, who'd both died last February. Alec's father, whose funeral we had attended at the beginning of the month, had promised to take us all out for Christmas lunch, to celebrate his golden wedding anniversary. He'd put the money to one side, so Alec and Lisa's Nan decided to use it and have lunch in his honour. For a widow of just one month's grieving, after fifty years of marriage, Nan was amazing. She cried just once, when the turkey was brought in, because she remembered how Grandad used to like to carve it. Of course, that set all the women off crying, but then Nan started laughing at herself for getting worked up over the silliest little thing.

At about 6:30 we arrived back at Patsy and Alec's house, in the mood for a dance. Lisa and I cleared out the wicker furniture from the conservatory and Alec pulled out a compilation tape he'd made for the occasion. It was a bizarre mixture, switching from Diana Ross to 'Knees Up Mother Brown' to Bill Haley in rapid succession. We all started dancing.

'Something for everyone!' Alec shouted, as we

ducked our heads and started twisting to Chubby Checker.

We finally went upstairs to bed at 3:30 A.M. I looked around at the other neighbouring houses: they were all quiet, with only the Christmas tree lights sparkling in the windows. I wished that Christmas could last forever. This hadn't been a white Christmas, but it had been a dream Christmas. I didn't want to go back to Singapore; I didn't want to go back to the real world – or the unreal world of my 88888 losses. I wanted to stay here with Lisa and her family, and drink and dance like an idiot and laugh as Alec roared out his Tom Jones impressions. I hadn't felt so happy since our wedding day – and then we'd been truly innocent. I cursed myself, because I just couldn't feel happy – even now. My 88888 account was hanging around my neck like a string of rotten fish-heads. I shut my eyes and tried to hold myself together.

'Hey,' Lisa said, lying back on the pillows, 'where have you put those black knickers?'

I opened my eyes and saw that she'd put them on.

THE day after Boxing Day, Lisa and I caught a plane to Ireland, where we joined our friends Mark and Val for two days. The only other people flying in the tiny Business Class section were Hugh Grant and Liz Hurley, and I kept nudging Lisa and trying to overhear what they were saying.

Christmas with Lisa's family had been drinking and dancing: this was straight drinking. Mark was legendary for never ordering just one bottle of beer, he always drank two at once. I wondered whether he could do this with Irish stout. He could.

'Oi! Shithead! What's yours?' Mark roared from the bar.

'A pint of Murphy's.'

'And I'll have a half,' said Lisa.

'Three pints of Murphy's and two halves please.' Mark came back from the bar and started lining up the pints on the table.

'How many pubs in this place?' I asked.

'Over twenty,' Mark said, 'and we're going to get through them all.'

'But it's late already,' I said.

'No, let's drink up and move on.'

I drank more Murphy's, beautifully black and creamy.

'Ready to go?' Mark had finished his pint – his tenth of the evening, I reckoned.

'Hang on, why don't we stay for a while? It's great here.' I looked around. We were the only people in the pub.

'Are you coming?' Mark asked.

'I'll catch you up,' I said. Mark then stood up and walked over to the bar.

'How much would you charge to shut down now?' he asked the barman.

'What do you mean?'

'Shut down. Close for the night. Go home.'

'But I might get some more customers.'

'How much would they spend?'

'I don't know. They'd just have a few jars.'

'OK,' Mark said, fishing in his trouser pocket and

pulling out some cash. 'They wouldn't spend more than £50, would they?'

'Er, no,' the barman said.

'Well, here's £100. I would like you to shut the bar and not serve any more drinks tonight, particularly to that gentleman over there,' he said, pointing at me.

'You can't do that!' I squawked.

'Oh yes I can, unless you want to outbid me to keep it open.'

But I knew Mark was not one to argue with. Once he'd got an idea, nothing would budge him. So with that the barman took the money and we were out on the street.

'Now, let's move on,' Mark said. 'You've really got to keep up.' And he led the way to the next pub.

'If I ever get my hands on that crapped-out piece of old junk you call a Ferrari,' I told him, 'I promise I'll take it for a nice drive and return it to you in a neat little square packet. Then you'll be able to carry it round in your pocket.'

'I think it's your round,' Mark said, utterly unconcerned. 'I'll have another Murphy's.'

We worked our way around half the pubs in town that night, then Lisa and I and Mark and Val all walked arm in arm back to the bed and breakfast we were staying in. The B & B was a quiet Georgian house on the outskirts of Cork, with a wide front door and a tiled hallway. The carpets were flecked with orange and brown, and in our bedroom we had a little tray with a kettle and some teabags, plastic spoons, sachets of sugar and pink and white cups. A framed picture of a little boy on a bicycle hung over the fireplace, and the curtains were pink and frilly. The whole atmosphere was one of an old people's home.

We stumbled into the hallway and made our way upstairs. The landlady was a rather imposing woman who'd told us to keep the noise down if we came in after 9:30 P.M. It was past midnight. We tip-toed up the stairs. At the top I noticed a fire extinguisher. I saw Mark looking at it at the same time, and I suddenly realised what he was going to do. I grabbed the key from Lisa's hand, pushed at Mark so he crashed back down the stairs, and yelled: 'Quick, Lisa, run!'

I dashed to our room, fumbled madly at the lock, opened the door and shot in. Then I slammed the door shut. I heard Mark come roaring up the stairs.

'Nick!' he yelled. 'Open the door!'

'Fuck off, you wanker!' I yelled back.

'Open that door now!'

I turned round and realised that Lisa wasn't inside with me. Where the hell was she? I also noticed that the pink frilly curtains looked hideous, and started laughing.

'Nick! Open the door!' It was Lisa.

'Is Mark with you?'

'No.'

'Do you promise? I'm not letting that crazy idiot in here.'

'He's not here,' she said. 'He's gone to bed.'

I heard some muffled giggling.

'Lisa, is Mark with you?' I said.

'No!'

'Mark Green is a complete tosser!' I shouted through the keyhole.

'Come out here and say that!' Mark roared, his voice inches from my ear.

Then I heard another voice: 'You open that door, young man!'

'Lisa!' I shouted with laughter. 'Don't put on such a crap Irish accent!'

'Open the door now!'

'Fuck off, you silly cow!'

'Mr Leeson, will you open the door?'

Too late I realised that this wasn't Lisa; this was the landlady. I opened the door.

'What in God's name do you think you're doing?' she demanded, a figure beside herself with indignation, wrapped up in her pink flannelled dressing gown.

'I'm most awfully sorry,' I said. 'I was trying to save your furniture.'

'My furniture!' she exclaimed. 'All of you: get to bed! Now!' She threw her arms up, Lisa slipped into my room and Mark made a lunge for the door.

'Too slow!' I said, slamming it in his face.

BREAKFAST was an amazing feast. We ordered porridge, bacon and eggs, and basketfuls of sour dough bread with marmalade. We were planning on kissing the Blarney Stone when the landlady came in, but she had other things on her mind.

'Mr Leeson,' she said excitedly, 'there's a young lady on the telephone for you. She says she's calling from Singapore.'

The telephone was in the hall, on a little table surrounded by leaflets on what to do around Cork. I picked up the black bakelite handset.

'Hello, Nick, it's Linda.'

'Hi! How are you?'

'I'm fine. As it's Friday I'm just phoning up about the balance on the 88888 account.'

I looked at my watch. It was late afternoon in Singapore. I looked at the newspaper on the table: it was Friday 30 December. Tomorrow was New Year's Eve. I couldn't believe I'd left the position so uncovered. I'd pushed it right away from me. Since we'd been in Ireland, I'd almost forgotten about it.

'What's the balance?'

'The equity balance this week is 7.78 billion yen.' Linda read it out with as little interest as if it had been the weather forecast or the colour of shoes she was wearing. I tried not to imagine how big 7.78 billion yen was, but unfortunately – since the yen was 100 to the dollar – it was all too easy: it was US $77.8 million, fifty million pounds.

AT the end of 1993, I hadn't had a problem. I'd been able to sell options and bring in a premium which exactly equalled the realised loss, bringing the account to zero. The value of the options was underwater to 4 billion yen, but that could be rolled over and carried forward. Last year the price of options had still been high, with their volatility around 30 per cent, and I'd known that I'd be able to bring in sufficient premiums to cover my cash balance.

Now, at the end of 1994, the figures had multiplied tenfold. I'd sold options all year, forced the volatility down to 10 per cent, the prices were too low and I'd finally run out of rope to hang myself. I now couldn't sell enough options to match the realised loss. I was 7.78 billion yen short. I'd paid 7.78 billion yen losses over to SIMEX, by way of variation margin payments which I'd received from London, but which had no corresponding entry on the balance sheet. There was a 7.78 billion yen hole.

'Linda,' I said slowly, almost improvising as I went along, 'please can you listen carefully. Book this trade through the system for me: sell 2,000 December 21,500 puts at a price of 7778.'

Linda repeated the instruction back to me.

'Good. Now print off the normal reports before and after that entry. Use the reports before the trade for everything *but* the trial balance sheet, use the report after that entry for the trial balance itself.'

'Fine,' she said, not really understanding what I was saying.

The impact of this instruction was that the trade booked at 7.778 billion yen would bring the account balance back to zero. However, in order to reconcile with SIMEX we would have to use the pre-entry reports. This was cooking the books just as surely as our Irish landlady was cooking our porridge.

By changing the *general* ledger (the trial balance of cash and debts owed to Barings) and not the *sub*-ledger (which reconciled with SIMEX's records), I was making the 7.78 billion look as if Barings was owed it by SIMEX. Of course the auditors would jump on it and ask where it was, but they wouldn't do that until I got back. In the meantime, I'd arranged for 7.78 billion yen, £50 million, to be owing to Barings from SIMEX rather than from inside my 88888 error account. I dreaded to think about the trouble it would put me in – but then I wasn't going to go back. I would never go back to Singapore. The books balanced at 31 December 1994, and that was the last they'd see of me. If I ever went back, they'd find out that SIMEX had no third party from whom it could claim the 7.78 billion yen, they'd find my fraud and hang me out to dry.

I put the phone down and went back into the breakfast room. Mark and Val were arguing about the Blarney Stone.

'You've got to kiss it upside down,' Mark said.

'Who's going to hold my legs?' Lisa laughed.

'Trust me,' Mark said.

'No way!'

'Nick'll kiss it,' he went on, turning to me.

'No way. I hate heights.'

I sat down at the breakfast table as we all happily argued. Our life looked so good from the outside – breaking the news to Lisa that it was all going to change was my last hurdle. We weren't going to go back. I hate heights – but I'd have preferred to have hung upside down and dangled over the precipice to kiss the Blarney Stone rather than tell Lisa. In fact, I needed to kiss the Blarney Stone to get the gift of the gab.

'OF course we're going back,' Lisa snapped at me. 'What in the world are you talking about? You're mad. You've got your bonus to collect in February. Surely to God you can hang on for two more months? What's the matter with you?'

'I'm cracking up,' I said weakly, aware that Mark and Val next door would hear every word through the wall if we shouted. 'I can't stand the pressure any more.'

'That's mad!' Lisa said. 'Ron's promised you four hundred grand, which will set us up for life! It's like winning the lottery. I don't see why you can't go back, take it easy, and we're there. We can clear out in March. And in any event we've got Richard coming out next month, and then Nadene in March. In fact my parents are planning to come in April. We can't let them down.'

March! April! It was out of the question. I didn't know what to say. Lisa was right. From her point of view she was entirely right. I couldn't disagree with her. But I couldn't tell her what I knew. I had this cata-strophic secret which was burning up inside me – yet I couldn't tell her. I simply couldn't open my mouth and say, 'I've lost millions and millions of pounds.' I'd have found it easier to tell Risselle, or Patrick, the Irish trader I'd got drunk with in New York, or the landlady of the B & B, but I couldn't tell Lisa.

She stood in front of me, her whole body arched with indignation and misunderstanding, so that she looked like a black question mark which demanded to be answered, but I shrank away from her. I loved her too much to admit that I'd lost such a vast fortune. I didn't want to shock her. And then, as I allowed myself to think a little more, I realised that I couldn't bear to be seen as a failure in her eyes. I had always succeeded at whatever I'd done, and I couldn't stand the idea of being a failure. I'd read stories about how some men pretend to their wives that they've got a job, and they go off to work in a suit every day but then sit around on park benches until five o'clock. Lisa and I had laughed at stories like that.

But now the ghastly truth was that *I* was the man leading a double life – and I couldn't tell Lisa what I'd done. I stared at her, and she stared back at me. I could hardly meet her eye. I felt as though it must be obvious to anyone that I'd lost millions of pounds. I felt as if it was written all over me, like a scorching red infected rash across my face, or like a sandwich board strapped across my shoulders emblazoned: 'THIS MAN HAS LOST MILLIONS!'

But Lisa couldn't see it. Nobody could see it. I just saw it in the mirror. It was an invisible loss to Barings – for the time being – and an invisible loss to Lisa.

'What's the matter?' she demanded, as I stood silent.

'Nothing,' I said defiantly. 'We'll go back to Singapore then. No worries. It'll be fine.' And we left the matter there. I had failed to tell her. Among all my failings, this was the worst. I'd hidden my losses from everyone at Barings, from my friends, and now from Lisa. I was tied hand and foot to that big balloon I had imagined, and now I was being lifted off out of control. We were going to return to Singapore. I was damned to return to my 88888 account, to a hidden loss which must now exceed £170 million, and to the small problem of how to get around the 7.78 billion yen which I'd now put into the system as a receivable from SIMEX. I had to conjure up £50 million from thin air.

* * *

WE fastened our seat belts. The plane banked and dropped steeply as it began its descent to Singapore. I looked out of the window and saw the familiar line of skyscrapers which bordered the harbour. In one of those offices there was a computer, and on that computer was my 88888 account, and in that account there were invisible losses which I knew I could no longer contain. They would erupt out into the world.

'Pleased to be back?' Lisa asked. 'Now that we're here?'

'It's fine,' I smiled. 'It'll be no problem.'

Some time between now and the end of February, when the bonuses were paid, I'd have to shit or bust.

7

January to 6 February 1995

'It's just a non-transaction. It's an error. It is a back office glitch. Don't worry about it.'

James Bax to Ron Baker, 3 February 1995

I WAS BACK ON the SIMEX floor wearing my blue and yellow striped jacket and everything was back to normal. I was making good money, I was busy, my traders were happy and professional, we had built up a nice long position and we were riding the market up.

'Nick! What gives, mate?' It was Danny.

I pulled out another tube of fruit pastilles and snapped them in half. I was kidding myself. My life was most definitely not normal. The market wasn't up, it was just moving obstinately sideways. I reckoned my year-end losses had topped £170 million, and they didn't look like getting any better.

'This market's driving me nuts.'

'It's a bummer. Catch you later, Nick. You want lunch?'

'Sure, I'll give you a shout.'

I walked from the JGB pit back to the Barings booth. The Union Jack had a bit more life to it. It was fluttering bravely with all the doomed energy of a crushed butterfly. I looked over at George and Spy in the Nikkei pit. I was the wrong end of £170 million. If I was to get out, I had to pull the trigger one way or the other. The only problem was that it could also blow up in my face. I knew that SIMEX and the auditors couldn't be far away now. I had seen the auditors, men in grey suits, up on the 24th floor, and they'd be working their way down soon. They were eating their way through filing cabinets and columns of figures with the unhurried, meticulous attention of termites, and soon they'd come up against the 7.78 billion yen fabrication – and that would be the end. In fact, more serious than that, they could flick a switch at any time to check my open position, see the 88888 account and its haemorrhaging losses – and that would be the end rather more quickly.

AT the year-end my only futures position in the 88888 account was 1,000 March 1995 contracts. I think they were showing a small profit. The options were showing a healthy profit of about £75 million since they'd been sold, but the losses I'd realised during the year were huge. Since I couldn't sell any options to bring in cash premiums to fund the margin, I had to use futures to swing the market and take the maximum benefit from the options position that I already had. Most of my options would stay in the money if the market kept at around 19,000. I had to protect the strike prices of my options positions. I had no Japanese Government

Bonds and no Euroyen in the 88888 account. I'd been unable to persuade Lisa that we needed to get out of Singapore. We were stuck here. The only weapon I could use to prevent my 88888 losses increasing was buying futures to prop up the market. In fact, if the market rose too much, I'd have to sell futures, because I didn't want the other half of my straddles being exercised on to me. I was ready for a final push.

From the moment we arrived back in Singapore in the first week of January I lost control. I stopped looking at the 88888 account balance. I knew that it was large, but I was just intent on surviving each day. I was juggling a number of problems: the year-end audit, and that ridiculous sleight of hand that I'd done on the 7.78 billion yen deficit; the fact that SIMEX were beginning to worry about the amount of funding the 88888 account needed to support it; and of course I had to continue to get London to send me over more than $10 million each day. I had to get out of trouble, but from the time we arrived back in Singapore on 8 January my top priority was just being able to get through each day and drive back to our flat and be with Lisa.

'WHAT's this fucking letter all about?' Simon Jones snapped down the phone.

I had read it with amazement that morning. Although addressed to Simon, it had been put in my in-tray since it was a SIMEX matter about futures. It looked straightforward, but I had digested it with mounting panic. The crucial passage read:

We understand from your staff that the Initial Margin requirement was the margin requirement of the positions held by the sub-account '88888' of BSL-CSA. Based on the information provided so far, it appears to us that your company had financed the trading margin of the positions held by sub-account 88888. If this is really the case, your company has violated SIMEX rule 822 which prohibits members from financing the trading margins of their customers.

Dated 11 January 1995, it was from the Audit and Compliance Department of SIMEX.

I had thought about hiding it or destroying it, but they would only write again, and then Simon Jones might pick it up himself. Surely someone would now turn on a computer and check my open position. Never mind the 7.78 billion yen fraud which I had to deal with, the 88888 account itself was blown open. It was all over.

I had stared at it and stared at it, and then realised that the only way to confront this was to bluff it out. So I scribbled a note on a post-it, 'Simon – let's discuss later', as if it was the most natural thing in the world, and put it in my out-tray so that an internal messenger could take it up to Simon Jones. And he had called me the second it hit his desk.

'I'm coming up,' I said.

'Right now.' And the phone clicked off.

'So what the fuck is this all about?' Simon exploded when I came into his office. It looked as if my tactic had backfired.

214

'Oh, they're just banging on about our intra-day funding limits,' I said, with a bored shrug of my shoulders. 'I wish they'd just get off our backs and let us do some business.'

'God, they're a pain in the arse.' Simon made a face. 'I mean it's as if they don't *want* us to trade. We're the number one trader in town, and they're trying to tie us up in red tape.'

'They've gone and muddled up our client accounts with our house position,' I pointed out.

'They're fucking idiots,' Simon agreed. 'And what's this calculation – it looks about £90 million out to me.'

'Yeah, I know. Look, I'll draft an answer for you,' I said, holding out my hand for the letter. 'Don't worry about it.'

'Yes, do that, will you? Get the reply on my desk by tomorrow.' Simon gave me the offending letter back. 'Now, what are you betting on Man United?'

'Bunch of celebs,' I shook my head. 'No soul. Nobody in Manchester supports Man U. All their supporters are yuppies from London; the only team in Manchester is City. As for this git Cantona – what a prize wanker!'

'Blackburn Rovers?'

'They're more like it.'

'Bet you $500 Man United win.'

'It's a deal,' I said, shaking his hand. Five hundred dollars was a cheap price to pay to keep his mind off the SIMEX letter.

Back at my desk I tossed the letter into my in-tray. I'd have to do something about that. I'd draft a reply which Simon would then change and edit and generally use as an excuse to exercise power over me. Well let him. It was like being a clerk back at Coutts, when I had to draft letters for my boss which were then changed so much there was no point in drafting them in the first place.

The response to the SIMEX letter of 11 January was sent on 25 January. In his reply Simon wrote: i) 'The yen 10 billion difference was partly funded by the excess yen funds in account 92000 [a Baring Securities Japan account] and the excess yen funds of account 99001' [another BSL agency account]; ii) 'The Baring Group's margin funding requirements in the Asian time zone were managed by inter-company loans' [in this case, loans from BSJ to BSL]; and iii) 'Ms Yong would be appointed the Regional Risk and Treasury Manager for the Baring Group, to be based in Singapore, with the specific responsibility of monitoring large exposures, regulatory requirements and liaising with SIMEX.'

Even before Simon Jones had replied to SIMEX another letter arrived, which at first looked very threatening. Dated 16 January, it talked about an improper segregation of client funds and improper computation of client funds to meet financial requirements.

Meanwhile my funding requests were becoming ridiculous. In early January I'd received an internal memo from Tony Railton, in which he asked how I came to the US dollar funding figure on a daily basis: 'A lot of figures do not appear to move very often,' he wrote. 'The ideal situation would be for us to reconcile the US $ figures. I think this would be good generally for us and also for SFA [Securities and Futures Association] requirements.' Poor Tony – he was right, of course, but it was the last analysis I would ever do for him. I told him that it was impossible, gave him some bullshit reasons and he believed me.

One of the key factors which helped me obtain this funding was that there seemed to be a big personality clash between two Barings groups: Mary Walz and Ron Baker in the Financial Products Group, and Tony Hawes and Tony Railton, Group Treasurer and Senior Settlements Clerk respectively. Mary and Ron were all gung-ho – they wanted to do the business, and if they needed the money then it should be there. The two Tonys were altogether more cautious. But Ron and Mary ignored poor old Tony Railton's request for a breakdown of the different fundings for Barings' in-house position – they now just wanted to gear up. They had their bonuses waiting for them at the end of February, and they were out to prove that they were the biggest rollers in town.

As each day went on, and my requests continued to be met, the explanation dawned on me: they wanted to believe that it was all true. There was a howling dis-crepancy which would have been obvious to a child – the money they sent to Singapore was unaccounted for – but they wanted to believe otherwise because it made them feel richer. I must be doing more business, there-fore we would *all* be richer.

However, every second or third day Brenda Granger called me up and made a complaint. One day I asked for $30 million.

'Nick? It's Brenda here. Look, buddy, you're asking for more money than I can collect in. It's now looking as if I have client debtors, which I don't.'

'Don't worry,' I assured her. 'Look, London's the

cash cow for this business. Without you, it folds. You're funding Singapore. We don't have access to any other kinds of funds.'

Soon enough Brenda began to communicate her bemusement at the money I was demanding.

'Just awaiting breakdown from my buddy Nick ... (once they creatively allocate the numbers),' she wrote in a memo to Tony Hawes. My numbers were unreal. I knew that, and I was the one asking for them. In London they were beginning to think they were unreal as well.

I WAS sitting at the Barings booth when the phone call came. Lisa had scarcely said a word before bursting into tears. I looked across at the trading pit and tried to shut my ear to the noise in front of me and concentrate on her.

'What's the matter?'

But she only cried and cried into the phone. It was horrible.

'What's the matter?'

'Nick,' she blurted out, 'I've had a miscarriage. That clot of blood was a baby.'

A few days earlier Lisa had suddenly started bleeding. She had spent yesterday in bed, and had kept a large blood clot to take to her doctor to analyse. I stared out across the trading floor and almost collapsed. All the madness out there on the floor – the shouting, the buying and selling, the thousands of contracts, the losses in the 88888 account – it all became absurd. It was meaningless. Lisa and I had desperately wanted a baby, and this blood clot was more precious to me than anything in the world. The whole dealing floor, the stupid world of

SIMEX and Barings, the pressure they'd put on me, all my crimes – they just dissolved away into nothing: to less than the tiny little blood clot which we'd lost.

I could hardly hear Lisa. I was sitting at the booth in my ridiculous striped jacket surrounded by a host of screaming men who were all living or dying for the next few ticks up or down on the Nikkei – and my wife was telling me that she'd lost our baby. I desperately wanted to cry, to hug her, to make love to her, to conjure up another baby and create a life for ourselves where we could be happy. But it couldn't happen here. Not in Singapore, where I'd lost – God knows – getting on for £200 million, if I stopped to think about it. Not here, where George and Din were already waving at me to ask what was happening and where, out of the corner of my eye, I saw the market move again.

'Shall I come home?' I asked. 'What can I do?'

'Nothing,' Lisa sobbed. 'You stay there. But can we get the hell out of here and get home? We'll have a baby at home. I'm going to book some furniture removers. Nick, I want to go home.'

When I put the phone down, something inside went numb. I had no feelings, no qualms about what I was going to do. I had dithered around for too long, living off my nerves and hoping that the market would move in my favour. I was now going to fucking well make it move in my favour. I couldn't care less if I was caught or not – I had to get out and get us both home. I was going to go for broke.

Then something happened that no one in the world, never mind Singapore, could have predicted.

* * *

'THERE's been an earthquake in Kobe,' was the first news I heard from Danny as I picked up the phone at 5:45 A.M. 'The market's going to fall out of bed.'

I practically fell out of bed myself. Earthquake! That was all I needed. The market had been steady for a few days, and I was beginning to think that it might have turned.

On Wednesday 18 January, as pictures of the earthquake dominated all television screens, the trading floor was absolute carnage. Everyone in Japan had family or friends in Kobe, and they were selling shares to pay for the damage. The market was butchered.

I stood by the Barings booth and watched the chaos. All the Japanese guys were talking about the cracks which had appeared in their walls, but funnily enough, I was pretty calm; I began to see this as an opportunity. The market was well down – 300 points – and, of course, markets around the world were tumbling, so my futures position had lost something like another £50 million, but I reckoned this could be the turning point. I waited for a day or two to see whether the market would really move, and then, on Friday 20 January, after the market had steadied at about 200 points below the pre-earthquake level, I went into the pit and spent all day buying over 10,000 March contracts. This was a massive purchase, the largest purchase I'd done in my life, but I did it with two utter convictions in mind. I had to buy it back up to try to push it towards 19,000, the price range of my option position, and I thought the market looked cheap.

At the weekend my brother Richard arrived from Thailand, and Lisa and I took him out on the town. I had no calls from anyone; the market had tossed about a little, but my 10,000 contracts were a good buy. Given the circumstances of Lisa's miscarriage and the Kobe earthquake, it wasn't a bad weekend, and I loved spoiling my brother.

'Can I come and see you on the floor on Monday?' he asked.

'Sure, give me a call and I'll arrange it.'

On Monday 23 January the market opened up 30 points. It was approaching 19,000. I sat at the booth and let it run. It rose another 30 points. I was making money – I'd made several million pounds. I watched the price with increasing satisfaction, kept an eye on George in the pit, and pushed the voicebox to Fernando in Tokyo.

'Anything doing?'

'Not much: steady.'

'Your lot didn't have any family there, did they?'

'No.'

'We've been trying to call our friends there all night. The lines are down.'

'It's chaos.'

'And no water.'

'Bit of movement here.'

I watched the screens and then heard the noise.

'Selling,' Fernando said. 'Hold on to your hat, there's some selling—'

The voicebox was open for the next hour, but we were too astonished to say anything. I watched the pit and watched the screens and saw the market drop over 1,000 points. I'd never seen it move so fast. Every five minutes I was waiting for a bounce which never happened.

Finally I flashed to George: 'Sell 2,000 at market.'

George sold them for me. I knew it was madness to try to sell more than that. He was getting no price at all. He could make whatever errors he wanted on this one, I thought, I'd lost an absolute packet.

The phone rang. It was Richard.

'Hi, Nick! How's it going?'

I'd forgotten all about Richard. He sounded so young and enthusiastic. He had no idea what I was meant to do all day, trading futures and options and arbitraging, and he certainly had no idea what I was really doing all day – trying to claw my way out of a black hole. For a moment I could hardly speak to him, I was so over-whelmed with shame. I felt ashamed that he admired me, his elder brother, so much. I knew that he'd have told all his friends that he was off to Asia to visit Thailand and then stay with me. All his friends knew that his elder brother was a hero in Singapore, doing really well. I'd left Watford and succeeded out in the big wide world. Nobody knew what I really did, but they all knew that Lisa and I lived in Singapore and that I jetted around to New York, Hong Kong, Tokyo. Richard would have told them about the weekend trips we did to Thailand or Bali. They'd have sat around the pubs in Watford and Richard would have told them where I'd been, and they'd have wondered what it was like to stay at the Oriental in Hong Kong or the Sheraton in New York. Or what it was like to fly First Class, and what you got in the little complimentary bags the air hostesses handed out.

'I can't see you today,' I heard myself calmly say. 'I'll see you back at the flat.'

222

'All right,' he said, after a pause. 'Let's have a good time tonight.'

'We will, the best,' I agreed.

I put the phone down, and knew that I must have lost at least another 7 billion yen on the options – a fucking yard of yen. What was 7 billion yen? US $70 million. I was down £50 million on the day. But more than that, I'd let my brother down. I should have made the time to see him. He'd have loved to have come on to the floor and watch the traders shouting at each other. He'd have seen where I sat, met Risselle and George and Eric, Maslan and Spy and Carol. He'd have been amazed to see the screens moving, the untamed chaos of the trading pit. He'd never have understood what it was all about – no visitor ever does – but he'd have remembered it and been able to tell everyone back home.

But I'd let him down – I'd forgotten about him. And if he'd come to see me, he'd only have seen the surface anyway. He'd never have guessed that I was cheating. He'd never have guessed that for all the apparent success I enjoyed out on the dealing floor, with all the dealers clapping me on the back and waiting for my instructions, I was a failure. I was a fraud and a cheat. If I could escape back to London, I would. I'd have loved to have been in his shoes, mixing up the plaster for Dad. That was a real job, an honest job. It was far more valuable than the mess I'd made of my life in Singapore. I remembered him at our wedding – he was so thrilled to be wearing a morning suit and top hat, and had crammed the hat down over his eyebrows to stop it blowing off, making him look like the Artful Dodger. From that magical day, when Lisa and I had been the golden couple, I had torn myself apart. I sat down, my losses buzzing around inside my head, wiping out any other thought. The only thing I could cling on to was that I had to get out, had to escape.

The market was down over 800 points. I would need around $40 million from Brenda Granger to meet my margin funding requests from SIMEX.

Strangely enough, by the close of business I felt rather elated. It was such a massive loss that surely I must soon be caught. I couldn't get out of this one; the numbers couldn't get worse. It would shake up two years of deceit and fraud, and do what I just couldn't do – bring it all to the surface. When I was on the trading floor I felt no sense of vertigo. I just concentrated on the minute-by-minute movements and traded in and out. Numbers just flew about, none of them seemed to matter; they all disappeared into the computer. It was when I left and returned to face the back office that I got scared to death. That was when the numbers emerged on the print-outs and I was confronted by them face to face. Sure enough, that evening the numbers started flying back at me.

'IT's Mui Mui for you,' Linda called out, holding her hand over the mouthpiece, 'from Coopers & Lybrand.'

This was the call which would kill me.

'Nick Leeson?' Her voice was quiet and soft. 'I've been trying to get hold of you. I'm compiling the year-end audit and we're working on BFS. I need to ask you about a receivable from SIMEX which I can't trace. It's quite a big sum: 7.78 billion yen.'

I stretched my hands behind my head and yawned.

So this was what it felt like to be caught – blank indifference. I was too tired to care. 'It's a fair cop; I'll come quietly, guv,' ran the cliché. I knew how the guy felt. I'd been nicked too.

'It's a little complicated,' I said. 'What do you need?'

'I just need an explanation of what happened,' she said quietly, 'and I can't find any paperwork.'

I'd prepared the only story I could think of. It wasn't much of a story. In fact it wasn't any story. No auditor would give it credibility for any longer than it took to describe. But what the hell; I relaxed my grip on the handset and gave it a whirl.

'It was an OTC [over-the-counter] trade between Spear, Leeds & Kellogg and Barings London which I did back in December,' I explained slowly, testing each word like a foothold as I went on. 'It fell through the normal computer system – we've had trouble with OTC trades before. I'll have a word with the systems manager and get something to you.'

I held my breath.

'OK,' Mui Mui said, 'just get me the documentation and I'll review it.'

And that was that. For a whole day. I didn't return a couple of Mui Mui's calls, and I was up in Simon Jones' office when he brought it up.

'What's all this about 7.78 billion yen?'

'It's a nightmare,' I said. 'It was an OTC trade last month which was incorrectly booked. The auditors are giving me a rough time over it.'

'I know,' he said savagely, 'they're a pain in the arse. They just don't know when to stop. What's their gripe with you?'

'They want all sorts of documentation. I can produce it, it's just a question of time.'

'What's the problem?'

'There was a computer mistake and Barings rather than SLK [Spear, Leeds & Kellogg] ended up paying BNP [Banque Nationale de Paris]. I'm getting the money back. But I suppose it messes up their balance sheet.'

'Send me a memo on it,' Simon said.

And with that I walked off.

I had to come up with something. As I whirred down in the lift, I realised that the good news was that Simon Jones hadn't lifted an eyebrow when I mentioned an OTC trade. He knew I had no authority for these, since they involve assessing credit risk: when you do an OTC trade, you do not have the security of an exchange like SIMEX to gather your money for you, so you have to assess the credit-worthiness of your customer yourself – a prolonged operation.

Coopers & Lybrand wanted an explanation of what had happened. I would produce something. I had a week.

By Friday 27 January I'd bought almost 30,000 futures and the market began to shift. On the same day Coopers & Lybrand, auditors to Barings Singapore, sent a status report to Coopers & Lybrand in London.

There is a ¥7.7 billion (S$ equivalent 115 million) trade receivable from a third party, Spear, Leeds & Kellogg (SLK). This represents refund of margin deposited with SLK for an over-the-counter Nikkei option which expired on 30 December 1994. The amount is still outstanding. We are awaiting the audit confirmation of the year-end balance.

We are informed by BFS that collectability of the said ¥7.7 billion is not envisaged to be a problem. Also, the contracting party with SLK is Baring Securities Limited (BSL), and that SLK's creditworthiness has been discussed with BSL. Could you confirm with BSL that SLK is an on-going customer and is credit-worthy?

This status report soon raised some eyebrows in Barings.

Monday 30 January 1995

On Monday 30 January the market reacted to my purchases and was squeezed up 700 points. I was up over £50 million on the day, and had recouped all my losses since the Kobe earthquake. I was buying the Nikkei and selling JGBs short, trading like a maniac and requesting about $10 million every day from London.

Soon enough the phones started ringing. First it was Brenda Granger, then Mary Walz, then Ron Baker. They all wanted to know what was happening. It was Ron who finally got through to me.

'The arseholes in Treasury are saying that the funding's getting a problem. They've got no idea. The old farts in ALCO [Barings' Asset and Liability Committee] have asked that you reduce the position. Can you bring it down?'

Another letter from SIMEX was waiting on my desk on Monday afternoon. Dated 27 January, the previous Friday, it was also addressed to Simon Jones, and it presented a table of positions held by Barings and Barings' customers. It officially reminded Barings of its responsibility to ensure that 'you have at all times adequate funds including standby credit facilities in order to be able to fulfil your financial obligations to the SIMEX clearing house'.

I looked down the letter and saw with a sickening feeling in my stomach that, unlike the previous letters, which we'd kept in Singapore, Simon had already copied this letter to Barings in London.

'Have you seen this letter?' Simon Jones came on the phone to me.

'Yes, it's a difficult position,' I agreed.

'There's an ALCO meeting tomorrow. I imagine they'll discuss it there.'

'Can I do anything?' I asked.

'Let's see what Tony Hawes wants,' he said, and we left it at that.

That day James Bax finally sent back a reply to SIMEX's letter of 16 January, which had asked us to confirm that there was no violation of SIMEX rules concerning the funding of positions. Dated 30 January, it gloriously missed the point SIMEX had made and contained the wonderful excuse: 'The underlying causes of the errors noted were largely clerical slips and typing mistakes.'

Tuesday 31 January 1995

THERE was a cc-mail message from Group Treasurer Tony Hawes on my computer, quoting the Coopers & Lybrand status report and asking me to explain the ¥7.78 billion receivable. I called him up and left a message on his voice mail.

'Hi, Tony, it's Nick. I got your mail and I'm dealing with it. It's actually Chinese New Year here today, so we'll be a little slow but I'll get back to you on that as soon as possible.'

Tony Hawes took the C & L status report to Mary Walz and told her that he'd asked me to explain it.

'God,' she said, 'you're the guy who's always asking these time-consuming questions.'

'Look, Mary, if you take this at face value, it could mean there's a £50 million hole in Barings' balance sheet,' said Hawes.

Lisa and I celebrated Chinese New Year with a whole restaurant of Chinese brokers. There was the traditional dish to begin with, where you're supposed to toss the food up in the air to welcome in the New Year, but our table was a bit more adventurous, so rather than tossing it and eating it, we were all wearing it on our heads. We were the guests of some Chinese friends, but were spared the trauma of having to eat the most sophisticated Chinese food, which is full of frog's bladders and stag's balls and stuff like that. We were given steak and chips and we were in great form.

As we enjoyed the amazing feast and admired all the tinsel and glitter, back in London the Asset and Liability Committee meeting had begun. ALCO is the

most senior credit committee in Barings, and decides
the bank's strategy and funding levels across the entire
network of operations. One of the items on the agenda
to be discussed was the SIMEX letter of 27 January.

Wednesday 1 February 1995

'NICK, it's Rachel.' This was odd – Rachel Yong, the
Financial Controller, never called me on the trading
floor. 'Mui Mui's been asking about this 7.78 billion
yen receivable. She can't find it.'

'Don't worry,' I said, 'I've got somebody working on
it.' This was no kind of answer and we both knew it.

'Nick, they want to tell Simon all about it. And they
want to sign off on the accounts next week.'

'I'll be back in the office at 5 P.M.,' I said. 'I've got a
meeting between now and then.'

I'd earned myself a couple more hours.

Back at the office I looked through my drawer of cor-
respondence with other brokers. Having mentioned
Spear, Leeds & Kellogg and an absurd OTC trade, I'd
have to stick with the story somehow. I knew that I
couldn't pass this one off. I flicked through a loose-leaf
file and found an original letter signed by Richard
Hogan at Spear, Leeds & Kellogg, which is a brokerage
house specialising in futures and options. I was lucky
that I had an original letter, since most of my corre-
spondence with other brokers was done by fax. I had a
signature – and a germ of an idea which was so dishonest I could scarcely admit to myself what I was thinking.
Then I started to compose myself for an eyeball-to-eye-

ball meeting with Simon Jones. I knew very little about over-the-counter trades, but I was relying on the fact that nobody else knew anything either. I was sure that Simon Jones didn't understand them, and I doubted that Coopers & Lybrand would.

The trade I had to describe was about as far removed from a normal OTC as was possible to invent. One immediate problem was that having mentioned Barings London to Mui Mui, I was in deep trouble, since as soon as Simon Jones thought that Barings London were involved he'd be on the phone to Ron Baker to ask what had happened. I needed to cover this. I had to tell Simon a double lie: I had to say that I'd lied to Coopers & Lybrand about Barings London, and that really it had been a trade between Spear, Leeds & Kellogg and the Banque Nationale de Paris, which I had brokered. This would stop Simon from calling up Ron Baker. Lies and lies: I was building up a towering pile of lies, and if one of them was found out, they'd tumble all over me.

I braced myself and picked up the phone.

'Simon, it's Nick. I'm just coming up to talk about SLK.'

'Look, put it off until tomorrow will you? I've got to go and play squash. Put a memo on my desk and let's meet about 7:30 in the morning.'

And with that I put the phone down and realised I'd won another twelve hours. Perhaps I should escape – catch the next plane to London and leave it all behind. But then how would I ever get Lisa to come with me? She never ran away from anything.

I settled down to write the memo. I tried out about ten different versions, and by the time I'd finished I was surrounded by screwed-up balls of paper, all of which had missed the bin. I'd never be Michael Jordan, that was for sure. Lisa called at 9 P.M., and I said I'd be home in an hour. Then I started on a fresh sheet of paper and wrote a bizarre note to Simon Jones about the fictitious trade between Spear, Leeds & Kellogg and Banque Nationale de Paris, which had resulted in a £50 million hole being blown in Barings' balance sheet. This is what I wrote:

Large option trade put through the system between SLK and BNP. Booked via the system between SLK and BNP with premium to hit at maturity. At this stage no impact on system. Customer side to hit at maturity. Broker side: no movement because holding both sides (Dr + Cr) impact zero – BFS were not to be involved at all. Payment would be between SLK + BNP.

ERROR in input of maturity dates. True maturity = 30/12, maturity for BNP leg 03/12. Subsequently BNP have received value for the funds 3/12 and funds have been effectively returned to them over a period during the normal course of business i.e. error not picked up. Therefore reversal of entries 30/12 has left us with a receivable of JPY 7,778,000.

As the trade was to have no impact, referral was not made – so blame me!

Subsequently received verbal communication that fund will be paid 2-2-95. Expecting written confirmation this evening circa 10pm

I stopped and thought for a while. That should fox him. It certainly foxed me. It was ridiculous. It was utter nonsense. Nobody in their right mind would accept this, but I was too tired to care. Then I carried on:

> There are obviously a lot of errors that I can be hung on, to which I will take full responsibility, but suggest that we tackle the matter with the auditor, show him receipt of funds value 2-2-95 and confirmations that we will receive this evening of balances. And hopefully then he will make London happy.
> See you at 7.30
> Nick.

I reckoned Simon would never understand the first half of the note but would be too embarrassed to ask me to explain it. He always prided himself on being the sharpest brain in the building. By promising that the money would come in tomorrow, I was giving him a lifeline to grab – he'd just want to ensure that the money was in and the auditors could sign off. I put it on top of a pile of perfectly innocuous papers and left it sitting there like a time-bomb.

Thursday 2 February 1995

THE next morning I took the lift up to Simon's office. I didn't know what to expect. I stopped in the kitchen to drink a glass of water, as some bile had risen in my throat. I turned the corner and was amazed to see him looking very normal, reading his mail.

'How was the squash?' I asked casually.

'James just beat me. My wretched knee started playing up halfway through.'

Simon had an answer for everything. He could never admit that he'd been fairly and squarely beaten by anybody. If he'd won, he'd have told everybody about it all day.

'Now, what's this fuck-up, Nick?' Simon shuffled his papers in an authoritative sort of way and scanned my memo again.

God! It wouldn't even stand up to a thirty-second read!

'I'm sorry, Simon,' I held up my hands in mock surrender. 'I didn't check the entries into the machine properly.'

I sensed that he was more worried about what London would think than the actual explanation of the problem. And he was always very determined to keep London off his back. He read the memo through once more, and in the silence I strained to read the notes he was making. Reading upside down I deciphered: 'Credit Risk – what approval?'; 'Documentation'; 'Profit to BFS???'; and then, at the bottom, 'BFS out of pocket SGD 115 million for 2 mths!!'

He'd seen through it. It was of course a laughable memo, and he'd seen through it. He was about to kill me where I stood. I tensed and waited for the blow. Simon looked up and I forced myself to meet his eye, trying to look both apologetic and keen to please at the same time.

'So what credit risk appraisal was there? Who did it?'

'There was none,' I apologised, 'I just went straight ahead with it.'

'You cowboy! And paperwork? The auditors will want some documents.'

'Yeah, I've got that,' I nodded.

'And no profit to BFS?'

'None,' I said, 'so no impact on the P & L account.'

'What about the interest on the 7.78 billion yen? We've been out of pocket for two months. That's a heap of interest.'

'SLK will pay it. They've had the money.'

Simon Jones called himself the 'King of Auditors'. He used to brag that nothing ever got past him – he could smell it a mile away. He paused and then pushed the memo into a corner of his desk.

'OK, Nick, can you sort it out with Coopers?'

And I walked out of the office a free man. I didn't breathe until I reached the lifts and was halfway down to the 14th floor. And it was still before 8 A.M.; the market hadn't even opened yet. I checked my desk for messages, and then disappeared off to the trading floor before Coopers could call me.

Mui Mui was on the phone by ten. She was becoming increasingly puzzled.

'I need documentation,' she said. 'I need to see three pieces of paper. I need confirmation from SLK that the 7.78 billion yen will be paid; sight of your bank balance tomorrow to show that the 7.78 billion yen has been received; and a note from someone in London, preferably Ron Baker, saying that he's fully aware of this deal and the credit risk and he approves it.'

I went back to Simon Jones.

'Coopers are on top of me again,' I said, leaning against his door frame.

'What's the matter?'

'They want the documentation about the 7.78 billion by today, and it'll take a little longer. I know they want to sign off the audit soon.'

'Look,' Simon said, 'they want to sign it off tomorrow. If you've got the documents, that shouldn't be too much of a problem.'

I went back to my desk and pulled out the loose-leaf file with Richard Hogan's signature. I found another with Ron Baker's signature. Then I scribbled two notes, one from Baker and one from Hogan. I had to do this quickly.

'As Head of the Financial Products Group I confirm my knowledge and approval of the Nikkei OTC option deal with Spear, Leeds & Kellogg.'

I wrote a note from Richard Hogan, Managing Director of SLK, which confirmed the outstanding balance of 7.78 billion yen and confirmed that payment would be made on 2 February 1995.

I passed these notes to Nisa in the back office and asked her to type them out.

'Just print them out for me on plain paper, please,' I told her.

It was easy to forge Ron's note, since we had some Barings London paper. I then took the printed letter, cut off the letterhead of Richard Hogan's original letter, cut off the signature, stuck them to the plain paper and photocopied the whole thing. This was much harder than I imagined. I stood at that photocopier for over an hour, trying to get the letters to look normal. I found a big black bin-liner, which was soon stuffed full of rejects. Finally the letter came out without any of the tell-tale lines where the papers had overlaid each other and with the signature in the right place. The memo was easier, but still took me twenty attempts to get it right. I went back to my desk, ignoring the looks of the girls – who clearly wondered what I was photocopying since I'd hardly ever used the thing before. My desk was covered with tubes of glue, scissors and cut-up pieces of paper. It looked so childish. I pushed everything back into my drawer and locked it. All I needed now was the 7.78 billion yen.

I left Barings and went back to the flat. On the way I called Nisa on my car phone.

'Can you get me the customer balance at Citibank?'

I held the phone, waiting.

'Three point four five billion yen.'

'And what about the house account?'

'One point four five billion.'

'Now listen to this carefully. I want you to arrange a transfer of 7.78 billion yen from the client account to the house account.'

'But it won't go,' she pointed out.

'I know, I know,' I held the phone tighter, 'you can reverse it immediately. But I want that transfer done, and then I want Citibank to send us a fax of the house statement showing that 7.78 billion yen has been paid in.'

'Fine,' she said neutrally. She must have thought I was mad. Like all the girls in the back office, she was unswervingly loyal to me. I had fought for their bonuses, treated them well, and they would do anything for me in return.

When I got home I rang the doorbell just to make

sure that Lisa wasn't in. I'd have run away if she'd been there. Then, feeling like a burglar, I let myself in and went to the fax machine. I took a deep breath, and then dialled my office number and sent the two forged letters from Ron Baker and Richard Hogan to myself. Then I left the flat and drove back to the office. I was ashamed: I'd been driven into a corner, where I was now forging documents like a petty criminal.

Throughout the grotesque build-up in the 88888 account I'd taken some comfort in the fact that I was trying to trade out of a loss which had been forced upon me. I could have admitted to the early loss, but I tried to trade out of it. I could have come clean, and Barings would have sacked us all and written off the loss and that would have been the end of the matter. But all along I'd traded and traded and dug myself deeper and deeper into trouble. Then I'd covered up the loss at month-ends, but that had been a rolling forward operation. I had avoided crystallising the loss, and so theoretically I could still be able to trade out of it. Under such prolonged pressure to make profits, I had allowed my sense of criminality to become warped, and the loss had become hidden. It was always invisible numbers, not real money, and the tricks to hide it had been elementary sleight of hand.

But once I'd forged these two documents, I knew that I was damned. These were forgeries. Up until now I had prevaricated, been economical with the truth, refused to separate out numbers which others could have easily found, and made outrageous claims for funding from London. If I had to stand in front of a jury, I'd have confessed to false accounting and probably obtaining property by deception. But now I'd added a new crime to this catalogue. I couldn't say that anyone else was responsible. I couldn't pass it off as a white lie, needed at the time. I had physically cut out somebody's signature, glued it to a piece of paper, taken it to my flat, faxed it back to myself, and now I was going to hand it to Rachel Yong to pass on to the auditors. And if the Citibank fax with the statement showing a 7.78 billion yen transfer wasn't there, I'd shout and curse until I got it. I felt hot tears of shame pricking behind my eyes: I was behaving like a criminal. I'd become a criminal and I couldn't stop it. I'd been caught up in my own web of deceit, and I was drowning in the tangle – a tangle of 8s. I needed something, anything, to get me out, and morals no longer mattered.

ON Friday 3 February, Coopers & Lybrand issued an unqualified audit report on the consolidation schedules of Baring Futures Singapore. I had been vetted and cleared.

I went out to fetch some water from the kitchen. When I came back the phone was ringing. Throughout the afternoon everyone who had anything to do with me had called about the SLK receivable. It had started to take on a life of its own. Each new person had a different version of it. I just played a very straight bat and maintained that it had been a booking error. Nobody asked me outright how on earth I had arranged for the 7.78 billion yen to leave Barings. I knew from my experience in Jakarta that when it came down to detail, no senior managers actually wanted to get their hands dirty and investigate the numbers. They always assumed that they were above that, and let other people get on with it. Luckily for my fraud, there were too many chiefs who would chat about it at arm's length but never go further. And they never dared ask me any basic questions, since they were afraid of looking stupid about not understanding futures and options.

The phone was still ringing, so I waited until the call transferred away from my desk and one of the girls picked it up. As soon as I sat down I picked up my phone to stop the call coming back to me and dialled a friend in Watford for a chat. Nisa walked over and left a yellow post-it note on my desk. 'Tony Hawes: Urgent,' it read. I carried on dialling and got straight through to Alan. I hadn't spoken to him in a while, and he told me his wife was pregnant. As we chatted I picked up the Tony Hawes note, screwed it up into a tight ball and then flicked it at the bin. To my astonishment it flew straight in. I told Alan about it.

'Six yards and straight in,' I boasted.

'No kidding!' he said. 'Jocky Wilson!'

'As long as I'm not turning into that other geezer, Eric Whatsisname.'

'You putting on weight then?'

'Sure am.'

'You can't be as big as Kath, though.'

'Yeah, but she's pregnant. That's quite an excuse.'

We chatted on until I looked at my watch and saw that I'd been on the phone for almost half an hour. I finally rang off, then remembered that a friend was coming to dinner and realised I was going to be late. I rang Tony Hawes in London.

'Hawes,' he said.

I always marvelled at his superb British accent. He sounded sublimely self-important. I also always had a fantasy that one day I'd ask: 'Is that whores and hookers?'

'Tony, it's Nick. I've just had a message that you needed to speak to me.'

'It's this SLK and BNP thing,' he spluttered. 'What's bothering me is where you got all that money to actually, ah, pay SLK. I mean it's the equivalent of $78 million. It just doesn't add up, you know.'

Of course it doesn't add up! I felt like shouting. A three-year-old could tell you that! I've conjured it out of nowhere! I was in Ireland and I didn't kiss the Blarney Stone and we just got pissed and I never intended to come back here. It's all bogus.

'It's obvious, Tony,' I said, in my most patient voice. 'It's part of the funding which we've taken from you over the last six weeks. So when it's paid off, you should see a reduction in the funding we require by an equal and opposite amount.'

'Yes,' Tony said hesitantly.

'The same figure will flow back to you.'

'So you're saying that some of the funding was used to pay SLK?'

'That's right, Tony,' I reassured him, as if he was finally getting there, 'and so we'll be able to pay it back to you.'

'That'll be good,' he said. 'Getting our funding down will be good. I'm having to juggle quite a few balls at the moment.'

'It's very difficult,' I demurred.

'OK,' Tony said.

'OK,' I signalled the end of the conversation, 'I've

got to dash. I'm running late and we've got company for dinner.' I knew Tony would understand an excuse like company for dinner in a way in which he'd never understand having to dash off and do some work.

I put the phone down and wrote a note to Nisa for her to book some futures sales into the system, which should more than balance the recent purchases I'd made for the 88888 account and so induce the SIMEX computer to calculate that SIMEX owed us money. This might result in some money being paid back to Barings London through Citibank. And if it didn't, so what? I'd just have to dream up another mad excuse and see if they'd swallow that one. I'd blame it on market conditions, which they'd never contradict. I left the office with my fingers crossed, and then pushed everything away to the back of my mind for another night. One less day to go.

Just before I went to sleep Mary Walz called me.

'What's this 7.78 billion yen all about, Nick?'

'Oh God,' I said. 'Look, everyone's on to me about this. It's an accounting screw-up. The auditors and Tony Hawes are all over me about it. I've learned my lesson – it won't happen again.'

'Is it sorted then?' she asked.

'As far as I'm aware the auditors are happy now.'

'Well, thank Christ for that. Now we can get on and concentrate on your funding. You'll probably hear more from Tony Hawes.'

'OK,' I said, 'I've got to go.'

'OK, Nick.'

And with that I put the phone down and switched it off for the night.

* * *

Some time while I was asleep, Ron Baker got to hear of the 7.78 billion yen in London. He was called up by Peter Norris, the company's Chief Executive Officer. It's never nice having your boss ask you about something you should know all about.

'Peter Norris called me,' Ron Baker said. 'He asked: "Was I aware that we had lent some money to a broker in Singapore? What was happening?" I had no idea what to say, I was just shocked by it.'

Ron Baker went to find Mary Walz and they phoned Peter Norris back. 'I got angry because I just couldn't believe the story,' said Ron.

Walz told Norris and Baker that she'd spoken to me earlier, and that I'd told her it was 'an accounting screwup' and that Tony Hawes was 'all over me about it'.

Walz and Baker called up Tony Hawes and Tony Railton and told them to pack their bags and go to Singapore to sort out the mess. Although the audit had been cleared, they were worried about the cash flow. Ron Baker then called James Bax to find out what had happened with the 7.78 billion yen and why I was doing completely unauthorised OTC trades. Bax knew that the audit had been passed, and thus by definition that the money must be back in the Barings account.

'It's just a non-transaction,' James Bax assured Ron. 'It's an error. It is a back office glitch. Don't worry about it.'

The senior management then began to cover up my mistake. They had taken fright that £50 million should have been owed to Barings by Spear, Leeds & Kellogg –

'somebody I'd never heard of', as George Maclean, Head of the Bank Group, described them. Geoffrey Broadhurst, Group Financial Director of Barings, went so far as to ask the internal Barings Credit Unit to check SLK out.

'I think they established that Spear, Leeds & Kellogg had minimal substance, a net worth of $2 or $3 million. It raised my concerns higher,' said Broadhurst.

In actual fact the Bank of England later found out that, at September 1994, SLK had a net worth of some $268 million. The Barings Credit Unit also established that back in the summer of 1993 a counter-party review had been prepared on SLK and that they had given a limit of US $5 million.

So it was obvious that the £50 million which SLK had apparently been owing Barings for two months was way off the credit scale. However, Barings took the decision – which gave me another month's breathing space and trading time – that they would cover up this mistake.

After London received confirmation from Coopers that the audit had been cleared on Friday 3 February, the question then arose as to whether the SLK issue should be mentioned in the audit review. Peter Norris told the Bank of England: 'Bax then expressed his wish to try and have the thing dealt with in a way which would not give him problems with the local regulator, SIMEX . . . which was the issue of that year's audit report or management letter. I agreed to see if we could put that in train . . .'

Norris justified this concealment by saying: 'I did so only on the basis that the transaction had been reversed, there was not an issue of exposure and also on the basis, as he told me, that the auditors were fully aware of it.'

The SLK matter continued to rumble on in London after it'd been cleared in Singapore. The last I heard of it was on 3 February – but on 9 February, Coopers & Lybrand in London had an audit meeting with Geoffrey Broadhurst, whom Duncan Fitzgerald, the C & L manager responsible for the Barings audit, remembered as being 'very categoric during the meeting that the issue had been resolved'. It was at this meeting that Coopers & Lybrand were asked about excluding the whole SLK fiasco from the management letter.

On 10 February Simon Jones replied to the SIMEX letter of 27 January, which had been discussed at Barings' Asset and Liability Committee. I was not especially privy to this last letter, since a directive had come from Tony Hawes in London to reply to it, and I'd played down the significance of it so much that people like Mary Walz had lost interest. Among other things, Simon Jones wrote:

> BFS is aware of the necessity of being able to meet its financial obligations to the SIMEX Clearing House at all times, and is confident that it is able to do so. BFS deals almost wholly as a broker on behalf of other companies in the Baring Investment Banking Group, acting either as agent or principal. BFS itself has no principal positions. Margin called from these Group companies is met immediately

245

through Group Treasury. The Group's external customer business is mainly transacted by Baring Securities Limited, minimising the exposure of BFS to customer default. BFS calls margin from Baring Securities Limited, which through Group Treasury will always pay in full. Any shortfall in customer payments falls on Baring Securities Limited in London, not BFS.

It is the policy of the Baring Investment Banking Group to ensure that risks of all kinds, including exposure to exceptional intra-day calls for settlement variation and advance margin, are managed actively. All risks are monitored daily by the Group's risk unit and reported to the Asset and Liability Committee. Immediate action is taken to correct situations where the Group is over-exposed to a particular risk. If open positions are such that an exceptional margin call by SIMEX might exceed existing overdraft facilities, additional funds are made available in advance to BFS's clearing bank to ensure that the largest anticipated call can always be met . . .

It must have taken SIMEX quite a long time to digest this letter, certainly longer than the cavalier excuse that the discrepancies were due to typing errors.

IAN Hopkins, the Director and Head of Group Treasury and Risk at Barings, wrote a memorandum for MANCO prior to their meeting on 13 February.

MANCO stands for Management Committee, and is the most senior management committee for the whole Barings Group, chaired by Peter Baring himself, at which all the most confidential and important matters facing Barings are discussed. Hopkins summarised the findings of ALCO, the Asset and Liability Committee, and circulated them to the MANCO members:

> The annual audit of Baring Futures Singapore brought to light a 7.7 billion yen (c.US $80 million) error arising from an incorrect payment made by us on 3 December to BNP Singapore relating to an OTC option trade brokered by us between BNP and Spear, Leeds & Kellogg, a futures broker for whom we provide clearing on SIMEX. The trade expired on 30 December, but the amount was not recovered until 5 February. We have yet to claim interest.

The discussion of Hopkins' memo wasn't minuted. Apparently Peter Norris made passing reference to it. Hopkins himself said: 'I was amazed that it did not cause more discussion, because $80 million worth of the Bank's money had gone walkabout for two months without anyone noticing.'

Not only did they all try to push it under the carpet – but nobody ever dreamed of asking what on earth SLK and BNP were doing with a premium of £50 million. It was a truly colossal deal for such a short time-frame.

Meanwhile, over in Singapore, I'd been given a new lease of life by the audit clearance, and since nobody questioned the amounts of money I asked for, I began to gear up. I had until 24 February, bonus day, to either trade out of the losses or leave. To make any inroads into my losses – which now towered over £200 million – I had to double up.

'WE used to joke about Singapore,' laughed Brenda Granger, 'and say "Why don't we send somebody's mother out there to run the department, since Nick's so busy now!"'

I never quite saw why that was meant to be such a hilarious joke, but they did something even funnier: they sent out Tony Hawes and Tony Railton. On Monday 6 February, the two Tonys walked into the office. Their immediate brief was to find out about my funding requests and sort out what had happened with SLK. With their jet lag they looked as punch-drunk as me. *My* immediate brief was to head them off the scent. If they'd done the elementary check and looked at the open positions on SIMEX, they would have seen the 88888 account and its horrendous loss. I knew that I only had a few days to play with until they found me out. We all sat down and chatted about their flight, and then mentioned the SLK transaction.

'It really did the rounds in London!' Tony Railton joked.

'Yeah, it was a bit of a cock-up,' I admitted, 'but thank goodness it's over. Now, how's your tennis? I've heard that you were a county player.'

'I've brought my racquet with me!' Tony smiled. 'I'll give you a game.'

8

Monday 6 to Friday 17 February

> 'Wow! That's impressive! You know if he makes \$10 million doing arbitrage in a week, what's that? About half a billion dollars a year. That guy is a turbo arbitrageur!'
>
> Mike Killian, February 1995

I WAS ASTONISHED THAT nobody stopped me. People in London should have known that I was making up the numbers. Brenda Granger, Tony Hawes and Tony Railton should have known that the daily requests for cash were totally wrong, yet they still paid them over. Mary Walz, Ron Baker and Peter Norris should have known that the so-called OTC trade with Spear, Leeds & Kellogg stank of rotten fish all the way from Singapore to Billingsgate. Simon Jones knew that I wasn't authorised to carry out OTC trading. Both he and James Bax in Singapore, sitting ten floors above my head, knew that something must be seriously wrong if £50 million could leave the Singapore office with only my say-so: I just didn't have that authority. I was not a recognised signature on any cheque book, let alone one which could move that amount of cash. And over in Tokyo, if Fernando had really thought about what I was doing, he'd have seen that it was impossible.

Mike Killian described me as a 'turbo arbitrageur' on the grounds that I'd made $10 million profit in the first week of February. He'd dreamed up the scenario whereby if I carried on like that I'd clock up half a billion dollars a year profit: $520 million. The whole of Barings was only making £200 million, half of which was given away in bonuses.

'If Nick's doing that amount of business for that amount of profit, then shut down the rest of the bank,' he said. 'We're just overheads.'

My numbers were hopelessly out of orbit, yet nobody stopped me. Although Barings in London discussed what might or might not be going on, for some reason they seemed to let the matter slide. They may have lost confidence in me and decided to send out Tony Hawes and Tony Railton to check on the numbers, but in Singapore my image had never been better. All the Barings staff, from London to Singapore, were on a roll. February was bonus month, and we were lined up for some whoppers.

Monday 6 February 1995

I SUGGESTED to Tony Hawes and Tony Railton that they might want to have a look at the intra-day funding requirements, which SIMEX was beginning to question.

This was a nicely complicated subject which should take up at least a couple of hours of their time. I hurried across the square to SIMEX, grabbed an orange juice at Delifrance and slipped inside just as dealing was starting. I had to bring down my losses now. It could only be a matter of hours before they asked to see a print-out of all our positions. This would include the 88888 account – with its hundreds of trades, gaping open positions and mountain of losses. The game would be up. I expected a call immediately.

As the first hour went on, and then the second hour, and then we broke for lunch, I began to breathe a little more easily and think that perhaps they wouldn't find it immediately.

And the market was strong. It opened 110 points up and stayed that way. Over the last three days of the previous week, I'd built up a long position of about 30,000 March contracts and suddenly it looked as if there was a chance. I hardly dared believe my luck: I'd got the missing 7.78 billion yen past Simon Jones, James Bax, Ron Baker, Peter Norris and the auditors, and I was now making good money. In the afternoon I closed out 1,100 contracts and was up £15 million on the day. My total loss was still over £200 million, but I felt that the market was turning. It had digested the Kobe earthquake and was now looking cheap. It had bounced up from 18,000 to 18,500 and – surely by now – was going to stay stable.

The bulk of the options I'd sold last year to bring in the cash premiums were in the money for me if the market stayed at around 19,000. The March contract was coming closer, and I had to buy or sell futures to push and pull the market to where I wanted it. And to really influence the market, you have to deal in bulk. I began to throw my weight around.

I started by throwing my weight around on the tennis court. To keep Tony Railton off the scent, I'd arranged a doubles match between Simon Jones and Eugene Marais from upstairs and Tony and myself for later that afternoon.

'Good shot, Tony!'

'That's 40–30.'

'Sorry, Simon.'

'Just keep it away from Tony at the net,' Simon scolded Eugene.

'Ready?'

I couldn't care less who won or lost. I was just intent on keeping Tony – and Simon – out of the office for as long as possible. They couldn't do me any harm out on the tennis court. It was five o'clock, and they could have been reading through Barings' files instead of whacking a ball around.

'Good serve,' I admitted to Simon as the ball flew past my racquet in a fuzzy yellow blur.

'Bad bounce,' Tony consoled me.

'Just a bit of slice,' Simon called. 'That's game. Four–one. Your serve, Nick.'

I bounced the ball twice and tossed it up to serve. I had no idea where it was going to go. Two double-faults later I could see that Tony was itching to tell me how to do it. Then I hit a smacker off the side of the racquet, which shot over the net wide of Simon's backhand.

'Ace!' Tony called from up at the net.

'Just out,' corrected Simon.

'Looked good to me,' persisted Tony.

'No, it was well out. Second serve.'

I served another double-fault. Love–40.

As I prepared for my last serve, I watched Tony as he hunched over the net. He was tensed, ready to pounce, dead keen to win at least a point, make a fantastic interception and show Simon Jones what a player he was. I knew that he was going to lunge across the court to intercept. Finally my serve plopped in. Sure enough Tony darted across to make the interception but Eugene shot it straight back down the now unguarded tramlines, and Tony was marooned in the middle of the court.

'Yours, Nick!' Tony bellowed, skidding to a halt.

I watched the ball thud into the netting at the back of the court.

'I didn't have that one covered, I'm afraid,' I said.

'Didn't you see me signal?' Tony said. 'I pointed behind my back like the professionals do. Come on, that's one–five. We've got to get this one.'

We didn't. Nor did we get any of the games in the second set. I didn't mind, so I was happy to take all the blame. I could see that Eugene and Tony rather fancied a game of singles – they were clearly the best two on court and had been eyeing each other up. Sure enough, as we sat and drank cold Tiger beer at the clubhouse, Tony leaned forward and said: 'Fancy a game of singles, Eugene?'

'I can't now, but same time tomorrow would be fine.'

They looked at Simon and me, worried about their tennis infidelity.

'Don't worry on our account,' I said, holding up my

hand. 'I'm just delighted to see you having a good game.'

'Squash is more my bag,' Simon said. 'A game where you need *really* fast reflexes.'

And we ordered another round of beers. The time ticked on, the 88888 position ticked on, and I was going to make it through another day. I drained my glass and looked up to see an aeroplane taking off from the airport; escaping up into the clear blue sky. I was going to have to keep my wits about me if I was going to follow it.

I WAS back in the office by 6:30 P.M. The coast was clear: Tony Railton had gone back to his hotel, Tony Hawes was nowhere to be seen. Nisa had stayed behind. My biggest problem was that Tony Railton had been given the spare desk right next to mine, and unless I was very careful he'd overhear some mention of the 88888 account, if only because the girls spoke of it so innocently.

'How did the game go?' Nisa asked.

'Fine. Tony and I were thrashed, so Simon was happy.'

'Here's the balance sheet.' Nisa handed it to me. 'And Brenda Granger and Mary Walz both rang, as did AP–Dow Jones.'

'Thanks,' I said, taking the messages. 'Are you off now?'

'Yes, unless there's anything else.'

'Nope, we're all set. I'll just make these calls and then I'll go too.'

After Nisa had gone I turned back to my desk. I opened the drawer to file away the balance sheet, and I saw the cuttings, shreds of paper and glue which I'd used to forge Ron Baker's and Richard Hogan's signatures. I couldn't believe what I'd done. I looked at the incriminating evidence of last Thursday, the final day of the Chinese New Year celebrations, when the market had been quiet and hungover, and I'd faxed through those letters from our flat. I bit my nails and remembered that Coopers had cleared the audit on Friday. It seemed too good to be true. It was so simple, and so patently unreal.

With my scissors, stick of paper glue and fax machine, I had created £50 million. Coopers & Lybrand, world-class auditors, had agreed the figures. Barings, a world-class merchant bank, was holed by £50 million. I had no idea what Barings' profits were going to be for the year just ended, but they couldn't top £200 million. People were talking about a £100-million bonus pool, and Peter Baring was in line for about a million-pound bonus as a retiring present. For the first time in two hundred years a non-Baring was about to become Chairman. And I, sitting at a formica desk on the 14th floor of a tower block in Singapore, had cut and pasted in fifty million quid.

My phone rang. Who the hell could that be? Mary Walz? Ron Baker? James Bax? My mind spun a little faster: Peter Norris?

'Hello?'

It was a reporter from AP–Dow Jones.

'I'm calling about the large positions you've been building up in March futures,' he said.

255

'Yes.'

'It's a considerable position.'

'I don't know what the client's going to do,' I hedged. I wish I'd hedged the position too, but that was another matter.

'Do you believe the market's set to continue today's rise?'

This was good news. I'd almost forgotten about today's rise. I pulled the statement towards me and scanned down the figures. Yes, the position was about £15 million better today; the market was beginning to rally.

'The market's looking better now that everyone's had a chance to come to terms with the earthquake,' I said.

'Off the record,' the reporter said, 'can you tell me who you're buying for?'

'Of course not,' I said. 'Is that all? I've got to go now.'

And we said goodbye.

I replaced the phone with a horrible feeling that he was beginning to see through me. Perhaps this reporter from Tokyo was going to do what nobody at Barings either in Singapore, Tokyo, or London, nor the auditors, were capable of doing: putting two and two together and looking at my purchases in Osaka and calculating that they were too large to be hedged in SIMEX. The SIMEX volume just couldn't take them. It would be like plugging a three-amp lamp straight into the overhead power line – it wouldn't just blow, it would disintegrate.

Ever since 1992 I had hidden the numbers. I'd hidden them from Brenda Granger, from Tony Railton and Tony Hawes, although I knew that they were very unhappy with the requests I'd made. They were the Treasury team, and they'd made a fuss. Luckily for me they'd been crapped on by Mary Walz, Ron Baker and probably even Peter Norris, who'd been fed Ron's story and saw me as a cash machine. So I'd unwittingly played the two sides of the London operation off against each other.

The Tokyo end was more straightforward, because Mike Killian and Fernando were so obsessed with their own trading that they never examined my trading books. They believed me when I told them I'd hedged the position, and they just saw my Osaka purchases removed from the Japan book and brought back to Singapore and that's all they thought of it. They didn't see themselves as my supervisor, more as partners.

As for Singapore: the traders knew that I was covering for them, they knew I put errors into an error account numbered 88888, but they never stopped to either think about where that led or actually thank me any more. It had just become a way of life. If they made errors, they were bailed out. We had a great team spirit, we all made money, they got their bonuses and their lives were everything they'd ever wished for. The girls in the back office never seemed to realise that I was doing something funny with the 88888 account, despite the balance sheet entries I asked them to push through – especially the 7.78 billion yen – but again, it wasn't really their job to ask me what I was doing. I was their boss and I looked after them.

Simon Jones was another matter. Like Ron Baker, he wanted to believe that I made money because that reflected well on him. But like James Bax, he wanted

Barings Singapore to be as independent as possible from London. He ran the ship, and he didn't want anyone else breathing over his shoulder.

I drew a circle on a pad of paper, and then added some spokes radiating out of it. I jotted down the names of the people I spoke to every day – Brenda Granger, Mary Walz, Ron Baker, Fernando, George Seow, Risselle, Simon Jones. For various different reasons they all wanted to believe that my profits were real. They all benefited from me, and in their different ways they all put me under pressure to create these profits.

Outside this circle of Barings staff I wrote down Coopers & Lybrand and the newspapers. They had no reason to believe that I was so successful. In fact they should be objective about my dealing and see through it. I crossed out Coopers – they'd been taken in by a clumsily forged fax, which I know had printed out with NICK AND LISA on the top since I'd sent it from our flat. But they had gone away now. They'd blithely agreed that since a Citibank statement showed a 7.78 billion yen transfer – albeit just from one Barings account to another – Barings must be 7.78 billion yen richer.

The newspapers were another proposition. I was well up today. The market was strong and I'd made good money. But I couldn't see how I was going to fool the newspapers in the way I'd fooled everyone else. I'd just have to leave that one as a question mark.

My phone rang again. I spun the wheel of possibilities and picked it up – it was Mary Walz.

'Hi, how's it going?'

'We're knackered over here. Tony Hawes and Tony

Railton have just arrived. They're going over the numbers.'

'I pity you.' Mary clearly didn't care for them, they were too old and crabby for her ball-busting style. 'Now, Ron and I are worried about the size of your position. It's pulling in too much funding. Shit, Brenda Granger's told me that Barings is borrowing all over Japan to channel the funds through to you. People are beginning to talk.'

'I'll try,' I said.

'Nick, Ron says that you've got to *really* try. If only for a little while.'

'OK, Mary.'

'And for God's sake don't pull any OTC trades out of the bag again. The fall-out is still echoing around here.'

'OK, Mary.'

'Catch you tomorrow.'

I put the phone down. These conversations were always the same with Mary. She tried to give me some kind of tough instruction, but I always deflected her so they ended with the promise of another chat tomorrow. This was fine by me. Each tomorrow I passed was another day. With the market set like this, I just needed to buy time. Ten more days' worth of £15 million profits would be £150 million. Then I'd be almost out of the hole.

The phone rang again. I was relaxed now. Mary had been a pushover. It was Lisa.

'What time do you reckon you're coming home?'

'I'm almost done.'

'What do you fancy for dinner? Mexican or stir-fry?'

'Let's have stir-fry.'

'Great, I've got some chicken, lemon grass and coconut milk. Good day?'

'Looking forward to coming home.'

'See you soon, darling.'

'I love you,' I said as she rang off.

I looked back at the circle of deceit I'd drawn. I picked it up, scrumpled it and threw it at the bin. Lisa. I hadn't put Lisa on it. I loved her, I'd die for her, but I couldn't tell her. Our argument in Ireland hadn't been revived. She must have sometimes wondered why I was so quiet at home, why I was so fat and why my nails were chewed-off stubs. But she still looked after me and made the best of life. God, I must be a revolting husband – fat and without fingernails. But she loved me. Yet I'd lied to her. I'd lied about my entire day's work. I couldn't tell her that I'd spent the whole day trying to keep Tony Railton away from my secret losses. I just carried on pretending that I was happy, that we'd work through until the spring and then leave in our own time. But something was going to snap.

The phone rang again. This was not so good. I looked at it for a few rings and then, against my better judgement, picked it up. It was Ron. Had he been shown his forged signature?

'Nick, how are you?' He sounded friendly.

'Knackered, just knocking off.'

'I don't want to talk about that OTC deal, I gather that's water under the bridge. I just wanted to say that I've agreed your bonus with Peter Norris.'

'What's the damage?' I tried to sound hopeful, but my heart sank. If I couldn't get out of these losses this time, I couldn't take it. I'd have to go.

'Four hundred and fifty thousand,' Ron said.

'That's great,' I said. 'Thank you, Ron.'

There was a silence.

'Now you've got to reduce your position,' Ron said. 'The funding requirements are too high at the moment. Those old farts in London are still worried.'

'I'll try, Ron, it's a tight market.'

'You'd better do more than try. Take a hit on some of it if you have to.'

'Understood.'

'All right, I'll let you get on then. Bonus day is the 24th of Feb.'

'Bye, Ron.'

I left the office and went home in a daze. Even Lisa meeting me at the door with a great hug and the smell of lemon grass and coconut didn't shake me out of it. I wasn't pleased by the size of the bonus, I was horrified by it. And bonus day of 24 February meant that I had less than three weeks left.

Tuesday 7 February to Sunday 12 February 1995

I WAS long of Nikkei futures, short of JGB futures and my options were out of the money since the index sullenly refused to budge from 18,500. I forgot all about my other clients, I forgot all about the funding I'd have to ask for from Brenda, I just concentrated on the market. I'd made £15 million yesterday, I needed another £15 million today. George and Maslan were in the pit, waiting. The hubbub was subdued. The market was about to open. Osaka had opened quietly. SIMEX was looking for a lead. The bell rang to open the business. I broke open a tube of fruit pastilles and was halfway through it before I signalled the first buy to George.

'Buy 500 at 510.'

He rapidly bought 500 and signalled that he'd filled the order. This was not good news. The market absorbed this large purchase without blinking. It was just gone. Nothing moved. The market stayed at 18,510.

Risselle picked up a few client orders and I left the futures pit and found Danny at the JGB pit.

'What's the action?'

'It's good, high volume, tight trading range, heading down, I'd say. Want a bet?'

I smiled and shook my head. I needed more than a bet.

The JGB market was trading closely between 108.50 and 108.75. JGBs are one of the costliest futures contracts in the world, with the value of just one tick on a SIMEX JGB contract being 5,000 yen (US $50) – compared with 2,500 yen (US $25) for each tick on a Nikkei futures contract. If the index moves from 108.50 to 108.60, a single contract increases in value by $500.

I was already 10,000 JGB contracts short, so my position was swinging into profit or loss by a factor of $500,000 for every tick movement in the index. The index would typically move about 40 ticks in either direction in a day's trading, so I was looking at $20 million swings. The attraction to me of playing in the JGB futures market, which needs exactly the same funding mechanism as the Nikkei futures, is that it is significantly more liquid than the Nikkei futures market – and the market had been experiencing bigger swings, so bigger profits were possible. As were losses. My position was so big in the Nikkei that I was becoming too obvious, and the market was beginning to discount my purchases and sell against them because they sensed I'd soon have to unwind – and they didn't want to be hung with me.

'I'm a seller of JGBs,' I said to Danny. 'I think that after the earthquake people will be drawn into the higher appreciation of the Nikkei.'

'Who knows?' Danny said casually. 'You could be right.'

I felt like yelling at him and insisting that I had to be right. It was a good theory and it should work. JGBs looked expensive; the Nikkei cheap. JGBs should fall; the Nikkei should rise. I refused to acknowledge that I was forcing myself to believe this scenario because it had to happen if I were to escape.

That day I sold another load of JGB futures short and the market didn't budge. By 2:15, when the bell rang for close of trading, I was utterly exhausted. Nothing had happened. My position was unchanged; the market wouldn't react.

'I'll have some tiramisu,' I said as Danny and I slumped into some seats at Il Fiore, 'and a pot of coffee.'

'Good day?' Danny asked.

'No comment.'

'What's happening with the football?'

'God knows, I've hardly had time to look.'

I wasn't great company that lunchtime. If Danny and Lisa had compared notes, they'd have realised that I was clamming up. The only way I could see out of this mess was to trade out of it.

Over the next three days I decided to double up. On Wednesday, Thursday and Friday – 10 February – I shorted another 10,000 JGB contracts to bring my exposure up to 20,000 lots; and I bought another 25,000 Nikkei futures to take my position to 55,000. This size of dealing was unprecedented in SIMEX. The trades all flew into the 88888 account since I was shoring up a falling Nikkei market and selling into a rising JGB market. I hid the trades in the 88888 account, and I hid from everyone at the back office by spending all afternoon in the dimly-lit Il Fiore – drinking coffee, eating tiramisu and refusing to call anyone back. But I couldn't hide the funding. I had to call Brenda Granger and ask her for $45 million. By Friday 10 February I'd gone through over $100 million – and I needed another $45 million, thirty million pounds.

'Forty-five million dollars?' she repeated.

'Yeah, we've had an advance margin call from SIMEX on all our client positions. They're worried about the market stability since the movements are now so radical,' I gabbled, 'and so they've calculated that our clients need to put up additional margin of $45 million. This will of course be returned when market conditions calm down.'

'So it's an emergency measure?'

'That kind of thing,' I said, 'although they call it more of a standard practice.'

'Isn't everyone squealing out there?'

'No, we're all reconciled to just stumping up.'

'OK, Nick, send over the request and I'll put it into motion.'

'Thanks, Brenda.'

The phone rang as soon as I put it down. Mary Walz, I predicted. It was.

'What's this funding request? Forty-five million dollars?'

'I've explained it to Brenda. It's an advance margin call. Do you remember that SIMEX did one at the beginning of the month, just before the Chinese New Year?'

'Yeah,' she said.

'Well, they're doing it again. It's purely a balance sheet receivable. It doesn't impact the profits at all.'

'OK,' Mary said, sounding slightly mollified, 'but the numbers are getting big, you've had over $100 million put through BFS this week.'

'I'm working on reducing the position; it's not easy in this market.'

'Sure, but let's get on with it.'

My purchases hadn't gone unnoticed by the press.

'What is all this?' the *Nihon Keizei* paper wanted to know.

'It's just a large block,' I said, 'nothing particularly unusual.'

'The size is unusual,' the reporter said. 'I mean, Barings is standing in the market and we reckon you speak for around 50,000 March contracts.'

'We're happy with it,' I said, and shook him off.

Ron Baker was far from happy with it.

'I know it's a hedged position,' he began, 'but people are beginning to talk. For fuck's sake, Nick, we've had the Bank of International Settlements in Basle on the phone asking whether Barings can meet its margin payments. It's not good for the image.'

265

'I'll reduce it,' I said. 'Tony Railton is out here and he's talking to Citibank about the letters of credit and with SIMEX about how the funding works.'

'OK,' Ron said, 'I'll leave it at that, but I know Peter Norris will want to talk to you next week.'

The odd thing was that although people were aware that the numbers were big, they weren't as frightened by them as they'd been by the small numbers. This was odd, since by the middle of February I'd absorbed something like £300 million of funding – when the entire share capital base of Barings Bank itself was just £470 million.

Monday 13 February 1995

I HATED Mondays. The weekend gave me respite both from the pasting I was given on the dealing floor and the threat of discovery in the back office. The weekend gave me two days when nobody was in the office – so nobody would pick up a balance sheet or the margin feed to SIMEX and ask me where the missing numbers were. SIMEX was shut so I'd receive no margin calls and I wouldn't have to make a request to Brenda Granger for more funding. I could stay at home with Lisa, or we could visit one of the islands off Singapore, or wander around shopping and choose a video. At weekends we were just an ordinary couple, and we talked about our family visits, where to eat, what we needed to buy for the flat. Sunday night was when I realised that I had to go back into the office, and Monday was the start of a whole new week. I had given up trying to work out when I'd be caught or how I'd escape, I was just hoping to survive each day.

The market had closed and I was back at my desk looking through all the deals. Tony Railton was at the desk to my left, looking through some papers. I hated that. I hated him looking at any papers and wished he'd take himself off to the tennis court, where the only damage he could do was a top-spin backhand down the line. His phone rang, and he looked over his shoulder at me and pressed the handset close to his ear as if trying to stop me overhearing. He caught my eye and smiled, waggled his forefinger to and fro between us and mouthed that he needed to speak with me. I smiled back, baring my teeth and nodding.

'Nick,' Tony said slowly after he'd put the phone down, 'Simon gave me a letter from SIMEX and asked me to have a look at it' – he waved the SIMEX letter at me – 'but I can't exactly work out how they've come to the conclusions they've come to . . . if you see what I mean.'

I saw what he meant. With the SIMEX letter in his hand I saw all too clearly what he meant. Thank God he didn't see what he meant himself.

'Let's see that letter,' I said sympathetically. He handed over the SIMEX letter. It was the one of 11 January, which I'd already discussed with Simon and to which I'd drafted a nonsensical reply. It was history. But of course it mentioned the 88888 account – in black and white, screaming at me like a tabloid's headlines. This had to be the end. Even Tony Railton couldn't let a letter like this go unheeded. He'd have to report it back to Tony Hawes, who'd have to mention it to some of the

Credit Committee in London and the wall of water I'd balanced over my head would come tumbling down.

'Yes,' I said, softening my voice to sound as relaxed and indifferent as possible. 'We've dealt with this one.'

'What's this account they mention: 8 . . . 8 . . . 8 . . . 8 . . . 8?'

I'd referred to this account as the 'Five Eights' account for so long with everyone on the dealing floor and all the girls in the back office that it took me a second to register what he was talking about. Then the penny dropped – and then the millions dropped. But I realised that he was asking me a question rather than accusing me of fraud and deception and wrestling me to the ground in a citizen's arrest. If he was asking a question, he might not know the answer.

'It's a consolidation account we use, something like the gross account reporting we do for you,' I said airily. This was gobbledegook. He couldn't possibly swallow this one. I put one hand out of sight below the desk and pinched my thigh to stop myself from smiling at my own idiocy. My explanation made no sense, but it was the best I could come up with on the spot. I switched tactics, to put myself in control of the conversation and stop him asking questions.

'What are you doing with it anyway?' I cut in on him as he opened and shut his mouth like a goldfish.

'Simon asked me to look at it and then re-format the figures as SIMEX has asked us to,' he explained meekly.

'Don't worry about that.' I tossed the letter carelessly back on to my desk, and let it lie there out of reach so he'd have to ask for it back. 'I've done that already. SIMEX are happy with everything. I'm sorry, I never told Simon.'

'Really?' Tony was relieved.

'I'll call Simon and tell him it's all sorted. Now, is there anything else I can do? Have you looked at that automated booking system yet?' This was a meaningless task which I'd mentioned to side-track him.

'Yeah,' he was defensive, 'I'm getting on to that. It's just I've been working on that SIMEX letter all day.'

I pinched myself hard. Tony had been working on this letter all day. He already knew that he couldn't ratify the cash which London had passed over to me, and he knew that the balance sheet was wrong, and he'd now been looking at a letter which mentioned a new and unexplained account, 88888, which had large positions in it absorbing millions of dollars, but he still couldn't see what they had in common. He couldn't see that he was looking at the root of my problem. I nodded to him to indicate that the conversation was over and the matter closed, and he duly rose and went back to his desk. I put the SIMEX letter in my drawer so that Tony wouldn't feel that he could just come and pick it up. And I knew that he'd be too scared to go and ask Simon Jones for another copy – he'd get his balls chewed off. I picked up the phone and called Simon.

'Simon? Nick here. Tony's just gone through that SIMEX letter with me and we're all set.'

'What about SIMEX though? What about them?' Simon asked.

'They're relaxed,' I said. 'I spoke to them today.'

'All right, see you later.'

Before my phone could ring again, I called Steve and said we should go out boxing now. I got up and wandered out of the door, as if I was just going to go for a pee. Then I slipped to the lifts and pressed the DOWN button. The lift came, I stepped inside, and the doors slid shut. I'd survived another day.

PETER Norris, Barings' CEO, passed through Singapore on Thursday 16 February.

'Nick,' Norris buzzed me on the phone, 'I'm up in Loh Siew Khang's old office. Do you want to come up?'

'Sure, I'll be right with you.'

I pushed back my swivel chair and walked to the lift. I didn't know what I was letting myself in for. Perhaps they had found everything out and Norris was going to perform the ritual sacking. Perhaps he was going to confront me with a print-out of the 88888 account and ask me to explain it. Perhaps he had a query on the balance sheet. Perhaps Ron's forged memo would be sitting there, and he'd have Ron on the speaker-phone asking me to explain it. Perhaps he'd had a call from Coopers & Lybrand. Perhaps Simon Jones had called Citibank about the 7.78 billion yen and been told that it didn't exist. Anything could have happened.

I walked out of the lift, past all the gleaming gold export awards which Barings Singapore had won, and slipped into the Gents opposite for a glass of water. Before I could drink the glass, I found myself bent over the lavatory, retching. My stomach was empty – as usual I'd just grabbed an orange juice for breakfast – so I retched and retched on an empty stomach and swallowed down the little dribble of bile which came up. I splashed some water on my face and rinsed out my mouth. I met my eyes in the mirror.

'Looking like shit, Nick,' I said to the face staring back at me.

'Feeling like shit, Nick,' I answered myself.

I hardly recognised the person who was supposed to be me. I was white and bloated. A sheen of sweat speckled my forehead. I met my eyes but wondered who this person was. It wasn't me: it wasn't the same person who loved Lisa, who'd got married one windy spring day at a little flintstone Norman church where Lisa had worn freesias in her hair, and where everyone had been laughing outside the church and clutching hold of their hats and skirts at the same time; it wasn't the same person who'd taken Lisa on honeymoon to Venice and cuddled her as our vaporetto sped away towards the Cipriani; it wasn't the bright young banker who'd been asked to set up the Baring Futures Singapore office, who'd been made General Manager and given the brief to make it into a profit centre. I'd turned myself into another creature. It was as if my body had been completely taken over from within – someone only had to tap me with a spoon and I'd crack apart and my secret would gush out.

I practised my smile. My skin felt dry and cracked, and my lips weren't stretching properly. I must look as if I was snarling. I walked into the kitchen and took another sip of water and then turned down the corridor along past the research department. At least I might avoid Simon Jones and James Bax, whose offices were on the far side of the building.

Siew Khang had been director of research, and her office had glass walls overlooking the research department. I tapped on the door and Peter Norris motioned me in. He was on the phone. I walked in and split my face into a suitable smile of welcome. He waved me to a chair and I sat in front of him while he finished his call.

'Hi, Nick,' he said, 'I've got just one more call to make. Do you mind?'

'Not at all,' I smiled again. And I didn't mind. I'd happily sit there for an hour with him on the phone. Talking to him – and being seen to be talking to him – was my perfect alibi. I also realised that if he was making calls back to London, he didn't have anything serious to say to me. I sat and waited. The call lasted twenty minutes. Peter Norris kept looking at me and motioning that he would be almost finished, that the guy at the other end was a bore, that I was his top priority, but I let it all go over my head. Keep talking, I urged him silently, just kept chatting away and I'll survive another hour. Finally he put the phone down.

'I'm so sorry, Nick,' he said. 'Now, how are you?'

Before I could answer, the phone rang again. This time he took five minutes. It was excellent. I looked at my watch. Peter Norris saw me do so and came off the phone.

'I know you need to get on,' he said, 'but I just wanted to ask you about the market. How is it?'

'Staying between 18,000 and 18,300, drifting a little,' I said, 'but it's settled after the earthquake.'

'It's funny how these things are so quickly worked through. The losses from the October '87 crash were almost completely recouped by the year-end.'

I waited, not daring to say anything. If this was all he wanted to ask me, it was too good to be true.

'What about the positions you're running? Are you happy with them?'

I wondered about telling him that I'd thrown up in the Gents before coming to see him, that I could still taste the bile in my mouth. I wondered whether I should fall on the carpet and tell him that no matter how important his phone calls might be, mine were even more so. But I just nodded.

'I'm relaxed. Most of them are now March contracts, so if it's too difficult to sell them in this market, I'll just let them expire.'

'Good, that sounds fine to me,' Peter Norris said. 'Now, we've had a lot of stick about funding.'

His phone rang again. I waited.

'Just hold on a minute,' Norris said into the phone. Then, to me: 'OK, look, I'm sure you want to get on. Let's speak later. You're coming tonight, aren't you?'

This was an invitation to the Polo Club for dinner. Simon Jones hadn't invited me, which had pissed me off but pleased me at the same time, since it would be a diabolically boring evening.

'Yes,' I nodded as I stood up. 'See you there.'

'Excellent,' he said.

I went back to the lift and hit the 14th floor button with glee. Back at my desk I looked at the cluster of post-it notes plastered to my computer screen: the usual names – Brenda Granger, Mary Walz, Fernando, Lisa.

'What's the SIMEX margin call?' I asked Nisa.

'Forty-eight million dollars.'

'Will you fax that through to Brenda with a 50–50 breakdown?'

'Sure.'

'Actually, make it 60–40, we did 50–50 yesterday.'

'No problem.' Nisa turned back to her screen to type up the request for the cash transfer.

'And can you call Mary Walz and Brenda Granger and say that I'm in a meeting with Peter Norris?'

I called Lisa and told her I had a dinner to go to and that I'd have a quick workout with Steve at Farrer Park beforehand. Then I called Steve and arranged to pick him up. Feeling light-headed at the madness of it all, I just walked out without returning either Brenda or Mary's calls. Let them hear that I was with Peter Norris and they'd assume that everything was fine. He was the perfect alibi.

I SMASHED him full wallop in the face – *thud!* Tony Railton crumpled in front of me, his head split open like a melon; then Ron Baker – kick, punch, *thud*, stone dead; Peter Norris – thud, thud, and he staggered back against the ropes, his nose compacted and bleeding down his green silk tie; then Tony Hawes – thud, that was a mercy killing; Simon Jones – smash, smash, smash, kick, left, right, upper cut and his jaw flew apart and his teeth scattered like pearls as he toppled backwards. I stopped, panting and sweating.

The punch-bag spun dizzily in front of me, and my chest heaved. Next I had all the traders to deal with, those fuckers who were squeezing me out of the market, a whole army of Chinese with short hair, glasses and red jackets. I flew into them, punching left and right. In between the blows I kicked out with my heels, savage thrusts into the lower part of the punch-bag. My head span and I stopped, desperately panting for breath, sweat stinging my eyes. The punch-bag was undented, still smooth and shiny, spinning slowly and ready for more. I was knackered. I was dead on my feet.

The punch-bag was impervious. Someone else could come and kick the shit out of it, and it'd never notice. It would absorb it all. Punchers came and went and the punch-bag just hung in there, plump and tempting. I couldn't do any damage to it – I could only destroy myself.

It was time to go to dinner.

I DROVE down Mount Pleasant Lane and passed by James Bax's house, set back from the road, a large colonial villa. I was pissed off at having to go to this dinner. I'd known about it for some time, as people were asking who was going. I'd felt both snubbed but also pleased not to be going. Now I'd been the last person to be invited, and I felt angry that they'd ignored me for so long and angry that it was going to be a complete waste of time – another entry on the Barings expense account. I turned up Thomson Road and passed through the entrance gates of the Polo Club, the most exclusive club in Singapore – if you like that kind of thing. I was apparently the last to arrive, and parked at the end of a long line of Mercedes and Jaguars which spent their lives guzzling petrol in the Singapore traffic.

I walked up the steps to the entrance and smelled the polo ponies in their stables over to one side. I took in the Barings crowd who were gathered around the bar. A circle of admirers pressed around Peter Norris, laughing at his jokes and nodding at his insights into Asia and the world at large; another circle stood around James Bax. It was a Barings hall of fame – everyone who was any-one in Barings Asia was there, including Tom Hester, the latest star in James Bax's team. I drained a couple of glasses of beer and longed to get completely smashed. But I had the car to drive back, and I knew that these guys wouldn't drink like me. I stared out over the large flat expanse of the polo field, thinking it must be one of the biggest places in Singapore which wasn't covered with artificial lighting.

'Nick.'

I turned to find Simon Jones at my elbow.

'How did it go with the auditors?'

'I think I got rid of them. But it wasn't easy.'

I was in no mood for conversation, so I nodded and left it at that. At a signal from James Bax we all pro-ceeded towards the restaurant, but instead of going up to the formal dining room we stopped at the terrace, where a large table had been laid for us. Small candles were set along its length. It could almost have been romantic – with the right person. I hovered around behind everyone while they all angled for the best places to sit, and finally swooped down into a seat well away from Peter Norris and James Bax. The conversation was about polo ponies and the cost of keeping one. I had no opinion on the matter and looked at the menu. As the waiter took orders, I saw that we weren't having any starters, so I went along with that as it would get me out of the place faster.

Everyone was talking around me, over me, across from me, but I stared at the pretty winking candles and just thought about my 88888 position. If they knew what I was thinking, they wouldn't be tucking into all these steaks and lobsters – they'd be choking on them. Over the last few weeks, my losses had exploded. I could hardly bring myself to pick up the 88888 print-out and read it, because I didn't want to be associated with it. I didn't want to get my fingerprints on it. It had leapt from a loss of tens of millions to a couple of hundred million.

A guy next to me tried to chat about the market, but I fobbed him off. I kept my head down, ate my food quietly and waited to leave. At least Ron Baker wasn't there – he'd have got up and started making some crass comments about how successful we all were. Peter Norris just kept chatting away and looking at his watch and everyone knew that he was on an evening flight back to London. I was delighted when he finally checked his watch again, whispered to James Bax and stood up to go. He waved to us all as if he was departing royalty, and then James Bax walked him back to the entrance of the club where his driver was waiting. He'd gone. I felt pleased that his visit hadn't caught me out, but I also knew that he was an excellent alibi. It'd been so easy to tell everyone not to worry because I'd sorted it out with Peter Norris, or was with Peter Norris, or Peter Norris knew all about it. Now he was gone there was one less person to use as a shield. We all filed back into the bar and everyone refused the offer of a nightcap. I looked back at the debris of the dinner table. The waitresses were clearing it up and blowing out the candles. The party was over.

Friday 17 February 1995

IN a blind fury I left the Barings booth and walked across to the Nikkei pit. Fucking George was useless. He was just fucking around in the market and nobody took him seriously. How could they when he looked such a wanker with that absurd haircut? The market was dropping through 18,000 and it needed a lift. It needed some serious buying. I pulled the dealing slips from my pocket and stood beside George, towering over him and looking at the sea of faces around me, all of them sellers. I'd take the whole pack of them on. They were just a load of tossers. What did Mark call them? Pond life. They were just a pool of scum and algae and they were in my way.

'Nine-fifty bid for a hundred!' I roared at them, holding out my arms and beckoning them on. Bang, bang, bang, bang, I bought four lots of 25 contracts and scribbled them down. The market fell again.

'Nine-fifty bid for a hundred!' I roared louder, and – bang, bang – I took two hits of 50 each and scribbled those down.

The market fell another ten points, as traders forgot who I was and sold more and more. I knew that they knew that I was long – very, very long – and at some stage they knew I'd have to cut my position. But I wanted them to believe that I was hedged in Osaka, and that I was just buying a long position to balance my book.

'Nine-forty bid for a thousand!' I roared, oblivious to George, who was standing silently beside me, watching as I bought up the entire market. Aha! This took a little longer; now I was planting seeds of doubt in their minds. There was a discernible pause as they digested this, and then I bought up some locals and turned to the big boys, Morgan Stanley and Nomura.

'Nine-forty bid for 500!' I roared again, my voice raw at the edges. 'Nine-fifty bid for 500!' I changed my bid as the market turned a tick higher. Nomura sold me a hundred and then I looked around the pit.

'Nine-sixty bid for 500!'

I took another hundred off Nomura but Morgan Stanley weren't interested.

'Come on, George,' I yelled at him. 'Move this fucking market!'

'Nine-seventy bid for 500!' George yelled beside me. We were both on the bid, both in full cry. The market was pushed up. We hoovered up any sellers, not just buying from them, but buying immediately – taking them off at the legs. They hardly had time to meet our eyes to confirm the price before I'd bought. I lost count of my purchases. It was insane. I was punch-drunk and reeling in front of the market, roaring and beckoning and only half aware that George was being very quiet, and that Risselle over at the booth was signalling some orders through to Maslan: mainly sell orders he was trying to net off in George's ear so he didn't over-buy.

'Five bid for 500!' I was bursting my lungs to chase the market up. It inched above 18,000.

I backed off away from the market, watching the overhead screens as I walked back to the Barings booth. I took a bottle of water off the counter and swigged it back, and then poured some over my head and ran my hands through my hair.

'Nick!' Tony Railton popped up like a ghost beside me. How the fuck had he got on to the floor?

'Hi!'

'Nick, I really need to go over some of these figures with you.'

'Sure,' I said, massaging my head. Then I saw the market slip back through 18,000.

'Back in a minute,' I said, and shoved my way to the pit, smouldering with rage.

'Nine-seventy bid for 500!' I screamed. 'Nine-seventy bid for 500!'

I took out a couple of offers and then chased the market up some more. It hit 18,050 and then came back. I could see Tony standing at the Barings booth. Fuck him! Let him stand there. I began to just shout mad things out, punching the air and howling: 'Fifty bid for 500! Fifty bid for 500!'

I was actually bidding with other buyers now, so nobody took me out, but I could stand and shout all day while Tony Railton stood like a spare part over at the booth.

'Fifty bid for 500!' I shouted and shouted until I heard a few more dealers shouting the same. Soon 50 became the mid-price and everyone was bawling 50, beckoning 50, signalling 50. Five fingers were everywhere. It was magic. They were doing my bidding for me. In a sudden blaze of inspiration I understood the expression 'do my bidding for me'. There they were, all those red jackets across the pit, literally doing my bidding for me. All over the world the dealers would now be going back to their linesmen, who would in turn pass on the message to their customers that there was a lot of support at 18,000 and the market wouldn't fall below that level. And if enough confidence could be whipped up, then the market would indeed stay above 18,000. The market confidence was self-perpetuating. And it had all come from me.

By the time I staggered out of the pit, Tony Railton had gone. He'd left some prissy note that he'd catch up with me in the office. I walked outside and headed for Il Fiore. Nobody knew my hiding hole. I could stay there until about 6 P.M., when I'd have to get back into the office to call London and make the funding request. In fact, money could be coming back today. The market had gone with me. I pulled my dealing slips out of my pocket and checked through them. I'd bought about 15,000 Nikkei futures contracts. I couldn't do the sums in my head, but the market was a touch stronger, so I'd receive some money from SIMEX on the rest of the position, but have to pay the margin on today's purchases. I'd probably be not far off even. That was a relief. Although I'd raised the odds dramatically by buying all those futures, I'd survived another day. If I hadn't bought, the market would have hit 17,500. Then the phone call to Brenda would be impossible – I'd be asking for $200 million and we'd all go up in smoke. As it was I needn't tell her about the buying, I'd be asking for no money from her and possibly even repaying some, and I could live through the weekend. I wouldn't speak to Mary Walz or Ron Baker.

I knocked back the dregs of the coffee and raised my hand for some more. Then I ate some tiramisu and felt my veins expanding and warming up. I was going to get away with it. This time next week was bonus day; and my birthday was the day after that, Saturday 25 February. I had just one more week to go.

9

Monday 20 to Thursday 23 February

I DREAMT THAT I was lying in the middle of the SIMEX trading floor. There was the usual chaos as everyone swarmed around, shouting and signalling and dealing as the Nikkei lurched up and down. But as I looked at the dealers' faces, I saw with horror that they had the heads of wolves, hyenas, stray dogs. They all wore their flimsy brightly-coloured dealing jackets, but their necks were broad and covered with fur, and their mouths were open snarling snouts.

My perspective changed and I began to be able to look down upon my body, stretched out in the middle of the Nikkei pit. I was alive, looking around me, and suddenly one of the hyenas leapt forward and snapped at my back. He tore a piece of flesh off me and went back into the scrum where there was a fight over this flesh. Another creature leapt out, and then I saw the entire dealing floor all converge on me and start tearing my body to pieces. I was still alive, writhing under their weight, but they kept stripping pieces of meat off me until I saw the bones glinting white under the lights.

'I'm not dead!' I shouted. 'You're only meant to eat dead meat!'

But the wolves and hyenas kept snapping and twisting at me, and then secondary markets sprang up as they tried to establish a futures price for the meat before it went rancid, and other dealers bought options to eat the meat.

'Market forces!' whispered someone in my ear. I saw that it was Ron Baker. 'We need another £2 million profit next week, no "ifs" or "buts".'

'It's not actually terribly difficult to make money,' said someone else, and it was Peter Baring.

'Seven point seven eight billion yen!' shouted Mui Mui.

'It's a glitch! It's a glitch!' shouted James Bax, but even as he continued shouting, the words changed from 'It's a glitch! It's a glitch!' to 'It's a girl! It's a girl!', and then I saw Lisa cuddling our baby and crying and looking so proud. But I wasn't beside her. I looked around. All I could see was my blue and gold jacket lying on the empty dealing floor.

'It's a girl!' cried Lisa. 'It's a girl!'

'It's a glitch!' shouted James Bax.

'Where's Nick?' Lisa sobbed. 'Tell Nick to come here.'

George Seow ran to the blue and yellow jacket and picked it up, but underneath he found just my splayed white skeleton. And then Lisa looked up and screamed: the baby in her arms had vanished and in its place was a tiny blood clot, staining the white muslin wrap with a deep spreading red blotch.

* * *

MONDAY and Tuesday were quiet days in the market. I had bought up so many Nikkei futures last week that there was a liquidity squeeze and it moved up to around 18,400. I didn't do much trading, I just sat on my 88888 account and watched it move with the market. I would have liked it to be higher – 500 points higher would have taken me off the rocks. But it clung to the 18,400 level and refused to budge. My JGBs, on the other hand, were losing money as the index rose from 109 to 110. I suspected that I'd lost around £30 million on those, but I was too scared to look. In any event, given that it was only just past the middle of the month, I needn't do anything immediately. In fact, given that I had to make or break by 24 February, I wouldn't have another month-end to have to cover. I spent Tuesday afternoon in Il Fiore and went back to my desk at five o'clock.

'Nick, hi, it's Tony Railton. Can I come down for a minute?'

Shit, I was caught red-handed at my desk. I'd managed to banish him up to the 24th floor for a couple of days to investigate some sort of automatic trade reporting, which was a complete waste of time – it was just an excuse to keep him away from me and stop him overhearing my conversations.

'Sure, come on down.'

I wondered what he'd uncovered. My list of deceit was too long for me to recite now. It could be anything from the balance sheet to the Citibank account to the 88888 account. I waited for him.

'Hi, how's life?'

'Good,' he said. He was certainly looking tanned.

'Must be nice to get away from London in February.'

'It's great,' he agreed.

I was pleased to see that he wasn't holding any papers in his hand. Anything written down would have been a disaster.

'I just wanted to tell you that I've sorted out lines of credit with SIMEX,' he said. 'Brenda Granger will be able to authorise up to $50 million from Citibank which SIMEX can draw down.'

'That's good.'

'Yes, it'll free up Brenda a lot.'

'How's everything else?'

'Well, I'm still needing an analysis of all the client positions.'

I felt like telling him to get a print-out of our declared SIMEX position. That had everything on it. SIMEX knew more about Barings' position than Tony did.

'I'm working on that, Tony. I promise I'll have something for you when I can.'

'Thank you. The other thing is the OTC trade you did back in December, the 7.78 billion one. Do you have any documentation on that? I just need to double-check through it and do a report back to London.'

'Coopers have all the papers,' I said. 'I gave them all to Mui Mui.'

'OK, I'll chase her then.'

'Anything else?' I pointedly looked at the post-its on my screen.

'No. Oh, you know they're having a board meeting at the moment?'

'Here?'

'No, a main board meeting in London. Friday is

bonus day, and they're just finally agreeing them all. I gather that Peter Baring is up for a million.'

'Lucky old him!'

'Very nice man,' Tony said. 'You know that he always goes to work on the Tube?'

'Bloody miser!' I joked.

'And I gather that Tuckey and Norris are on line for a million each.'

I didn't want to sit here and salivate at other people's bonuses. I wished the phone would ring.

'Are you moving here permanently?' I asked.

'Yeah, I hope so. I don't know how to negotiate the right package though. There's lots of tax implications.'

'It's quite easy,' I said. 'London should be able to help.'

'What about housing allowance though?' Tony persisted. 'Is that taxable? And what will they give me?'

I looked again at my phone. Poor old Tony was trying to ask about his salary. I'd be giving him advice on his pension soon. At last the phone rang. It was Danny. I pressed the handset tight to my ear so that Tony wouldn't hear.

'Really?' I said.

'Nick, come and have a drink,' he said.

'What, right away?'

'Yeah, everyone's getting nicely smashed here.'

'A settlement problem?'

'Problem my arse, get over here.'

'You're at SIMEX?'

'SIMEX?! What the fuck are you on about?'

'I'll be right down.'

'Damn right you will.'

I put down the phone. 'Sorry, Tony, there's a problem with one of the tickets. George is at SIMEX.'

'No problem, see you tomorrow.'

And with that I walked off in the direction of SIMEX and met Danny in Il Fiore.

Wednesday 22 February 1995

I was awake to hear the first planes coming into Changi airport. They whined and roared as their engines strained back. I knew the time would be 4:30 A.M. Hearing the first planes is always a bad sign – especially when you didn't get to sleep until 2 A.M. Then I listened out for the cars. The traffic began to build up at about five, and then over and above the noise of cars I heard the birdsong in the trees outside. I was always amazed that the birds knew when dawn broke, given how much overhead street lighting shone around them all night. But they somehow detected the dawn through the orange fluorescence and sang their hearts out at it. In my unnatural life, which I spent on the air-conditioned, halogen-lit dealing floor, then in the dimly-lit recesses of Il Fiore, then lying awake in bed feeling my veins beat, this birdsong was the only natural thing. It was a tiny, reedy sound, but for a moment the birdsong rose triumphant over the city. Then it was lost under the growing rumble of traffic and bleached out by the glare of the sun.

As I shaved and shiftily avoided meeting my eye in the mirror, I was envious of those birds. For them, each day was a new one. The birds had such tiny brains that – rather like goldfish, who were meant to be eternally interested in each new circuit around their glass bowl – they were ecstatic at each new dawn because their lives started off again. For me, each day was a series of cumulative nightmares which by now had almost engulfed me. I had fought losses for long enough now to have nothing left to fight them with. I had until the weekend. Something had to happen. I hated each new dawn.

I tied my tie in the mirror without acknowledging myself. It was an odd way of dressing – ignoring the person in the mirror, refusing to meet my eye or smile at myself. The person in the mirror was in trouble, and *I* didn't want to get involved.

The market opened quietly. All through the morning I sat with my stomach eating away at itself and munched sweets and watched the market hover around 18,400. I was desperate for it to move up to 18,800. Anything could happen if only I had enough time. I slipped away from the trading floor at the ten o'clock break and stocked up with sweet black coffee.

I immediately knew that the market had crashed. The noise was a hysterical babble, which meant that people were straining and shouting at the tops of their voices to deal, but nobody was dealing with them. The mounting frustration and panic has a steely-edged sound to it; it's not a normal human voice at all. Gathering my thoughts I made my way to the Barings booth. Nobody had the time to smile or wave at me. I felt rather light-headed and distant from it all.

The market had fallen below 18,100 – well below

18,100. It was now 18,000, and I'd need at least $30 million to pay the 88888 daily margin if it didn't recover.

I didn't trade at all on Wednesday afternoon, I just sat and watched the market and tried to remember how it would have felt if I'd just stuck to my job of arbitraging: I'd be making loads of money on a day like this. I'd be in and out, screaming at the traders, on the phone to Fernando and making money all afternoon. Fernando was keen to trade, but I didn't have the heart – I gave him the prices in a lacklustre way and he soon cooled off as well.

Back at the office I asked Linda to fax the request for $30 million through to Brenda. I then called up Steve and arranged to go boxing. I didn't want to be around when Brenda came back on the phone asking me to explain why I wanted $30 million. At least Ron Baker was on holiday, so she wouldn't check with him. I left the office early on Wednesday and missed Simon Jones, Tony Railton and all the newspapers.

Thursday 23 February 1995

I DIDN'T tell Lisa that anything was wrong. I went through the motions of getting dressed and ready for work as if it were a normal day. I listened and nodded as she recited her plans for my birthday on Saturday: we were going to an Italian restaurant with four or five others. I barely understood a word she said. I was just praying that the market would bounce this morning. She dropped me off at Delifrance, and Danny and I drank an orange juice and bought some chocolate Kinder eggs. I found a toy penguin in mine.

'Hey! You lucky sod,' Danny said, 'those are really rare.'

We duly smacked hands over a nonsensical bet and made our way to the SIMEX lifts. The bell rang for the start of trade, and straight away the market was sold down. I waited, refusing to buy, hopelessly unable to sell, as the market fell 400 points without pausing for breath. Nobody looked particularly worried about this. The Nikkei index hit 17,600 and I snapped another tube of fruit pastilles in half. They were sickly sweet on my tongue, cloying with the bile I kept having to swallow.

Then I couldn't stand the inertia anymore. I had to do something about the market. I walked to the edge of the pit and replaced George. I began shouting. I had a lot to shout about, and I shouted my head off. I began to take on the big dealers in the pit, ignoring the locals who were just trying to ride on my shirt-tails, and concentrating on the big players who might relay a message back to their bosses in Japan or London that the Nikkei was bouncing and that they'd better jump in before they missed it.

The orders kept coming at me, and I swayed and nodded, and held out my arms and took the weight of the market on my shoulders. I wouldn't have been able to sell a single contract with the market as it was. I knew that I was flying in the face of Ron Baker's and Mary Walz's instructions to sell and wind down the positions, but the market was looking for any excuse to tumble, and I was the only support.

After buying around 3,000 contracts, I left and walked over to the JGB pit. There the scene was a mirror image of the Nikkei futures – the index was inexorably creeping up; had already risen 20 points. My short position was so huge that I was losing £8 million for each 10-point rise: I'd lost £16 million. I dodged my way back to the Nikkei pit and looked up at the screens: I was losing £20 million for every 100 points down on the Nikkei, and even as I watched the numbers flashed again, down 50 points, and I'd lost another £10 million. The Nikkei had opened 50 points down – today was its worst day of the year, and it looked as if it was heading more than 400 points lower. Putting my losses on the Nikkei together with my losses on the JGBs I was already £40 million down today, and I hadn't even broken into my third tube of pastilles.

I went back to the JGB pit, mainly in order to hide. I felt safe on the SIMEX floor. Just as I'd felt when Ash Lewis had come to start her internal audit, I felt that nobody could get me on the SIMEX floor. It was so busy and full of people that I could hide from anyone I didn't want to talk to. But more than that, anything could happen. Right up until the bell went, the market could soar up or collapse. I might get out of trouble yet. I checked the time: 12:15 P.M.

Then I ducked back to the Nikkei, picking up a handful of sweets from Connie on the way. The Nikkei was going down more, and I wondered whether they were ganging up on me to force me out of the market. The market was down over 300 points. I stood and watched the red jackets as they dealt furiously. I was past dealing. I felt like a ghost on the edge of the pit. I seemed to be fading away from it. I went off to find the Gents and ducked over the filthy lavatory, my stomach retching and my mouth full of slimy green regurgitated fruit pastille.

In forty-five minutes' time the trading floor would be deserted and I'd have nowhere to hide. Tomorrow, Friday, was bonus day. Saturday was my birthday. I had to get out of Singapore.

I hunched over a desk and looked at the screens. To the outsider I looked like Nick Leeson, the trading superstar who moved the Nikkei this way and that, the gambler with the biggest balls in town. The other dealers would see me and wonder what I was planning: was I working out some sort of eight-dimensional option hedge, which would derive profits off the back of the Nigerian copper price when put against the tomato price in Chicago? What a joke! I couldn't even get the straight Nikkei market right – it had bust me. No, I was sitting hunched over the Teletext screens looking at the football games for Saturday, trying to forget that I had lost hundreds of millions of pounds and had run out of rope.

Then, in the last half-hour, when the market was still falling down past 17,800, over 300 points down, I went back into the pit and bought another 1,000 futures to support the market. The bell rang as I was in full flight – one more figure in the crowd, whom nobody would think was doing anything any differently from all the others. But the one figure had now blown himself out of the water. I staggered off the trading floor and smiled at the other faces hovering in front of me, sweating and grinning. I realised I had to escape. I had no idea how I was going to get through the next few hours, but I knew that I couldn't sleep another night in our flat. We had to get out of Singapore.

I only had a few hours to go. The Nikkei had closed 330 points down. I'd made it bounce once or twice on the way down, but basically I'd only half stopped it. It wanted to fall further. I was now scared to death. I had to get out of here. I had no idea what the numbers were, but I knew they were overwhelming. I bit my lip and looked ahead over the next few milestones: I'd have to see Simon Jones and probably Tony Railton back at the office; I'd have to ask Brenda for perhaps a $40 million cash transfer for the margin call; Tony Hawes was coming back to Singapore over the weekend; tomorrow was bonus day and Saturday my birthday. And God knows what SIMEX might do. With the market down over 300 points I didn't have any room to move. I wasn't going to let them catch me, so I decided to get out now and enjoy my birthday.

'Nick, we're going to Escape,' George yelled at me. 'Danny's coming, what about you?'

Escape! Of course I was going to escape.

'I'm coming,' I smiled as I registered the pun. Escape was a local dive where the windows were tinted. You could sit looking out at the street, but nobody could see you. It was a perfect place to hide for three or four hours while I worked out what I needed to do.

We sat in a corner table and I ordered a beer, but then changed my mind and had a Coke. I needed to think. London was still open, and I knew that when they found my JGB positions, they'd have to unwind them and the liquidity in the March contracts was too tight. They'd take a real pasting if they had to run around and buy JGBs for cash settlement and immediate delivery. It'd be far better if they had a little more time to unwind the short position. It would be easier for Barings if I rolled the position over from March until June.

I pulled out my mobile and called Willow, the JGBs dealer at Tullets on LIFFE in London.

'Willow, it's Nick. Where are the JGB spreads today?'

'Hold on, let me get them up on the screen. You've had the hots for them this week all right. You've bought around 5,000, haven't you?'

'Don't remind me. I've got a bad March position and I want to roll it over into June.'

'The spread is bid at 92 and offered at 95.'

'OK, listen Willow, I'm 93 bid for as many as you can lay your hands on. If the size is there just keep on buying.'

'That's ballsy,' Willow said, clearly trying to overcome his glee at the potential commission. I hoped Barings would pay it, but that was another matter. But even as I listened to the clicks on the line as Willow left me hanging on, I knew that I wouldn't have to organise it any more. It'd be someone else at Barings who would have to unwind this position, probably Fernando.

'Exactly how many do you want?' Willow came back to me.

'Just don't stop buying,' I said. 'Buy as many as you can. You'll never complete my order.'

Willow must have thought I was pissed.

'Come on, Nick.'

'Call me on my mobile when you've bought 2,000 and we'll see.' I clicked him off and sipped my Coke.

'What are you doing in London?' Danny asked.

'I'm getting out of some March spreads.'

'I need to as well,' Danny said. 'Roger's been kicking my arse all week trying to get me to move. The fucking market has risen all week, I've had no chance.'

'OK,' I said, 'I've got to get back to the office.' I drained the icy, watery remains of my Coke and pushed the glass away from me. I had to see Tony Railton and Simon Jones again. God knows how I was going to cope with the funding for tomorrow. Right at this moment SIMEX would be calculating my losses for the day and preparing a request for the daily margin. It was going to be huge.

Back at the office everything looked normal. The girls were bent over their computer screens, the telephones were ringing, and there was no sign of Tony Railton. This looked promising. I looked at the post-its on my screen – again, the usual suspects: Mary Walz, Steve, Brenda Granger, Simon Jones. It was like a mantra. I could die and be sent to hell and these names would still spin around my head, with the bigger names behind them: James Bax, Ron Baker, Tony Hawes, Peter Norris, remaining unsaid but always implied. I'd hardly sat down when the *Nihon Keizei* called, wanting to know what I was going to do with my position – 'The Baring Overhang', as the reporter called it. I'd no sooner shaken him off and put my phone on 'Divert' than two more phones around the office rang, and the girls held their hands over the handsets and called out:

'AP–Dow Jones?'

'Brenda Granger?'

I shook my head and opened the locked drawer of my

desk. Among the scissors and paste which I'd used to forge the 7.78 billion yen receivable I found the 88888 statements.

I scribbled in the day's trading and looked at the figures: at today's Nikkei close of 17,885 I was long of 61,039 Nikkei futures contracts, short of 26,000 JGBs and had a mixture of Euroyen and Nikkei options which were devastated. All month these figures had been exploding but I'd pushed them away from me.

'Nick!'

I swivelled round and gathered my papers in one move. It was Tony Railton. I smiled and motioned him to a chair. I was delighted that he didn't have a piece of paper in his hand. He clearly still hadn't found anything.

'How you doing, Tony? Good day?'

'Great day, Nick, great day. How was the market?'

'Brilliant.' I flashed him my bullshit smile.

'Nick, I was talking with Simon about this hole in the balance sheet – I'm so sorry to bore you with it – but we wondered whether you could make a quick meeting this afternoon? And then James wants a meeting on Saturday, as you know.'

'God! Look, Saturday's out. I mean, it's my birthday, and Lisa and I want to enjoy it. Sunday would be fine, but not Saturday. And sure, let's meet later this afternoon. Lisa's just called to say that she's sick right now so I'm going home to check on her. I'll get back to you about 4:30?'

Simon Jones then made his appearance. When he turned to Tony I checked the time: almost 4 P.M. I had just a few minutes to play with. I had to get out. I pushed back my chair and headed for the door.

'See you later!' I called out to nobody in particular. In the lift I called Lisa and told her I'd pick her up in five minutes. I put my phone back in my pocket and it immediately rang. I pulled it out and looked at it. Then I switched it off.

It was time to run.

10

Monday 27 February to Thursday 2 March

Out of the corner of my eye I saw the thick black ink headline: BRITISH MERCHANT BANK COLLAPSE.

'Lisa,' I whispered, 'buy that newspaper. I can't read this. Barings is bust.'

As Lisa picked up the paper and started reading the article, which mentioned a missing trader, I looked out at the hotel. We were in the middle of nowhere, halfway along the north coast of Borneo. We were trapped. How could we get out of here? Lisa went up to the cash till and was about to sign for the paper and the biscuits.

'Pay cash,' I said. 'Don't sign anything.'

We blundered out of the shop and back to our hotel bedroom. Lisa sat on the edge of the bed and read out the article. I tore open the biscuits and started munching them, and then went into the bathroom and ran a bath. I couldn't read the paper myself. Lisa read it out three times, and when we looked at each other I felt as if she must be staring at a stranger.

'Is this missing trader you?' she asked.

'Yes. It's what I've been trying to tell you about. I've lost them money. I had no idea it was this bad.'

'What are we going to do?' Lisa said. 'I know, let's call Mum – she'll tell us what's going on.'

I couldn't bear to listen to the conversation, so I lay in the bath and concentrated on relaxing – while every time I closed my eyes the world spun upside down around me.

'We're fine, Mum,' I heard Lisa say. 'We'll try to get home. I'd better not tell you where we are so you don't have to lie to anyone who asks.'

There was silence while Patsy told her what was going on. To my amazement Lisa started laughing.

'He didn't!' she shouted with laughter. 'God help us.'

Then there was another long pause.

'OK, Mum,' Lisa took control of things, 'we'll call you when we can, but I'd better go. We love you.'

Then Lisa came into the bathroom and sat on the floor.

'There's been a House of Commons debate,' she said. 'The Chancellor of the Exchequer has called you a "rogue trader", and Peter Baring has gone on the news and said there's been a conspiracy. Barings is bust and has lost more than £600 million.'

I fumbled for the soap at the bottom of the bath, and felt irritated at the fact that bars of hotel soap are always so small.

'And Mum says that we've knocked Charles and Di off the front pages of the tabloids. Everyone's looking for us. There's a man-hunt going on across Asia, and some people think we're in our yacht sailing around Indonesia.'

I digested this for a moment. I couldn't see any obvious jokes, apart from the yacht.

'What was so funny? What were you laughing at?'

'Mum had called your dad to find out how he was. While they were on the phone, there was a knock at your dad's door. He said that he'd just open it. Then down the line she heard this scuffle, and then Harry shouting "Fuck off, scum!", then there was silence. Your dad knocked out a *Daily Mirror* photographer. Laid him out cold on the doorstep.'

'That's all we need,' I said. 'I get done for busting Barings and Dad gets done for GBH.'

I looked around the windowless bathroom, with its white tiles and shower curtain. It was about six feet wide by six feet long: a cell. I got out of the bath and Lisa and I sat on the bed.

'I'll call Danny and find out what's going on in Singapore.'

I called Danny at First Continental. It was a Monday afternoon and the market had crashed. The Nikkei had opened 880 points down and closed 645 points down at 16,960. The JGB market had soared up 50 points on news of my short position since everyone knew that Barings would have to buy to close it off. I couldn't work out exactly what my position would have lost, but if they hadn't sold anything on Friday, they might even have doubled.

I couldn't begin to think straight – sod it, the bank was bust and I was up to my neck in it.

'Bubble,' I said.

'Nick! Where the fucking hell are you?'

'Malaysia.'

'Look, we can't talk long in case anyone's on our case. Just listen to me: it is as bad for you as it possibly could be. You don't have any friends here. Get the fuck out of Asia and get to London or even Australia. If they catch you here, you'll both be banged up in the Bangkok Hilton.'

'We'll try.'

'Barings employees have been banned from SIMEX, George Seow is shooting his mouth off, and there are so many knives sticking out of your back that you can't even see your shoulder blades. Get yourself a good lawyer. And get the fuck out of wherever you are.'

'I'll call you when I can.'

'Listen, Nick,' Danny said, 'good luck, mate. If you need me, call. Any time.'

I put the phone down. It was our lifeline to the outside world. But despite being a nice soft shade of grey, it could be treacherous. It could enable the police to trace us to our room. I wondered whether anyone had put a tap on Danny's phone. I even wondered whether he'd been sitting there with a detective beside him, trying to get me to talk as long as possible so they could trace the call.

Lisa and I looked out of the window at the leaning palm trees and the sea beyond. We had to escape somehow. It should be so easy. We should be able to get into a rowing boat and vanish. We'd signed Green Cards at the hotel with our names and address, so I was sure the hotel would right now be checking all their guests, fingering our cards with mounting excitement and lifting the phone to the police.

I tried to imagine where we were on the map. The north coast of Borneo. It's about as remote and cut-off

302

as you can get. We could either set off into the forest
and go and hide up-river with some tribesmen, or try to
get to Brunei. Otherwise it was either Kuala Lumpur or
Singapore. It would be madness to return to Kuala
Lumpur, since they would certainly catch us – and it
was too close to Singapore.

Lisa picked up the phone and started calling travel
agents.

'We'd like to get a flight to London,' she said. 'We'd
like the earliest one. We don't mind which airline.'

There was nothing much doing. Indonesia is the
nearest country to Borneo, but there was no transport
there. Jakarta would have been ideal, since I could have
called up some old friends and fixed ourselves up. But
the only international flights out of Kota Kinabalu were
to Singapore or Brunei.

There was an eight o'clock flight the next morning –
Tuesday – to Brunei. It was full, but they said there
might be some cancellations and that our best chance
was to go to the airport the next morning and try to buy
a standby.

We kept to our room and ordered room service for
supper, then lay in bed and cuddled each other. I tried to
bury myself in Lisa's arms, feeling that if only I could
stay with her I'd be all right. I was terrified of us being
separated. With her there, I knew we'd be fine. We might
be wanted, or in trouble, but she'd sort something out.
If we were forced apart, and I was put in an Asian jail
on my own – my head just span out of orbit.

WE were up early on Tuesday. We packed in silence,

aware that we had to get out as quickly as possible. We were afraid to talk. At the hotel reception I paid for our expenses in cash, and watched the girl tear up my American Express slip, which I'd given as a deposit.

'There's so much fraud about now,' she said, 'you can't be too careful.'

Then we were gone. We took a taxi to the airport and went to the Royal Brunei and Malaysian Airlines counters. Both flights to Brunei were still full. It was the Hari Raya Puasa holiday, and everyone was travelling to be with their families. As the long queues formed at the ticket counters I felt like offering $3,000 to anyone who'd give me their seat. But I didn't have the bottle.

'Let's check into another hotel,' Lisa said. 'We can't camp here.'

We took a taxi to the Hyatt Hotel, checked in under Lisa's maiden name, Sims, and paid in cash. We couldn't stay in our room. We decided to go to the Royal Brunei ticketing office, which was on the far side of town.

'Let's walk,' I suggested. 'We've missed today's flight, so we've got all the time in the world.'

We walked through the little town with the sun high overhead. Knowing that policemen in Malaysia and all across Asia were looking for me felt very odd. I should be in a hurry, running somewhere, or driving for the border. But I was caught in a hole and couldn't do anything about it. To the local Malaysians we must have looked like any young happy Western couple: the girl was blonde, tanned and slim; the man running to fat, and wearing shorts and a baseball cap. They'd seen us and our kind many times before – two utterly normal holiday-makers. We walked along on the shady side of the street. The street dust rose in the sun as the cars and motorbikes roared past. A few dogs lay sunning themselves on the concrete pavement. They were the type of scabby mongrel which is endemic in Malaysia – but never in Singapore. In Singapore strays are cleaned off the streets like all the other vermin. But in Malaysia these mongrels – with their tails curling over their backs, their tawny black and brown fur and open sores – are allowed to roam freely. As we walked past, I took in the normal street life around me: the shops selling rice and tinned food; the bars with Coca-Cola and Tiger Beer signs and white plastic chairs; boutiques selling T-shirts and baseball caps. It was a small dusty town selling crappy souvenirs to the few tourists who made it here, and otherwise offering the normal chicken rice and Tiger beer that you get all over Asia. Life was cheap – but free.

'Do you have any flights to London?' Lisa asked.

The girl's fingernails clattered over the keyboard. I'd last heard that noise when I'd asked Linda to check the 88888 balance. I bunched my fists, embarrassed that my fingernails were raw little pink stubs.

'There's one to London later,' she said.

My spirits soared. We were going to get home. We'd be on that flight and nothing could stop us.

'Can we buy two seats, please?'

'But it's from Brunei,' she said, 'and there are no more connecting flights from here to Brunei today. It went this morning.'

'What about somewhere else in Europe?' Lisa asked calmly.

'There's one tomorrow to Frankfurt,' the girl said. 'It's via Brunei, Bangkok and Abu Dhabi.'

I nudged Lisa.

'We'll take that one,' I said. 'How much is a one-way ticket?'

'It's 1,500 ringgits. There's an eight-hour wait in transit at Brunei.'

'Please can we reserve it? We'll go back to the hotel and change some money.'

We walked out of the air-conditioned Royal Brunei office into the baking midday heat.

'Do you want to walk again?'

'Why not? We've got time to kill.'

'We'd better check the ferry to Labuan as well,' I said.

'It can't be a real choice,' Lisa pointed out, 'it'd get into Brunei too late. We'd never catch this evening's flight to London.'

'No, but they might not check our passports so thoroughly.'

'And if they did, they might decide to hold us hostage or something. You never know what might happen on a boat in the middle of Malaysia.'

The tiny wooden jetty showed few signs of life. There were some boxes of dried fish buzzing with flies on one side, and a man in a dirty vest sitting inside a cabin reading a porn mag.

'What time are the sailings to Labuan?'

'Eight o'clock in the morning and one o'clock in the afternoon,' he said, barely looking up.

'How long does it take?'

'Four hours.'

We walked back along the dried-out wooden boards. I paused and touched the salty splintered wood. I was the most wanted man in the world, and I was trapped between a slow boat to Labuan and a flight to Brunei with an eight-hour wait in transit.

'It's got to be the Brunei flight tomorrow morning.'

We walked back to the hotel, changed the dollars into ringgits and then walked back to the Royal Brunei office. The girl counted out the money, and then entered all the details into the machine. When the tickets came out I noticed that she'd misspelled Leeson as Lesson.

'I'm sorry,' she laughed, 'I've learnt my lesson. But it won't matter.'

I put the tickets into the side pocket of my shorts and we wandered outside. The name 'Lesson' on the tickets might help us if all passenger lists were being checked – a computer might just bypass it.

The flight was due to leave the next morning, Wednesday. We killed time all day. We walked back to the hotel, the fourth time we'd made our way across town. Then we sat around the Hyatt roof garden, where there was a highly chlorinated pool and the noise of traffic and horns beeping from the main road below. We both tried to read our books. I was stuck on my Tom Clancy, re-reading every page and forgetting where I was. Lisa was doing rather better with *Disclosure*, and seemed to be turning the pages.

'I'm hungry,' I said. 'I'm going to get a bun. Do you want one?'

'Thanks,' Lisa said.

I walked to the little shop in the lobby and bought two buns. The *Borneo Post* was for sale on the counter. I didn't expect to see myself on the front cover – but there I was: 'Nick Leeson, the general manager of Baring (Futures) Singapore, is missing . . .'

At least there wasn't a photograph.

'I'm still hungry,' I said, unable to sit still. 'Do you want to come for a walk?'

We walked around Kota Kinabalu again. This time we killed time by walking all the way along the town shoreline, where the grubby beach was covered with litter. We found a market and wandered among the stalls, looking at the dried octopus and fish-heads for sale, smiling 'no thanks' to the lady trying to sell us durian fruit – which smells so bad you're not allowed to take it inside restaurants or hotels – and haggling over a bunch of mangosteens. Then, munching the mangosteens and spitting the pips into the piles of rubbish alongside the road, we cut up through a cheap area where the bars all looked as if they'd fill up the moment a boat came in. It was getting dark – almost five o'clock – and the car headlights speared through the exhaust fumes and made us realise just how bad the air quality was. It hadn't looked so bad in the sunshine. We found a McDonald's at the bottom of a shopping mall, and bought a coffee. Neither of us could eat when actually faced with food. Then we walked further and passed a group of kampong, houses on stilts, where the rubbish was piled up below them, and we saw chickens and cats, dogs and rats all scratching around the mountain of coconut husks. Children crowded at the open door and peered out at us.

'Let's get back,' I said. 'We've done well. It's seven o'clock.'

We walked through the dark and the fumes back to the Hyatt. I'd stretched my legs.

That night we lay in each other's arms and I knew

that it would be for the last time. I didn't know when the arrest would be made, I was expecting police at our door all the time, but I knew that sometime between now and the end of our flight I'd be arrested. I thought through the possibilities. We had left a trail to Kuala Lumpur. I'd even faxed my resignation from the hotel. The police knew we were in Malaysia. Malaysia is a small country, with only one real international airport – Kuala Lumpur – and a few flights from Kota Kinabalu out to Brunei or Singapore. It was so easy to cordon off the country. And all the customs officers had to do was be on the lookout for Leeson, and we would be caught. They'd had since Friday to activate all emigration points. I lay in bed and shut my eyes. It was past three in the morning. I slowed my breathing down to match Lisa's. I didn't know if she was asleep or just pretending like me so that she wouldn't wake me up. I didn't want to whisper to her in case she *was* asleep and I did wake her. So I lay there, mulling over this double bluff, trying to work out whether she was asleep or not.

I tried to imagine what was going on in London, and what Barings going bust really meant. I wondered what Ron Baker and Peter Norris were up to, and whether Simon Jones had worked up a good excuse yet. Then I realised that Friday had been bonus day. I wondered whether the bonuses had been paid. People across the world were looking for me. As I lay there with Lisa, a host of unknown policemen were searching across Asia to find me, checking papers, hotel bookings, airline and boat tickets. They were like auditors – but they would find me in the end. I might have been able to hide figures, but I couldn't hide myself. They couldn't trace us to this hotel, since we'd paid cash, but they'd be able to pick up the Green Card at the Shangri-la and also pick up the flight ticket off the Royal Brunei airline computer. They would know when I was planning to fly and be ready to arrest me at the airport. While I was lying here with Lisa I was safe. I squeezed my eyes tightly shut to drive away the world outside. As soon as I moved, I'd be caught.

'WHAT are you wearing those for?' I asked Lisa, who was putting on a pair of thick jeans.

'It's going to be cold in Frankfurt,' she said. 'It's February. It's going to be freezing.'

'Don't tempt fate.' I put on my shorts and a T-shirt. At the airport we presented our tickets at the counter and were given boarding cards. Our baggage was checked all the way through to Frankfurt. I looked at the suitcases disappearing along the conveyor belt and envied their simple journey. They'd trundle along, get picked up, dropped down, bashed around a bit and find their way on to the Frankfurt carousel. The next-door desk was for the flight to Singapore, full of happy Westerners and probably bankers and dealers, one of whom might recognise me. I kept looking the other way, and then we approached Customs. This was where we'd be caught.

The Passport Control Officer wore a brown uniform with yellow epaulettes and a badge on his shirt pocket. I watched him stamping the passport of the people in line ahead of us and knew that he would catch me. He'd have my name and photograph stuck to his desk in front of him. He'd register the name, look at me, look back down to my passport and know that he'd caught the big fish. He'd be a local celebrity. He'd probably get a bonus. At least his wife would be happy and proud of him. Lisa went first. He stamped her passport without a second look. I gave him mine. He looked me in the eye. I was so frightened that I took a step back. With one look he could arrest me. What would he do? Blow a whistle? Push a button under his desk? In the end he just stamped my passport, flicked it shut and gave it back to me. I walked on air as I joined Lisa on the far side of the X-ray machines.

'God, I wish we'd gone by boat,' I said. 'We'd still be able to jump overboard and swim for it.'

'What about the sharks?'

'We could have tossed them some burgers,' I smiled. 'But now we're in transit. We can't get out of this.'

'We'll be fine,' Lisa smiled brightly.

We filed on to the small Fokker, and I waited until the doors shut before admitting to myself that we would actually leave Malaysia. The plane took off and heaved into the air. I looked down and saw a fleet of fishing boats spread out below us. For a while I could see miles across the open sea, which glittered in the morning sun like beaten silver, but then we flew up and the clouds closed around us.

EVERY television set at Brunei Airport was discussing the Barings collapse. Pictures of me, Ron Baker, Peter Norris and Peter Baring were flashed up, but, above all, me: the 'rogue trader' last seen on Thursday, known to have flown to Kuala Lumpur, now missing. I sat in the corner of the transit lounge and listened as journalists talked into microphones and gave their latest up-to-date assessment of how the situation had changed since their last assessment five minutes beforehand. I buried my head in a newspaper and tried to keep out of sight. As I sat there, I realised that the police had not tracked me down to the Shangri-la. Despite filling out the Green Cards at the hotel, these hadn't come up on anyone's computer.

'Lisa, that guy's staring at me,' I whispered.

'No he's not.'

'Yes, he definitely is.'

'That's because you've got your baseball hat on. He's trying to read the slogan.'

'We're here for eight hours, right?'

'Yes.'

'Well, let's check into one of those rooms where we can hide.'

Lisa went off to find whether they had any short-stay rooms, and came back with a key.

'It's over here.'

We went down a concrete spiral staircase and let ourselves into a tiny square room. There was a small double bed, and a bathroom. No windows, no telephone, no television. Only yesterday I'd been walking around Kota Kinabalu. It hadn't exactly been London or Paris, but I'd been outside. I'd been free. I'd had the choice of turning left or right along a small dusty street full of lorries and motorbikes. I'd had the choice whether to buy durian fruit. I'd smiled 'no thanks' to the lady, but I could have bought some. Now I was in a cell. As soon as we'd passed through Customs at Kota Kinabalu we were in an official system. I knew I'd be stopped. And then we'd be separated.

Lisa and I lay on the bed together and cried. She didn't ask me any questions, she just started sobbing in my arms, and I cried with her. I clung on to her, knowing that our life together was over. All that madness on the dealing floor which seemed so unreal – and had seemed so unreal at the time – was now going to destroy the only reality I had, my love for Lisa. I wasn't interested in Barings going bust; I wasn't interested in putting errors into the 88888 account and trying to trade out of them; I couldn't care less about Brenda Granger transferring all that money over to me or Simon Jones and the 7.78 billion yen. They could take all that away from me, take all my money away from me – but I was scared to death about what would happen when they took Lisa away from me.

'We should have gone by boat,' I cried. 'Boats don't have CNN everywhere and racks full of newspapers. We'd have been free.'

'No, they haven't traced us here,' Lisa said, 'there's no reason to think that they will.'

'But we've got eight hours to spend here, that's a full working day. It'll be Thursday by the time this flight lands in Frankfurt.'

'Look, we've got to get out of Asia,' Lisa said. 'If we'd been in a boat, we'd be stuck around Indonesia. If we'd been caught there, God knows what would have happened.'

'Can you go and get some biscuits?' I asked. 'And just see what's in the newspapers now?'

Lisa came back with a *Herald Tribune*. My photograph was on the front cover. I couldn't read the story. I just saw 'Nick Leeson' and £600 million losses. I wanted to speak to someone on the phone to find out what was going on. I had a mad wish to call up Brenda Granger and ask her to transfer some more money. And I wanted some sweets to chew. I couldn't ask Lisa again. If we didn't make it back to Frankfurt or London, if I was arrested, I was going to have to get used to not being able to pick up the phone whenever I wanted, and chew sweets whenever I wanted.

Seven hours later Lisa went out and watched the Frankfurt flight board. She noticed that there was no particular security, no policemen checking passports, just the normal air hostesses. She came back to get me when the last boarding call was made.

'OK, I think we're going to get on.'

We left the room and handed our boarding passes to the air hostess. She barely looked at them. We walked down the tunnel and into the aircraft, exchanging a small square cell with a double bed for a long slim tube full of seats. We squeezed our way to the back of the cabin and I sat by the window. Everyone on the plane was reading newspapers. Every paper had my picture on the front cover.

'Newspaper, sir?'

'No, thank you,' I mumbled, turning away and pulling my baseball cap down over my eyes.

'Take that off,' Lisa hissed. 'Talk about being conspicuous – you're sticking out like a bloody sore thumb!'

I pulled a blanket up to my chin and twisted my face

around so that I was half buried in cushions. At Bangkok we filed out and I sat slumped in the corner of the departure lounge until boarding was announced. I was not going to the Bangkok Hilton and the policemen would have had to wrestle me away. We were first back on the plane, and no policemen came on board. Eventually all the other passengers came trickling back on, holding their boarding cards in one hand and peering at the seat numbers as they came down the aisle. Lisa squeezed my hand as the engines whined and pushed the plane forward into the night sky. We'd left Bangkok; we'd left Asia.

'Only one more to go.'

'Yeah, but that one is Abu Dhabi. Don't they cut off your hands there?'

'No, don't be ridiculous,' Lisa said, 'they'd just stone you.'

We tried to sleep. We stopped talking. I was too tired and scared to tell Lisa what I'd done. She never asked me. The last time we'd been on a plane together had been when we returned to Singapore from London.

'Pleased to be back?' Lisa had asked. 'Now that we're here?'

We had to get out of the plane at Abu Dhabi. We had no idea what time it was any more. We'd flown west for ten hours and it was the middle of the night. Pale and exhausted, we wandered around the Abu Dhabi duty free shop and drank a glass of water. The Arabic newspapers could have been covered with Barings stories, but I couldn't understand them, and best of all there were no photographs. The *Herald Tribune* was the same issue as the one we'd seen in Brunei. When our flight was called, the flight next door was a Singapore Airlines plane going back to Singapore.

'Christ, look at that!' I said to Lisa. 'It's probably full of Barings people going to sort out the mess.'

We backed off and waited at the far end of the lounge until the last call was made. Then we surged past the Singapore queue and marched back down the tunnel to the plane. As the plane took off for the last time and headed through the night to Frankfurt, I still couldn't work out whether we were unlucky or lucky to be on this flight.

'Surely they'll arrest us at Frankfurt?' I whispered to Lisa.

'They might – or they might fly us straight on to London.'

'They won't fly us straight back to Singapore, will they?'

'No, that's illegal.'

'Should we get a lawyer at Frankfurt? Should we ask for a lawyer to meet us at Heathrow?'

'No, if we're going that far, let's get Mum and Dad to meet us. They can sort anything out.'

'They must know that we're on this flight,' I said, 'they've had a full day now. They knew that we were in Malaysia so they just needed to check all flights out of Malaysia.'

'Maybe that misprint saved us.'

The plane tunnelled on through the darkness. Lisa fell asleep, her fair hair falling over my shoulder. I sat awake, trying to read my book in a pool of artificial light, the only person awake as the full plane shuddered its way through the night sky. The whole world was looking for me. I alone had the secret of the Barings collapse, and I was sitting in seat 43A, obscure and invisible to everyone except to some silent flickering computer which would be sifting through the names and destinations of all passengers leaving Malaysia.

'As is customary with flights arriving at this hour of morning, the passport checks will take place immediately outside the aeroplane,' the captain announced.

We had landed in a murky grey dawn and it looked freezing outside. Lisa was warm in her jeans. I wrapped the blanket around my legs. We'd been travelling since we left Kota Kinabalu in that tiny Fokker, and now I was going to be arrested. I remembered when I'd flown to Frankfurt for a football match and seen the pictures of criminals posted up all along the airport corridors. It was an efficient, grey airport, and they were going to catch me.

'I love you, Lisa,' I said. 'Whatever happens – I love you.'

I didn't know when we would ever be able to say anything to each other in private again.

'You be strong,' she said.

We were going to wait until the end, but some people just took forever to sort themselves out, so we walked out and down the steps on to the wet black tarmac with a queue of ten people behind us. Lisa went first. The policeman was wearing a suit and had a gun on his hip. He looked at Lisa's passport, looked at her, and motioned her to one side. I saw an airport bus crammed with passengers. Their white faces were all pushed up against the window, watching the policeman. I had a wonderful image in my mind of the bus toppling over and capsizing, like a boat, but then the policeman said to Lisa: 'Where's your man?'

I stepped forward right under his peaked cap and said, 'I'm her man.'

We were led into a green police van, and the doors shut behind us. At least we were out of sight of the other passengers. I was freezing cold in my shorts, and hugged myself to keep warm. We waited in a room where we drank coffee and watched as they searched our suitcases. They asked me if I wanted to change my clothes and I gratefully agreed. One policeman pulled out a T-shirt which had a picture of Geoff Hurst in the 1966 World Cup final, scoring the goal against Germany with the score board showing 2–2.

'Good game,' I said to him.

'Gazza?' he asked.

'Geoff Hurst!'

I was taken downstairs for my mug-shot, and then we were taken across to the border police. Up until then everything had been very relaxed. I imagined that they'd traced me on the computer and arranged a quiet arrest at dawn. I was hardly watching where we were going, but suddenly I heard a noise and realised that we were walking very fast. We were led along a corridor past a line of photographers, who were all craning to see us and take pictures. Flashbulbs went off and I could only hear a scream of voices. It was like the trading floor. I felt like saying: 'Two-fifty bid for 100! Two-fifty bid for 100!' and flicking them the hand signals, but they wouldn't have got the joke and the photographs would have been awful.

318

'Any comment? Any comment at all?' shouted one American, his voice whining and grating above the uproar.

I was about to tell him to fuck off, or dive forwards and smack him in the mouth, but then I realised that that was just what Dad had done. I could see why.

It was clear that Lisa was not under arrest. It was clear that I was. The British Consul was called and he arrived with a list of lawyers.

'I can't officially recommend any at all,' he said, with his finger tapping one name, 'but some are much better than others.'

And so I called Kingsley Napley.

THE British Consul went out into the airport and brought us back a McDonald's for lunch. Some of the confusion began to clear itself up. We'd been in the police interviewing room at the airport all day. We hadn't seen any daylight. We'd chosen a German lawyer, Eberhard Kempf, who'd come in to see us wearing a green woollen suit, and we'd chosen an English lawyer who promised to come out and see me as soon as possible. We understood that I was under arrest on the basis of a warrant from the Singapore Government, and there was no question of bail. We had received over twenty faxes from English newspapers offering to buy my story.

By about 3 P.M. the mood started to change. Rather than talking about me, the conversation switched to how we were going to get Lisa out. The police had told us that the press had booked seats on every flight out of Frankfurt in order to be able to get hold of Lisa whenever she flew. We spoke to Patsy and Alec again, and they had been besieged by the press as well, and told us that the *Daily Mirror* had offered to fly them out to pick up Lisa in a private plane as part of the price of the story. We were aware of the massed troops of press outside, so we agreed to go with just one paper and get Lisa safely back home.

By 8 P.M. we realised there was nothing more to discuss. Lisa was going to have to go and leave me. I had to stay in police custody until the Singaporean charges came through.

'What else is there?' Lisa asked.

'I think you'd better go,' I said.

We stood up and hugged each other. I couldn't speak. It was over. She was going to go and I was going to stay.

'I love you,' she said.

'I love you too.'

And with that I was led away by the police out of the interviewing room. I knew that I was going to have to live with my own company for a long time. I couldn't cry – I had nobody's shoulder to cry on. Everyone started speaking German around me and I was rushed down a secret staircase in the airport and into a police car, which drove off around the far runways and into the American airbase. I couldn't see anything except a blur of yellow neon lights as we drove through the barrier and then out on to the motorway. I held on to my little bag which held some toothpaste and my toothbrush, shampoo and a sweater, and my Tom Clancy book. We'd been on the go since six in the morning, when the plane touched down in Frankfurt and I'd been arrested – fourteen hours ago now. I hadn't slept on the flight over, and I had no idea what the time in Singapore would be. I found out from the policeman that I was going to a police station. Upon arrival I was given a paper plate with some bread and jam, which they told me to save for *frühstück*, and shown into a freezing cold cell.

The moment I'd walked through the X-ray machine at Kota Kinabalu airport I had entered a different world – a world of locks and doors, X-ray machines, no entry, no exit, no fresh air and no choice. It'd be a long time before I could haggle over the cost of mangosteens in an open-air market.

I sat down on my cell bed. There wasn't much to look at. There was a little desk with a black formica top, a wooden varnished chair, some open shelves, a window with opaque glass which looked a foot deep and had wire mesh running through it, and of course the door, which was metal with a peephole. I had no idea where Lisa was; I had no idea what the Nikkei was doing – my two previous obsessions. I hadn't been near a telephone since we'd parted. I didn't know who was going to come and see me. I didn't know what my visiting rights were. I didn't know what the newspapers were saying.

Sitting in this quiet lonely pool of ignorance, I stood up and pulled my T-shirt from my bag. It was one which Lisa had worn when we were sitting around the pool at the Hyatt Hotel. I squashed it in my hands and held it up to my face. I breathed deeply and smelled the faint smell of Lisa, a smell of fresh green apples. I sat back on the bed and buried my head in the T-shirt, breathing her smell. It was all I had left of her.

I tried to remember what she looked like. To my horror I could only remember separate pieces of her, not the whole picture. I could remember her eyes, I could picture her hair, and of course I could remember her voice, or something which I thought was her voice. But I couldn't remember what she was wearing – I didn't know what she was wearing right now. I didn't know what she was doing or who she was with. I hoped that she was with Alec and Patsy, but I couldn't be sure. Perhaps she was already flying back to Heathrow. I could remember the pitch of her nose and her mouth and lips, and her teeth, and I tried to remember when we had last kissed and what it felt like. I tried to remember when we had last made love and what that felt like. I tried to remember what we had last eaten together. Most of all I tried to remember when we had last been free together, and I managed to piece together a photofit picture of Lisa walking down the hot dusty streets of Kota Kinabalu, in white shorts and a T-shirt, with her hair shining fair in the sunshine, slouching slightly with her hands in her pockets as she looked into the shop windows and then turned back to me and smiled. What had she been saying? She was joking about us having to buy a German phrase book.

I clung to that memory and tried to prevent it from fading, but as I lay on my cell bed, Lisa's image in my mind kept changing and warping and I couldn't hold it still. I burst into tears when I realised I just couldn't remember what she looked like at all.

11

Höchst Prison

THROUGHOUT FRIDAY MORNING THE guard kept coming up to my cell. With a heavy rattle and clanging of keys he would swing open the white steel door and announce: 'Another lawyer.'

In Germany any lawyer can visit any prisoner, so a stream of Frankfurt lawyers made their way to see me. I had already appointed Eberhard Kempf, but at least these ambulance-chasers gave me the excuse to get out of my cell and sit in the interviewing room. I even had a cup of coffee at one meeting. But for the rest of the morning I sat alone in my cell and tried to concentrate on feeling as positive as possible. In order to look to the future, I tried to banish my feelings of guilt and remorse. I tried to stop thinking about what was going on in SIMEX and with Barings. I had to let all those thoughts go. I was now by myself and I had to learn to live with my own company in a tiny cell. I had never thought about how much space I liked to have around me before, but I'd been used to walking around the large SIMEX floor and having thousands of people all around me. I'd also never been out of reach of a telephone. And for the last two years I'd been living a life

323

which was busy in itself and a double-life which was crammed full of deceit. I now had to focus on myself and the fact that my life was utterly empty. I needed that golden Buddha in my hand.

The worst thing for me to deal with is uncertainty. As long as I know what the procedure is, I am happy to follow it. Thus as long as I knew what my 88888 losses were, I was able to absorb them and get on with the problem of how to hide them. Now, alone and in silence, I had to work out an approach to my life in prison. I had to find out what would happen to me at each stage. This started off with a desperate urge to know when lunch was, when dinner was, when I would be transferred somewhere else, and when I would see Eberhard Kempf and the lawyers from Kingsley Napley. But it soon grew into an obsession over what would happen to me, and how I could fight my defence. I knew that I was guilty, but I didn't know what the charges were or where I would face them.

At around noon the guard brought me lunch – a paper plate with some fish (it was Friday) and potato salad. I threw away the fish and ate the potato salad. Then I heard the same clanging of keys and I was taken out of the prison and led into a green police van. I heard the photographers shouting at the van, and lots of flash-bulbs went off, but I sat tucked away beneath the window out of sight. Each little victory was important. I was taken to the court and led into a tiny white cell, pure white with a table and a chair screwed to the floor. It was freezing cold and I couldn't get comfortable on the chair or table and I couldn't get warm in the cell. After an hour or so I was led up to see the judge, and there I met Eberhard Kempf. The judge's office was on the ground floor, and at one stage a gang of press photographers streamed across the lawn outside and tried to take pictures. They looked like animal rights protesters. The judge pulled down a blind to cover the window. He asked me whether I would voluntarily accept extradition to Singapore on the basis of the single charge they had provided to date – the forgery of Richard Hogan's signature – with the prospect of unlimited further charges being added when I arrived there. It wasn't a difficult decision. I shook my head and said 'No', and that was that. It was late Friday afternoon, and Eberhard told me that he had agreed to meet the Kingsley Napley lawyer on Tuesday, and they would come and see me together. In the meantime I was going to be taken to Höchst prison, where I had the whole weekend to get through.

I STOOD by the window and peered out into the prison yard. Most of the window was thick opaque glass, the sort of glass you sometimes see in sections of pavement. But a thin strip of the window opened and I stood in the chilly draught of air and watched the prisoners exercising. It wasn't a great spectator sport – they just walked around – but I could see a game of table tennis in progress and one or two of the prisoners did some arm-stretching as they wandered about. Then I looked upwards at the sky and tried to see the sun, but I was on the wrong side of the building. All I could see was the bricked-up prison exercise yard and a cold grey winter sky which promised snow. Bored with the view I shut the window and turned back to my cell.

All through the previous night the guards had come and turned on my light by the switch outside and peered through the peephole. It had been difficult enough to sleep, but this made it impossible, and I shouted out that I wasn't going to escape or commit suicide so could they please leave me alone? But they carried on anyway. I was exhausted, but I had all of Saturday to kill. Saturday was normally my favourite day, with the market closed, a long lie-in and cuddle with Lisa, lots of sport to keep up with, and then the prospect of going off to wander around town and meet up with friends. But this Saturday was the Saturday from hell. I knew that I had one hour's exercise that afternoon, but otherwise I was alone in my cell with nothing to do. I still had my Tom Clancy thriller, which I'd brought with me all the way from Kota Kinabalu, so I read that straight through from the beginning, starting it all over again.

Mid-afternoon I was rushed over to the far side of the exercise yard. Apparently the press had rented rooms overlooking the yard, and I had to keep to the shelter of the far wall. Luckily this was where the table tennis was, so I picked up a bat and motioned to a black guy, asking him if he'd like to play. It was very cold, with snow on the ground. We stood there playing a desultory game and the white ball kept flying on to the ground where we couldn't find it on top of the snow. Ernest was Nigerian. I asked him endless questions about how long he'd been in this part of the prison, 'Neubau' as it was called, and when we could expect to be transferred to the bigger prison. The hour was soon up, and I was back in the cell. Ernest had told me that I should ask to go to the library, so I did and the guards took me there on my way back from the yard. There were scarcely any books, but I picked up a copy of *Tess of the D'Urbervilles* by Thomas Hardy.

Back in my cell I was engrossed in the wretched tragedy of Tess, whose continual suffering as a milk-maid and potato-picker seemed roughly equivalent to mine as a futures trader. I read it without pause, well into Saturday night. But just after she had murdered the baddie and started to escape with her lover, with the police closing in on them in Stonehenge, the book finished because the last four pages were torn out. I lay there in shock: did she get away with it? Did she get caught? Was she executed for murder, or tried for a crime of passion? How much time did she serve?

Sunday was just as long. I re-read Clancy again and reflected what great value for money it was: £5.99 had kept me quiet for hours and hours. I'd had the book when we went to Kota Kinabalu, had taken it with me as we got on the plane and held on to it through all the cells I'd been in. *The Cardinal of the Kremlin* was the title, and I was just beginning to understand the plot. But I kept having to stop reading because I repeatedly burst into tears and lay sobbing on my bed. I was so lonely, and so frightened. I had no idea what was going on any more. I couldn't make the time go any faster. Nor could I make it go backwards. I couldn't start again. I couldn't get Lisa back. I couldn't speak to anybody over the telephone. I didn't have a television to watch. I was alone – in a white prison cell in silence – and I didn't know when it was going to stop.

On Sunday I discovered that what I'd thought was an alarm system of some sort on the wall was actually a radio. It had two channels, a German one and an American one, which still carried on broadcasting even though the American troops had all gone home. It must have acquired cult status in Frankfurt. I listened to the German one, and almost jumped out of my skin when I heard the disc jockey say 'Nick Leeson'. It was some kind of dedication. The track was a German song called 'Geld, Geld, Geld', and was sung in the way that Monty Python used to sing about Spam. I felt a wave of indignation that I was such easy prey, cooped up in here so that they could make fun of me, but then I quite liked the song.

The weekend passed. My T-shirt, which used to smell of Lisa, was returned to me and now smelled of disinfectant. I put it on anyway. I saw Eberhard again on Monday, when he gave me some newspapers, and on Tuesday he came with my English lawyer, Stephen Pollard. My first question to Stephen was: 'Who the hell is this Max Clifford I'm supposed to have employed?'

And then I told him my story from the beginning. After I finished he asked a few questions.

'So there was no yacht?'

'No.'

'And no Porsche?'

'No.'

'Did you have two passports?'

'No.'

'I think I'd better give a press conference to stop some of these rumours, then.'

And so began the long process of explaining who I was to the press.

* * *

Lisa was due to visit me on Friday. I lay on my bed and tried to stop myself from crying again. I knew that seeing her was going to be the most difficult part of being in prison. I was desperate to see her, but then I knew how awful it would be saying goodbye to her. We'd only have an hour together. And it'd be in the same room as the room where I saw Eberhard Kempf and Stephen Pollard, a little whitewashed room with a tin ashtray on the table and uncomfortable metal chairs which scraped on the floor. I hadn't seen her for a week. I remembered our wedding day, when I hadn't seen her for the day before and I'd suddenly doubted whether she would turn up. At the church I was amazed that she had actually wanted to marry me. And lying on my cell bed I was amazed that she'd actually want to come and see me. Surely I was beneath her contempt. Surely she'd take the opportunity and declare to the world at large that she never knew what I was doing and I wasn't the man she thought she loved. She would be well shot of me. What did my life hold for her? I couldn't see it. I dreaded seeing her, and I dreaded her not coming. She could kill me with one look.

The door opened with the usual clang of keys, but then I was told: 'Your visitors are here.' I followed the guard through the floor-to-ceiling barred gate which blocked off the corridor to our cells, past the controller's room which monitored the closed-circuit television screens, and down a flight of stairs. We waited in a time-locked cage, and then I was shown through into the interviewing rooms. I could hear Lisa talking outside, and realised that she was with my dad. Then the door opened and she flew in and hugged me. We both burst into tears and clung on to each other. Over the mass of fair hair which piled on my shoulder I saw my father and my brother Richard. We were all crying.

'God, look at us!' my father said, and we started laughing and crying together.

'Now don't forget who we are,' Lisa said. 'Let's not waste time talking about Barings. They've got their problems, we've got ours. And my God I could clout you one, Nick Leeson. Just you wait until you're out of here. You're going to be in such deep shit from me I can't even tell you about it.'

With this we sat down. Lisa and I held hands, and she told me about her week, when she'd been chased by the press around a Sainsbury's car park and couldn't go back to Alec and Patsy's house.

'You're better off in here,' I joked, 'it's lovely and quiet.'

Looking at Lisa I knew we were going to survive this. It was just a matter of time. We both just had to think positively. Back in my cell I sat down on the bed and re-lived every second of our meeting. She was going to come back next week. She'd promised to come and see me every week. She'd get a part-time job to pay for the flights. She still loved me. I shut my eyes and imagined her sitting beside me again – in the privacy of our own room. I almost succeeded in bringing her to me, but then I heard a guard shouting in the exercise yard outside and I opened my eyes. I noticed one of her hairs on my sleeve. I picked it off and looked at it. I held it between my finger and thumb and twisted it in the light from my window. It shone in my cell like a thread of gold.

* * *

Iᴛ was difficult to think positively with the Serious Fraud Office on my case. Throughout the long hot summer, as I tried to understand the legal arguments for extraditing me to Singapore versus those for extraditing me to London, I became increasingly aware that the SFO weren't really that interested in me. They must have been delighted that I didn't quite make it back to London and present them with a problem in Britain.

As Stephen Pollard explained the case to me, it seemed that the Singaporeans were just charging me for crimes committed in the last three months of my time in Singapore. The twelve charges comprised four of forgery, two of amending prices, and six of implementing cross trades which had reduced my variation margin payments to SIMEX. I was not being charged with anything I'd done prior to Christmas 1994. Also the Singaporeans were not charging me for the false accounting which had led Barings to transfer so much money over to me.

I had caused the collapse of Barings by a variety of deceits, but the most crucial of these was my persistent demands for cash from London. By the end of February Barings had transferred something like $600 million over to Singapore to pay for my margin calls at SIMEX, and at least three-quarters of that was to fund the 88888 losses. I had sent false statements through to London every day. The false entries I had made to reduce my position in SIMEX – which comprised the basis of half the Singaporean charges, six out of the twelve – were tiny crimes in comparison with the real cash I had asked for from Brenda Granger.

I was prepared to plead guilty to a wide variety of

charges from the SFO, but they refused to listen to me. I offered to tell them everything, but they kept telling the press that I would only talk to them on the condition that they extradited me to London. This was not the case. I assumed that once I'd told them my story, they would have to extradite me since I had committed crimes over which they had jurisdiction.

Stephen Pollard sent me the exchanges with the SFO and I began to worry that he was too soft on them. I wondered whether he himself was part of the Establishment which wanted to keep me away from London. As Stephen's fight grew more and more desperate to make the SFO understand what was going on, I realised that he wasn't. In June he advised me to take the unprecedented step of releasing my Proof of Evidence – my written account of what had happened – to the SFO, so they would understand what I had done.

'They're just becoming a bureaucracy,' he told me. 'The SFO have lost so many prosecution cases they're frightened to put their head above the parapet. They've stopped investigating.'

As Stephen gradually pushed the SFO harder, they asked whether he knew of any medical or psychiatric problems I had, as presumably they feared I would plead insanity or something to undermine my evidence. Despite apparently carrying out an independent investigation into the Barings collapse, they didn't show any real knowledge of what had happened. James Kellock kept repeating that the information available to the Director led him to the view that the criminal conduct alleged against me was, predominantly, a matter relating to Singapore and should appropriately be tried there.

On 29 June Stephen wrote to the SFO and set out the crimes I had committed which fell under British jurisdiction. They were far more serious than the crimes for which I was being charged in Singapore. Stephen had asked the SFO to be a little more specific regarding the areas they were investigating, but had been brushed off. So he gave them my Proof of Evidence and compiled a list of my crimes as follows:

1. The communication of false information by Mr Leeson to the auditors of BFS in relation to the sum of 7.7 billion yen . . . This false information was accepted by the auditors and resulted in incorrect financial information being forwarded by them to Barings in London.

2. The exclusion by Mr Leeson of Account Number 88888 from the consolidated record of accounts sent daily to London. In this way the month-end balances could be manipulated by Mr Leeson to hide the losses appearing in that account and thereby give the false impression of profitability to Barings in London.

3. The repeated requests by Mr Leeson to Barings London for further sums to be paid to SIMEX by way of margin. These false requests resulted in sums being provided by Barings in London for one purpose (the payment of margin on authorised trades),

that money actually being used in addition for another purpose (the payment of margin on unauthorised trades in the 88888 account).

4. The false indication by Mr Leeson to his superiors in London that he was trading in conformity with the restriction that he maintain no overnight positions.

5. The false indication by Mr Leeson to his superiors in London that his trading was no more than arbitraging through a balanced book between Singapore and Osaka. Barings in London repeatedly and regularly received reports indicating that Mr Leeson's overall trading was profitable, whilst in reality it was making losses.

6. The entering by Mr Leeson or on his behalf of false prices in relation to account number 92000.

7. The false manipulation by Mr Leeson of the month-end equity balances on the 88888 account as communicated to Barings in London.

I looked at Stephen's letter and realised that the Singaporean charges were much less serious than the British ones. While I was being charged with four counts of forgery over the SLK 7.78 billion yen receivable, which affected both the London end and the Singaporean end of the operation, the other charges were small beer in comparison with what I was agreeing

to plead guilty to in London. This was the full catalogue of my crimes. Set out in black and white, they
looked appalling. I tried to remember the pressure I'd
been under to perform and produce profits, but then I
realised that this was just looking for excuses. These
were my crimes, and I had to acknowledge them, plead
guilty to them, and then put them behind me and get on
with my life.

I didn't want to force anybody else in Barings to be
tried alongside me, but I knew that nobody came out of
the collapse well. There was a line of people, ranging
from Peter Baring and his comment about how 'surprisingly easy it was to make money', through Peter
Norris, Ron Baker, James Bax, Tonys Hawes and
Railton, Mary Walz, Brenda Granger, Simon Jones and
Mike Killian, who could all have seen through me and
stopped me in my tracks. I didn't know where their negligence bordered on criminal negligence, or what
responsibility these people were meant to take for me,
but I did know that I could never even have begun these
crimes in any other bank. And since most of the cash
transfers from London to Singapore happened well
after they received the letter from SIMEX on 11
January, which mentioned the 88888 account, let alone
had a call from the Bank of International Settlements in
Basle, Barings needn't have gone bust if they'd hauled
me up even as late as the middle of January.

I put my head on a platter for the SFO, but they
didn't want it. On 6 July James Kellock wrote back to
Stephen Pollard and said that the information supplied
by me had not altered the Director's view that the matters concerning me predominantly related to Singapore.

On the contrary, he said, it had strengthened the Director's view that Singapore should take priority.

Given the lack of interest shown by the SFO, I wrote a letter to the press which Lisa read out at a press conference on 12 July. I pointed out that I was prepared to serve a British prison sentence for crimes which had brought down a British bank and caused British people to lose their money. I was prepared to plead guilty, I'd explain the whole story and I wouldn't pull any funny tricks like pleading senile dementia to get off the charges. I wanted to be in a British prison to remain close to my family – and I reminded them that at the time it looked as if the maximum prison sentence I might serve in Singapore was 84 years.

Despite Lisa's tearful reading of the letter, the SFO was unmoved. Later that day they issued a press release, in which they announced:

> The SFO's enquiries have not uncovered any evidence to suggest that individuals based in London were involved in fraudulent activities. It remains the case that the SFO does not have evidence which warrants an extradition application being made for Mr Leeson.

Stephen said in response: 'The SFO appears not to want to uncover evidence. It has not taken up the invitation to interview Mr Leeson, the principal participant. Its interpretation of the events leading to the collapse of Barings is very narrow and ignores the exchange of information between London and Singapore and the transfer of monies from London to Singapore which made it all possible.'

On 18 July the Bank of England's report into the collapse of Barings was released. Eberhard Kempf brought me in a copy, and I read it over the weekend while confined to my cell. It was difficult for me to agree with their figures, because they seemed to have put the 88888 account and its trading at the top of all my priorities, looking exclusively at the losses incurred there without netting off the genuine profits I made for other Japanese books. But apart from that, I marvelled at how every single Barings person blamed somebody else – especially me – rather than themselves. It was as if they needn't have been employed at all. If Treasury was not there to supervise cash payments, then it needn't be there at all.

My favourite quote, which made me laugh out loud, came on page 154. Coopers & Lybrand, the auditors, were meeting Peter Norris in London on Thursday 23 February at 2 P.M. London time – the very day I escaped from Singapore. Two in the afternoon in London is ten in the evening in Singapore, so Lisa and I had already booked into the Regent Hotel in Kuala Lumpur and were probably asleep. The meeting was described as follows:

Davies [the London partner of Coopers & Lybrand] has told us that he had met Norris to discuss matters relating to the audit at 2 P.M. on Thursday 23 February 1995. Davies told us that at this meeting he had asked: 'Is there anything that you [Norris] know of that would have a bearing on our audit that we have not discussed in this meeting?' Davies continued: 'He [Norris] said, "No, nothing."'

The report went on in the next paragraph:

Norris has given us his account of this meeting, saying: 'I only met the auditors once in the context of the 1994 audit which was, ironically enough, on 23 February, when Gareth Davies (who was the audit partner) arranged to see me to give me his debrief.' We asked Norris whether the SLK receivable was discussed specifically. Norris replied: 'No. In fact very little was. I can remember thinking that the previous year we had spent two and a half hours going through various things and this was literally half an hour of tea and biscuits really.'

Given the extraordinary chain of events which surrounded that 7.78 billion yen receivable, I was astonished that Peter Norris gave Coopers & Lybrand the go-ahead for the audit. He must have relished those biscuits. I wondered whether they were Rich Tea or Chocolate Hobnobs.

The Bank of England report concluded:

a) the losses were incurred by reason of unauthorised

and concealed trading activities within BFS;
b) the true position was not noticed earlier by reason
of a serious failure of controls and managerial confusion within Barings;
c) the true position had not been detected prior to
the collapse by the external auditors, supervisors or
regulators of Barings.

'What do you think?' I asked Stephen. 'Does it
improve my chance of extradition?'
'Difficult to say,' he told me. 'The press think so.'
He pushed across an editorial from the *Daily
Telegraph*:

The report reflects badly on the Bank of England,
badly on Mr Leeson, but worst of all on the senior
management of Barings. It defies the comprehension
of an outsider that a single individual could have
wreaked such havoc for almost three years without
detection. Mr Leeson is neither a victim nor a hero,
merely the latest in a long history of young men
entrusted with responsibilities for which they proved
unfit. But it is those who sat on the board of Barings
who emerge from this story as almost sublime
incompetents, blithely counting their own booty on
the promenade deck, oblivious of the torrent cas-
cading into their ship below the waterline . . . If Mr
Leeson goes to prison while the former board of
Barings continues going to Glyndebourne, this sorry
saga will leave the bitterest of tastes.

'I didn't know the *Telegraph* had it in them,' I said to Stephen, impressed. 'I'll start reading it when I get out.'

'But there's not a squeak from the SFO,' Stephen said. 'They're just not prepared to bring you over to London. There may be other political pressures being put on them. The legal case is definitely there. Obviously you could be tried in either Singapore or Britain, but your charges in Singapore have no relation to the role of the other managers, so they're very isolated incidents.'

'They'll keep their boxes at Glyndebourne then,' I said, staring at the opaque glass and wondering whether it was a sunny afternoon outside. 'At least they know they won't get mugged there.'

I flicked open the cover of the Bank of England report again. I saw a letter on the inside cover and stared at it. It seemed to be addressed from the Bank of England to the Bank of England.

'Hang on,' I said to Stephen, 'this doesn't make sense. Look: the headed paper says "Bank of England, Threadneedle Street, London EC2R 8AH" and the letter is addressed to "Bank of England, Threadneedle Street, London EC2R 8AH." The letter says: "Dear Sirs" and it's signed by Eddie George, the Chairman of the Board. You can't write to yourself, can you?'

'Well,' Stephen smiled, 'it's hardly independent, is it?'

'It's fucking outrageous!' I said. 'It's like being in charge of the trading floor and the back office at the same time. These guys are like me. They're cooking the books!'

'They're hardly going to fall over themselves to resign,' Stephen said.

I stared at the Bank of England report in astonishment. It wasn't worth the paper it was printed on. It was a scandal that they'd written it themselves to themselves, and only some obscure middle manager, Christopher Thompson, had resigned.

Good old Peter Norris – I hoped he enjoyed his million-pound bonus. He'd earned it by such breathtaking chutzpah in dealing with the auditors on 23 February. If I'd been able to emulate him, and had breezily told the auditors that there was nothing to worry about, as I helped myself to another Hobnob, I might have lasted a little longer and be a great deal richer.

On the same day as the report was issued, Stephen wrote to the SFO pointing out that they had accepted that they had jurisdiction over alleged offences, and that an interview with me would provide them with admissions in relation to such allegations. He pointed out that he had difficulty in understanding why the Director persisted in the view that the most appropriate place for trial remained Singapore.

At the beginning of August the SFO agreed to interview me, but they needn't have bothered. I was interviewed by two police officers who were seconded to the SFO and by an assistant director of the SFO. They clearly knew very little about the collapse of Barings, and I doubted they'd done very much research. Their questions showed how utterly at sea with the whole concept of futures and options they were.

The interviews were extremely exhausting for all of us, because they had to be tape recorded and also translated into German for a German stenographer to write them down in short-hand. I finally realised I was wasting my time when they turned to my handwritten note to Simon Jones, explaining the OTC trade between BNP and SLK. They asked me who had made the margin notes alongside it. They thought the comments written in the margin were 'Credit risk needs approval', which I corrected to 'Who approved?', and 'Denomination', which I pointed out actually read 'Documentation'. I was rather depressed that they hadn't read this note a little more carefully, since Simon Jones' and James Bax's handwritten comments on it were crucial proof that they had seen it and had taken my OTC trade on board.

The only time I felt that I was getting remotely close to being extradited was when one of the detective inspectors produced some of the dollar margin demands which I'd used to ask for cash transfers over to Singapore.

'I just want to be absolutely clear,' he said, 'that these documents are both central to your use of the 88888 account, and that they are, on the face of it, false and misleading. They're marked already, CS 4, 5, 6, 7, 8, 9 and 10. The CS stands for Christopher Steane, who is or was a director of Barings in London and who supplied these documents to the SFO.

'The bank was asked to provide documents which had been prepared by yourself, or at least on your instructions, which were demonstrably false. When the documents were produced, the following immortal description was used. They were handed to him and he was told: "There you are, these are bollocks."'

By 'bollocks' I understood that everyone was saying that these were false and dishonest documents. Looking around the room, everyone laughed and all agreed that this was very funny. I couldn't see the joke: if they were bollocks, which I agreed they were, and they had been handed by some guy in London to a detective of the SFO, then surely that meant they had evidence in London that I had committed a crime which affected London? But the joke was on me. Yes, it did mean that they had evidence that I had committed crimes under the SFO's jurisdiction. But no, it didn't mean that I was going to be extradited. It meant that they would choose to ignore that evidence.

Stephen tried to prevent the SFO from sliding away from their responsibilities in a final last-gasp letter, in which he said that, as my detailed admissions were made, it became ever clearer that the offences over which the SFO has jurisdiction dealt with the essence of the collapse of Barings – and he pointed out that the same could not be said of the Singaporean charges.

But the next day, 13 September, the SFO washed their hands of me. The SFO claimed that Singapore was the best place to try me, but they never explained why. They had all my evidence, given under oath and admissible as evidence in court, which showed how my fraud was practised on the London office of Barings and which would have led to me pleading guilty to some much more serious charges. Bizarrely, they were keen for me to go to Singapore. As Stephen Pollard announced in his press release in response to the SFO's decision: 'It makes no sense, unless there is a non-legal explanation and they are coming under political pressure to resist his extradition here.'

* * *

It's another weekend. Lisa has been and gone on Thursday and has left her sheets behind for me to sleep in. They still smell of her, and I prolong this smell by stripping them off my bed and wrapping them up in a ball in the cupboard. But the bare mattress, with its brown and black striped cover, gives the cell a totally different feel to it. I have one hour out in the yard today, and another hour out tomorrow. From Friday night to Monday morning is one long downhill ride into depression. I keep the television and radio on together to drive away the silence. Soon I know that I'm going to have to start training myself to get ready for Singapore. I've already started to get fit, and I do 5,000 step-ups on to a box every night. But the silence is something I dread. I know there will be no television or radio in Singapore.

The hour's walk outside is a bleak interlude. We walk in a slow circle. Most of the prisoners wear regulation blue prison kit, but I always make an effort and wear civvies. Today Christophe the Italian is dressed up in his Sunday best, wearing a suede trenchcoat with a cigar clamped between his teeth. We nod at each other and patrol around the yard. We can only walk fifty feet in any direction, so doing figures of eight is impossible. I want to fight the slow series of circles, but it's too difficult – I'd only piss off everyone else – so we fall into step and walk slow predictable circles like donkeys round a well. It's hardly exercise.

Back in my cell I try to make the time pass. I think of going to sleep. I watch the television and try to understand German. I try to read a book. I sit down at my desk and write to Lisa. I start crying again, and the tears fall in perfect drops on to the page. I never cried when I was trading; I never cried when my mother died. Lisa always accused me of being emotionally uptight, and unable to show my feelings. She wouldn't say that if she could see me now. Nobody can see me now. People think they've seen enough of me, because I've been in the papers and the Barings story has attracted lots of media attention. But I only ever see the papers three days late. And nobody can see me now.

ON Monday 25 September Stephen came to visit unexpectedly. He told me that Barings' bondholders, the outside investors who held the 9.25 per cent Perpetual Bonds in Barings, worth £90 million, and who had lost everything, were going to prosecute me privately. They were going to the City of London Magistrates' Court to issue a summons requiring me to appear in court.

'This is your last hope,' Stephen said. 'It means that for the first time someone other than me and Lisa is saying that you should be brought back to be tried in London. The bondholders are making exactly the same case as we are – that the collapse of Barings can only be properly assessed and those guilty established in an English court of law.

'They want to prosecute you, and use your trial and the subsequent publicity to bring in other potential defendants, such as the directors and the auditors. That is the only way they can see of getting their money back. Apart from the Baring Charitable Foundation, they are the only people to have lost money.'

'And of course Peter Baring didn't claim his £1 million bonus,' I said.

'But you have to confirm that you'll be prepared to give evidence.'

'I will, but only if it doesn't jeopardise my case in Singapore,' I said.

Stephen left the prison and tried to call John Koh, my Singaporean lawyer. He called him from the airport, and finally tracked him down in Islamabad. John Koh assured him that it wouldn't have any impact on my case in Singapore. The next day a lawyer from the bond-holders came to obtain my signature.

'How do you do?' I asked, extending my hand when he came in.

'I'm afraid I cannot talk to you,' the lawyer said. I signed the paper and he asked to leave immediately. I went back to my cell.

Sadly for the bondholders, who might have been able to pursue their case and sue me for fraud and a few other people for negligence, their case was diverted from the Home Office, to which they had applied for my extradition, back to the SFO. The SFO are able to squash any private prosecution which they feel is against the public interest. The SFO took it upon themselves to pick up the bondholders' application to extradite me and throw it in the bin: they suffocated it.

'I'm amazed that the SFO have done this. They've never used their powers to kill off a proper case before,' Stephen said. He looked gutted. 'This was a real hope – real people have lost real money and they've got a right to prosecute somebody to try to get it back. But the SFO have just canned it.'

'It was never going to happen, Stephen,' I said. 'They just don't want me there. I'd upset too many people.'

The next week, on Wednesday 4 October, the German court announced that it had accepted 11 of the original 12 charges from the Singaporean Government for my extradition. I had one month to appeal against this decision – or I was going back.

'That's a mad decision,' Eberhard Kempf told me. 'It's intellectually and logically wrong. The court's reasoning appears to be inconsistent and wrong in law. Why drop just one forgery charge? There are clear grounds to appeal against at least eight of the other charges.'

But I refused. I wanted to start my prison sentence. For all their legal arguments – which I knew were right – I knew I was going to go back to Singapore. Why would the Germans put their entire trading policy with Singapore at risk just over me? Why would the SFO risk losing yet another financial fraud trial? Everyone needed to put me away, and there was no better place than Singapore.

LORD Starkie came storming out of his cell at the open hour. I was leaning up against the wall, chatting to Keith, and we both turned to listen.

'If this noise continues, I'm checking out of here and I won't tip the staff!' he roared, throwing his book down on the floor. 'That bloody Turk was kicking his door again last night!'

We'd all heard it. At four in the morning there'd been a frenzied kicking as the Turk, a massive muscle-man built like the genie in *Aladdin*, had tried to kick down his door. It happened most nights and always scared the shit out of me. I could never get back to sleep after that.

Lord Starkie was actually Allan Starkie, one-time partner of John Bryan, the former financial adviser and toe-sucker to Fergie. Allan seemed unaware that he was actually in a prison and not a five-star hotel. Today he was wearing a silk dressing gown and velvet slippers with fox-heads embroidered on them.

'Have you beaten up any more sex offenders yet?' he asked Keith.

Keith was a little embarrassed. He had taken a great dislike to one prisoner who he thought was a child-molester. He had three children himself, and missed them a great deal, and sex offenders were people he really hated. The day before, Keith had picked a fight with this man and had beaten him up quite badly. In the evening he was told by a rather bemused guard that the man wasn't a sex offender at all, but was in prison for tax evasion. Keith still didn't believe it, and had taken to calling the man an 'ex-sex offender'.

Lord Starkie was in a fury with the Turk. It was one of the four days in the week when we showered together, and Starkie waited until he saw the enormous Turk coming out of the shower room. Starkie was less than five feet five inches tall; the Turk over six feet five. The Turk never even saw him coming – Starkie slipped in under his radar.

'Hold this for me will you, Nick?' he said, giving me his watch.

I looked on, impressed, as Starkie threw himself at the Turk and pummelled him to the ground. He sat on his chest, happily punching him until the guards came running and pulled him off. The Turk lay there groaning, bleeding from the nose and looking astonished.

'Don't kick your door again!' Starkie shouted as he was taken away by the guards, his tiny legs swinging beneath him. I handed his watch back to him and he was carted off back to his cell, his slippers still immaculate on his feet.

The next day we reconvened. The Turk hadn't kicked his door that night.

Lord Starkie had strong faith in me, which gave me great confidence.

'Barings is to blame just as much as you,' he'd say. 'It was a fucking dinosaur and you killed it. So what? It was a mercy killing. If you hadn't done it someone else would've.'

Our other friend on the block was Manny the Knife, a rather effete murderer who'd stabbed a lover to death. He kept complaining to us about the nightmares he had, in which the stabbed corpse fell out of his clothes closet.

'You're just an amateur,' I'd tell him. 'In the paper there's a sixteen-year-old Filipino girl who stabbed her employer thirty-four times. You're not even close.'

Manny would go into a depression when I told him this.

He carved things in the workshop and gave Starkie a wooden egg. Starkie promptly painted his girlfriend's face on the egg, and the likeness seemed so real to him that he began talking to it. At one point he was convinced that the egg smiled and winked at him. Manny offered to varnish it, to keep the paint from chipping off, but Starkie was worried that this would stop the face from smiling. However, it was varnished in the end, and Starkie was so pleased he spent the rest of the day making a woollen hat for it.

Starkie worked in the library, with a Bangladeshi we all referred to as The Indian. The Indian smoked over a hundred cigarettes a day, and often smoked himself into a trance in which he believed he was being visited by lawyers, practising attorneys, and occasionally even the judge – each bringing him tidings of impending release. In addition to reciting these fantasies, he also read the palms of other prisoners and sometimes even the guards. There was often a queue of guards outside the library, all waiting to have their hands read. The Indian had been arrested in connection with some incident over goulash soup. None of us could work out what could be so serious about a bowl of goulash soup, and I finally concluded that he must have been dealing in vast quantities, so vast that the police thought he must be a big-time goulash dealer.

When I came to have my hand read, The Indian promised I would be out of here soon.

'I know that,' I said, 'but how long before I'm out of prison?'

He bent over my hand again and traced some lines on it.

'In the not-too-distant future,' was all he would say.

THE Singaporean Report into the collapse of Barings was published on Tuesday 17 October. I didn't expect it to be much more than another blasting away at me, the single scapegoat, in the way that the Bank of England report had done. I couldn't have been more wrong. I flicked through the opening pages, the timetable of events, a list of abbreviations and definitions and then sat up with a jolt when I read on page 5:

> The Baring Group's management proffered many explanations as to how account 88888 purportedly escaped detection. However, we do not accept their contention that account 88888 was an unauthorised account that they had no knowledge of. In our view the Baring Group's management either knew or should have known about the existence of account 88888 and of the losses incurred from transactions booked in this account.

I read on with increasing delight:

> Barings London Settlements knew, or should have known, that the margin feed constituted a complete breakdown of the margin calls that were being made by BFS on its clients. Yet Barings London Settlements claimed that it never used the margin feed, a simple one-page document, to resolve the unreconciled balance.

I could have written that myself – it had been my main worry for two years. I had never been able to believe that this simple reconciliation was never done.

The Singaporeans castigated Barings over the

internal audit: 'The internal audit report had not in fact uncovered new ground. The Baring Group had known from the outset that Mr Leeson had a dual role as head of the front and back offices. The internal audit report served primarily to re-focus attention on this point. However, the Baring Group continued to act recklessly.'

The report really began to focus on the senior management's role, especially during the episode of the missing 7.78 billion yen.

'None of the senior managers of the Baring Group at any stage asked how and from where Mr Leeson had obtained the ¥7.7b to make such unauthorised payments.' There was a bizarre footnote alleging I'd committed forgery as far back as 1992, but most of the flak went Barings' way. And then the report came to the individuals: 'Both Mr Norris and Mr Bax have denied being involved in any plan either to underplay the significance of the discrepancy or to discourage independent investigations into the matter. However, we are unable to accept their denials.'

I was beginning to warm to their use of the word 'however'.

The report concluded:

In retrospect, it seems probable that until February 1995 the Baring Group could have averted collapse by timely action. By the end of January 1995, although substantial losses had been incurred, these were only a quarter of the eventual losses.

The Baring management could have remained ignorant of account 88888 up to the time of the collapse only if they had persistently shut themselves from the truth. Mr Norris' explanation after the collapse, namely that the senior management of the Baring Group believed that Mr Leeson's trading activities posed little (or no) risk to the Baring Group, but yielded very good returns, is implausible and in our view demonstrates a degree of ignorance of market reality that totally lacks credibility.

I sat back on my cell bed and leaned against the wall. For the first time in six months' imprisonment I didn't envy the Barings managers' freedom. They must be feeling wretched. I was probably the person they envied – I had come clean. I had done the frauds, been caught and was now going to serve a prison sentence. I was going to do it in Singapore because the SFO was spineless, but so what? I'd get through it. And then I'd come out on the other side and put it all behind me.

But these Barings managers were being damned as reckless and ignorant and they'd have to live with that. The only good thing about serving time in prison is that it is a punishment – and after you've done it you're back in the land of the living. But assuming these Barings managers carried on with their lives, going to Glyndebourne, seeing their friends – they were being consigned to the realms of the living dead. I had to accept and atone for my crimes and then put them behind me. But they were being accused by the Singaporean inspectors of being 'wilfully blind to the truth', reckless, ignorant.

Of Peter Norris, the Singaporean inspectors said: 'We

do not accept Mr Norris' version of the facts. It follows from this that Mr Norris has been untruthful.'

Of James Bax they wrote: 'In our view, Mr Bax's evidence, though given under oath, was false in material respects, and this also gives rise to an adverse inference being drawn against him.'

Of Simon Jones they wrote: 'Mr Jones' attitude to SIMEX's two letters reflected an unacceptable degree of apathy on his part. We are unable to understand how Mr Jones, as BFS Finance Director, could have simply signed replies drafted by Mr Leeson in response to SIMEX's concerns about Mr Leeson's activities, without independently looking into the matter in detail.'

For the first time since my arrest, I realised that I was glad to have played my part in this fiasco rather than theirs. I was happier in my prison cell than they were, sitting at home nursing their credibility back to pieces and always knowing what their friends were saying behind their backs. Fuck 'em! I thought. I could face all my family and friends and look them in the eye. I had nothing to hide. I was a free man in that respect. I'd get out of prison and get on with my life. They'd never be able to go to a single cocktail party without someone whispering behind their backs: 'That's Peter Norris . . . That's James Bax . . .' and they'd know that everyone thought they were stupid. I could correct my crimes – I certainly would never do anything like them again. But they couldn't correct the criticisms that the Singaporean report had made of them.

* * *

ON Sunday 29 October, just before the deadline for my appeal to the German Federal Court to delay my extradition, I announced that I would voluntarily go back to Singapore. On Monday 20 November I was given forty-eight hours' notice that I was leaving.

POSTSCRIPT

Nɪᴄᴋ Lᴇᴇsᴏɴ ᴡᴀs ʜᴀɴᴅᴇᴅ over to Singaporean custody and flew back to the Far East on Wednesday 22 November 1995.

On Friday 1 December he pleaded guilty to two offences of deceiving the auditors of Barings in a way 'likely to cause harm to their reputation' and to cheating SIMEX.

The following day, Saturday 2 December, Nick Leeson was sentenced to six and a half years in prison. He is currently serving his sentence in Tanah Merah prison, Changi, Singapore.

LIST OF ABBREVIATIONS

ALCO	Asset and Liability Committee (Barings)
BFS	Baring Futures Singapore
BNP	Banque Nationale de Paris
BoE	Bank of England
BSJ	Baring Securities Japan
BSL	Baring Securities Limited
CEO	Chief Executive Officer
C & L	Coopers & Lybrand
ETB	European Trust and Banking Co.
FCT	First Continental Trading
FPG	Financial Products Group (Barings)
JGB	Japanese Government Bonds
LIFFE	London International Financial Futures and Options Exchange
MANCO	Management Committee (Barings)
OSE	Osaka Securities Exchange
OTC	over-the-counter (transaction)
OUB	Overseas Union Bank
P & L	profit and loss
SBC	Swiss Bank Corporation
SFA	Securities and Futures Association
SFO	Serious Fraud Office

SIMEX	Singapore International Monetary Exchange
SLK	Spear, Leeds & Kellogg
TSE	Tokyo Stock Exchange

GLOSSARY

ARBITRAGE: The process of exploiting temporary price differences which open up between two markets.

BACK OFFICE: The department of a financial institution (e.g. BFS) responsible for the settling of trades.

BLOOMBERG: A computer-based financial information service.

CALL OPTION: A contract which gives you the right, but not the obligation, to buy from the writer of the contract at a specified price and within a specified time period. Call buyers expect the price of the product to rise. See also OPTION, PUT OPTION.

CLEARING MEMBER: A member of a futures exchange (e.g. BFS) authorised to clear trades through the clearing house.

CROSS TRADE: A transaction whereby a trader buys and sells orders of corresponding prices on behalf of two or more of his customers.

CUSTOMER ACCOUNT: An account held by a member of an exchange for the booking of trades done on behalf of its customers.

DERIVATIVE: A financial instrument (e.g. futures contract, option).

ERROR ACCOUNT: Officially, an account used to manage monies for the reconciliation of errors. In the case of Error Account 88888, its function went far beyond this.

EUROYEN CONTRACT: A Japanese futures contract based on the three-month interest rate for Euroyen.

FIMAT: The Singapore brokerage arm of Société Générale.

FRONT OFFICE: The department of a financial institution (e.g. BFS) responsible for dealing with the firm's customers.

FUTURES CONTRACT: An agreement to buy or sell a specified quantity of a commodity at a specified price. The details of the deal, and date of transaction, are agreed between buyer and seller on the floor of an exchange or on a dealing screen.

HEDGING: The protection of an open position to minimise risk (e.g. by betting that derivative prices will move the other way as well, to try and cover potential losses). A position where this has not been done is called UNHEDGED, and is a riskier position to maintain.

HOUSE ACCOUNT: An account held by a member of an exchange for the booking of trades carried out on its own behalf (PROPRIETARY TRADING). It is used to prevent confusion with trades held in the customer account.

INITIAL MARGIN: The minimum payment required by a

member from its customers for each contract undertaken.

INTRA-DAY ADVANCE MARGIN: The extra payment that may be required by a clearing house from a clearing member during a trading day.

JOURNAL: A record of transactions carried out by a member.

LONG POSITION: A position usually established when a trader has bought a financial instrument (e.g. futures contract), in expectation of a price rise.

MARGIN: The payment made to a clearing house by a member, or to a member by its customer, to act as security in the event of losses. As the value of the asset bought or sold changes, further payment may be needed.

MARGIN CALL: A demand for payment by a clearing house or a member. This is prompted by changes in the market value of the assets traded or new positions being undertaken.

MARK-TO-MARKET: The daily adjustment of the value of positions to reflect current market prices.

NIKKEI 225 INDEX: An index based on the values of the leading 225 stocks traded on the Tokyo Stock Exchange.

OPEN OUTCRY: A system of trading which takes place in a 'pit' (a designated area of an exchange). Traders shout out or signal their proposed trades, find a willing counter-party, and agree a trade which is later recorded on a trading card.

OPEN POSITION: A position in futures or options, long or short, which is not covered by equal and opposite transactions, and is therefore UNHEDGED.

OPTION: The right to buy or sell futures contracts on a set date, granted in exchange for an agreed payment. If the right is not exercised by the agreed date, the option expires. Option buyers take a small risk and can make huge profits; option sellers (writers) can expect limited profits and potentially disastrous losses. See also CALL OPTION, PUT OPTION.

OVER-THE-COUNTER: A transaction which takes place by telephone or computer between two parties, and which is not listed by an exchange.

POSITION: A trader's overall stake or interest in a certain market. See also LONG POSITION, SHORT POSITION, OPEN POSITION.

PREMIUM: The cost of an option.

PROPRIETARY TRADING: Trading done by a member on its own account, rather than for a customer. Such trades would be booked to the house account.

PUT OPTION: A contract which gives you the right, but not the obligation, to sell to the writer of the contract at a specified price and within a specified time frame. Put buyers expect the price of the product to fall. See also OPTION, CALL OPTION.

SETTLEMENT: The recording of a trade into the books of all parties involved in a transaction, prompting payment of any outstanding balances.

SHORT POSITION: A position usually established when a

trader has sold a financial instrument (e.g. futures contract), in expectation of a price fall.

STRADDLE: An option position created by combining the same number of put and call options at the same strike price.

STRIKE PRICE: The price at which the buyer of an option may buy or sell under the terms of the option contract. The strike price is invariably set when the contract is written.

TICK: The minimum unit of price change in a futures contract.

UNHEDGED: See HEDGING.

PICTURE CREDITS

All other photographs are from private collections.

Warner Books now offers an exciting range of quality titles by both established and new authors. All of the books in this series are available from:

Little, Brown and Company (UK),
P.O. Box 11,
Falmouth,
Cornwall TR10 9EN.

Fax No: 01326 569555
Telephone No: 01326 569777
E-mail: books@barni.avel.co.uk

Payments can be made as follows: cheque, postal order (payable to Little, Brown and Company) or by credit cards, Visa/Access. Do not send cash or currency. UK customers and B.F.P.O. please allow £1.00 for postage and packing for the first book, plus 50p for the second book, plus 30p for each additional book up to a maximum charge of £3.00 (7 books plus).

Overseas customers including Ireland, please allow £2.00 for the first book plus £1.00 for the second book, plus 50p for each additional book.

NAME (Block Letters) ....

....

ADDRESS ....

....

....

☐ I enclose my remittance for ....

☐ I wish to pay by Access/Visa Card

Number ☐☐☐☐☐☐☐☐☐☐☐☐☐☐☐☐☐☐

Card Expiry Date ☐☐☐☐